Critical Acclaim for Rapid Contextual Design

Although Contextual Design is one of our most powerful design tools, there has been a gap between theory and practice. With this book, the gap disappears. Here are those little gems of advice that a skilled mentor who peered over your shoulder would tell you. If you lack such a mentor, this book is the next best thing, explaining just what you need to do in a straightforward, easy to read, easy to understand manner.

—Don Norman, Nielsen Norman group, Professor, Northwestern University, Author of *Emotional Design*

Having had the opportunity to work with Karen in several CD projects, I learned to understand the value of Contextual Design both as a reference model of how design works in general, and as a pool of helpful and scalable tools to facilitate and drive good product design.

Rapid CD makes this experience now available to everyone. The new how-to guide boosts the value of the original Contextual Design book by transforming a design method into pragmatic advices of how to run a contextual design project in your own environment.

—Joerg Beringer, Director, Strategic Product Design, SAP AG

A wise guide to interface design dos and don'ts, from people with experience. They create a new language for thinking about design processes–combining a compelling structured process with sufficient freedom for innovative excursions.

—Ben Shneiderman, University of Maryland

My organization has used the Contextual Inquiry field research and design methods to put users at the forefront of how we consider, approach and develop our Web sites. As a result, our sites are becoming increasingly more effective and useful for users. Rapid Contextual Design provides a further step in innovation by providing detailed, practical advice on how to conduct successful research projects and to fit the project to the need. My team welcomes these new advances and the flexibility they will provide when we conduct future projects using this method.

—Terry Austin, User Experience Group Manager, Microsoft

RAPID CONTEXTUAL DESIGN

A How-to Guide to Key Techniques for User-Centered Design

The Morgan Kaufmann Series in Interactive Technologies

Series Editors:
Stuart Card, PARC
Jonathan Grudin, Microsoft
Jakob Nielsen, Nielsen Norman Group

Rapid Contextual Design: A How-to Guide to Key Techniques for User-Centered Design
Karen Holtzblatt, Jessamyn Burns Wendell, and Shelley Wood

Voice Interface Design: Crafting the New Conversational Speech Systems
Randy Allen Harris

Understanding Users: A Practical Guide to User Requirements Methods, Tools, and Techniques
Catherine Courage and Kathy Baxter

The Web Application Design Handbook: Best Practices for Web-Based Software
Susan Fowler and Victor Stanwick

The Mobile Connection: The Cell Phone's Impact on Society
Richard Ling

Information Visualization: Perception for Design, 2nd Edition
Colin Ware

Interaction Design for Complex Problem Solving: Developing Useful and Usable Software
Barbara Mirel

The Craft of Information Visualization: Readings and Reflections
Written and edited by Ben Bederson and Ben Shneiderman

HCI Models, Theories, and Frameworks: Towards a Multidisciplinary Science
Edited by John M. Carroll

Web Bloopers: 60 Common Web Design Mistakes, and How to Avoid Them
Jeff Johnson

Observing the User Experience: A Practitioner's Guide to User Research
Mike Kuniavsky

Paper Prototyping: The Fast and Easy Way to Design and Refine User Interfaces
Carolyn Snyder

Persuasive Technology: Using Computers to Change What We Think and Do
B. J. Fogg

Coordinating User Interfaces for Consistency
Edited by Jakob Nielsen

Usability for the Web: Designing Web Sites that Work
Tom Brinck, Darren Gergle, and Scott D. Wood

Usability Engineering: Scenario-Based Development of Human-Computer Interaction
Mary Beth Rosson and John M. Carroll

Your Wish is My Command: Programming by Example
Edited by Henry Lieberman

GUI Bloopers: Don'ts and Dos for Software Developers and Web Designers
Jeff Johnson

Information Visualization: Perception for Design
Colin Ware

Robots for Kids: Exploring New Technologies for Learning
Edited by Allison Druin and James Hendler

Information Appliances and Beyond: Interaction Design for Consumer Products
Edited by Eric Bergman

Readings in Information Visualization: Using Vision to Think
Written and edited by Stuart K. Card, Jock D. Mackinlay, and Ben Shneiderman

The Design of Children's Technology
Edited by Allison Druin

Web Site Usability: A Designer's Guide
Jared M. Spool, Tara Scanlon, Will Schroeder, Carolyn Snyder, and Terri DeAngelo

The Usability Engineering Lifecycle: A Practitioner's Handbook for User Interface Design
Deborah J. Mayhew

Contextual Design: Defining Customer-Centered Systems
Hugh Beyer and Karen Holtzblatt

Human-Computer Interface Design: Success Stories, Emerging Methods, and Real World Context
Edited by Marianne Rudisill, Clayton Lewis, Peter P. Polson, and Timothy D. McKay

RAPID

CONTEXTUAL

DESIGN

A How-to Guide to Key Techniques for User-Centered Design

KAREN HOLTZBLATT

JESSAMYN BURNS WENDELL

SHELLEY WOOD

ELSEVIER

AMSTERDAM • BOSTON • HEIDELBERG • LONDON
NEW YORK • OXFORD • PARIS • SAN DIEGO
SAN FRANCISCO • SINGAPORE • SYDNEY • TOKYO

Morgan Kaufmann Publishers is an imprint of Elsevier

MORGAN KAUFMANN PUBLISHERS

Publishing Director	Diane Cerra
Publishing Services Manager	Simon Crump
Project Manager	Sarah M. Hajduk
Editorial Assistant	Asma Stephan
Cover Design	Ross Carron Design
Cover Image	Figures Gathered Around Circle © The Image Bank; Will Crocker photographer
Text Design & Composition	Jessamyn Burns Wendell
Technical Illustration	Dartmouth Publishing, Inc.
Copyeditor	Adrienne Rebello
Proofreader	Jan Cocker
Indexer	Michael Ferreira
Interior printer	The Maple-Vail Book Manufacturing Group
Cover printer	Phoenix Color

Morgan Kaufmann Publishers is an imprint of Elsevier.
500 Sansome Street, Suite 400, San Francisco, CA 94111

Library of Congress Cataloging-in-Publication Data
APPLICATION SUBMITTED

ISBN: 0-12-354051-8

For information on all Morgan Kaufmann publications, visit our Web site at www.mkp.com or www.books.elsevier.com

Transferred to Digital Printing 2009

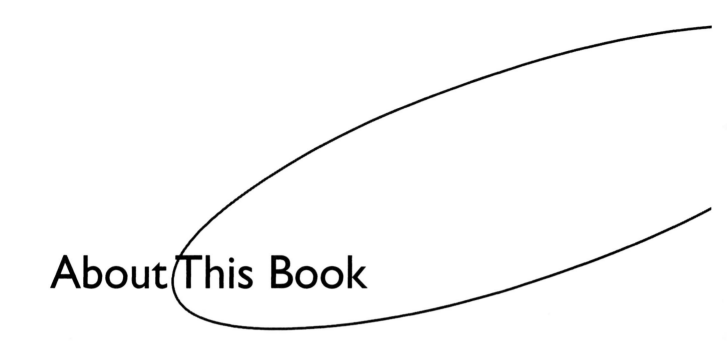

About This Book

Throughout this handbook you will notice several recurring features.

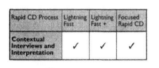

At the start of chapters four through 14 you will see a chapter guide box. This box will indicate whether or not the chapter's content applies to your type of Rapid CD project (see Chapter 2: Planning Your Rapid CD Project for type definitions).

This handbook is full of examples from real projects. We call out examples both in the main body of the text and in shaded boxes. Both use the same example icon.

Throughout each of the chapters you will notice information called out in shaded boxes. Each type of box is represented by an icon.

This icon indicates additional commentary from author Karen Holtzblatt on CD process issues.

The question mark icon represents boxes that answer frequently asked questions from our clients.

This icon is used to indicate a box with ideas for communicating out to your organization.

The "i" icon represents general information topics; information we wanted to share with you.

Contents

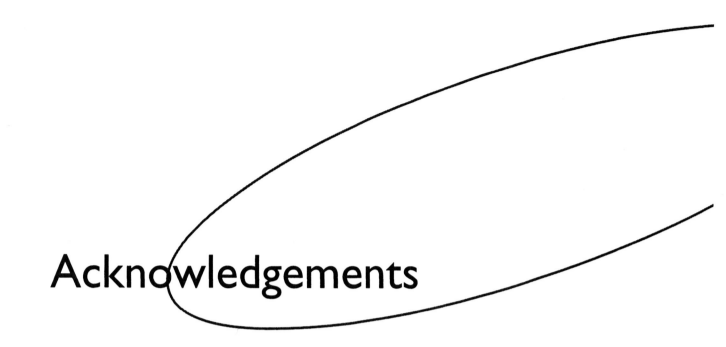

Acknowledgements

Many thanks to everyone who has made this book possible. First, to all the teams who have used Contextual Design over the years making it a living process. Because you adapted it to suite your needs and company procedures we have been able to learn from you and further guide you in adapting the full Contextual Design process effectively.

A special thanks to all the teams who contributed examples to this book letting others learn what to expect from your experience. Thanks to the entire team at eChalk for their end-to-end examples especially Charlene Noll, Torrance Robinson, Daniel Watts, and Alberto Garcia. Thanks also to Dave Wallace from Apropos, Lisa Baker from LANDesk, and Linda Doherty from Agilent for allowing us to share their data and design artifacts with the larger design community.

A big thank you to everyone who helped organize, edit, and contributed content to this book. Thanks Hugh Beyer, co-founder of InContext, for the first cut of the Persona chapter, compiling the examples, and providing content for selected information boxes and chapters. Thanks to David Rondeau, InContext's Design Chair, for clarifying design artifact and cleaning up illustrations.

Thanks also to our editor Diane Cerra and the team at Elsevier. Finally, a grateful thank you to all the reviewers of this book whose comments gave us the kind of real reader feedback that we needed to make what we hope is a thoroughly usable and valuable book.

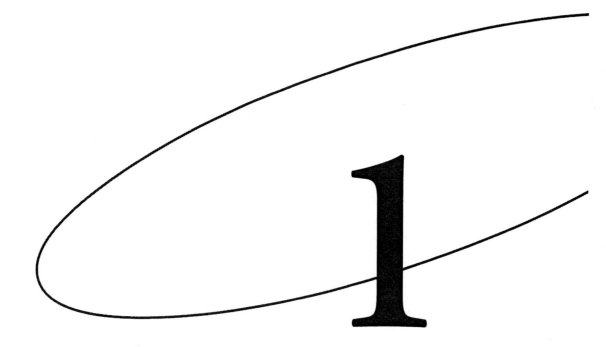

Introduction

This handbook is a how-to companion to the main Contextual Design book, *Contextual Design: Defining Customer-Centered Systems*.[1] Over the years, we at InContext[2] have worked on many projects of many types, with many teams in many different organizations. Contextual Design (CD), our customer-centered design process, has been used in many ways depending on the needs of the project. Contextual Design often has been called a scaffolding for user-centered front-end design—techniques can be used or skipped and different techniques can be added.

Rapid Contextual Design is a guide for practitioners of the most frequently used CD techniques. Like any new process adoption, certain techniques are adopted first and others come later. This handbook focuses on the core Contextual Design techniques that most easily drive customer data into the corporate design process. So, you should be able to use and adapt these techniques to your particular situation.

To help you understand how to use CD techniques on your projects, *Rapid Contextual Design* contains step-by-step instructions of how to use each technique, real examples of user data from our clients' and our own projects, schedules, and tips for using the process. We also discuss many of the issues that team members have raised over the years. And because some of you are integrating CD with other techniques like personas, Agile or Extreme Programming (XP), and use case generation, we include a discussion of how CD connects to these methods throughout this handbook.

Over the years teams have asked us, "Why can't we use a tool for Contextual Design?" Well, now you can—CDTools™ is InContext's software tool designed specifically to help you organize, analyze, track, and share user data. Because we have designed many other software tools by studying the people using them, we know the advantages and pitfalls of providing tool support for what was previously a paper process. So, in *Rapid Contextual Design* we highlight where and how to use CDTools within the context of the design process. And of course we designed CDTools with Contextual Design! We hope that these discussions will help you plan tool use into your own project process.

Finally, although *Rapid Contextual Design* can be used on its own, for a deeper discussion of the CD method and the philosophy of Contextual Design refer to the original book, *Contextual Design: Defining Customer-Centered Systems*. Throughout this handbook, we reference the appropriate sections of the main Contextual Design book. Because *Rapid Contextual Design* is a practical guide to the daily practice of Contextual Design, we spend little time on the *whys* of the process, and instead concentrate on the *hows*. And if you want to understand all the CD techniques, go back to the main text.

What steps of Contextual Design are covered in Rapid Contextual Design?

Rapid Contextual Design will take you from the start of a CD project all the way through to the finished design, addressing different project types and organizational needs. We cover defining the project scope, deciding on the number and type of interviews, and setting up interviews. We provide tips on conducting the interviews and running the interpretation session afterward. Once the data is gathered and interpreted, we guide you through the affinity building process and consolidating sequence models. Finally, we help you with visioning, storyboarding, and testing your system with paper mockups. Throughout we help you understand how to get a quality result from your variant of the CD process.

Depending on the type of Rapid CD project you choose, you may use several or all of the processes covered in *Rapid Contextual Design*. Chapter 2 covers planning your project and picking the type of Rapid CD process appropriate for your project.

An overview of the techniques in the full Contextual Design process, along with what we are covering in this handbook, follows. Throughout *Rapid Contextual Design* we will reference the more extensive discussions of techniques found in our original book on Contextual Design.

Contextual Inquiry. Field interviews are conducted with users in their workplaces while they work, observing and inquiring into the structure of the users' own work practice. This ensures that the team captures the real business practice and daily activities of the people the system is to support, not just the self-reported practice or official policies.

We cover setting up field interviews in Chapter 3, and how to run a field interview in Chapter 4.

Interpretation sessions and work modeling. Team discussions are used to retell the events of the interview, key points (affinity notes) are captured, and models representing the user's work practice are drawn. Five models provide different perspectives on how work is done: the *flow model* captures communication and coordination and the roles people play, the *cultural model* captures culture and policy, the *sequence model* shows the detailed steps performed to accomplish a task (task analysis), the *physical model* shows the physical environment as it supports the work, and the *artifact model* shows how artifacts are used and structured in doing the work.

This disciplined, detailed debriefing allows the team to share the findings, build a common understanding of the user, and capture all the data relevant to the project in a form that will characterize the population to be supported and drive the resulting design.

We cover interpretation sessions in Chapter 5. The work models recommended for Rapid CD, primarily the sequence model, are covered in Chapter 6.

Model consolidation and affinity diagram building. The data from individual users is consolidated to show a larger picture of the work of the targeted population. The notes from the interpretation sessions of all users are brought together into an *affinity diagram*, a hierarchical representation of the issues labeled to reflect user needs. Work models are consolidated, showing the common work patterns and strategies across all users. The sequence model, the key model for Rapid CD, shows the tasks that the system will support. The consolidated sequence model is equivalent to a task analysis or the "as-is" use case in process modeling.

Sequence consolidation is covered in Chapter 7, and affinity diagramming is covered in Chapter 8.

Personas. In addition to the basic Contextual Design techniques, in Chapter 9 we discuss how to use contextual data to build personas, popularized by Alan Cooper. A persona describes typical users of the proposed system as though they were real people. Personas help the team communicate the needs of the users by bringing them to life. Good personas are built from rich contextual data. When a persona is based on field data collected from many users, it's much richer and more complete than a description of any actual real user could be.

Visioning. Together, the team reviews the consolidated data by "walking" the data, sharing the personas if they were created and capturing key issues and hot ideas. This stimulates the team to start thinking broadly. After the "data walk" the team runs a *visioning session* to invent how the system will streamline and transform the work users do by applying technology. The *vision* is captured as a hand-drawn sketch on flipchart paper. This vision represents the big picture of what the system could do to address the full work practice. Subsequently, it can be broken down into coherent subsets to be implemented over a series of releases as may be required in a Rapid CD process. Alternatively, in a smaller project the team simply may brainstorm solutions.

We cover the data walk in Chapter 10 and the visioning process in Chapter 11.

Storyboarding. The vision guides the detailed redesign of user work tasks, which is fleshed out in more detail using pictures and text in a series of hand-drawn cells. A storyboard includes manual practices, initial user interface (UI) concepts, business rules, and automation assumptions. Storyboarding is equivalent to future scenarios, high-level use cases representing the "to-be" state of the work process, and becomes the basis for user stories in XP. Storyboarding is covered in Chapter 12.

User Environment Design (UED). A single representation of the system that shows all functions and how they are organized into coherent places in the system to support user intent. The UED is built from the storyboards. This ensures that a large system is coherent and fits the work. It provides a basis for prioritization and rational segmentation of the system. The UED is a customer-centered way of representing the system requirements.

Rapid Contextual Design does not include a discussion of the UED. Companies often have their own standards for recording requirements that will take the place of the UED in a Rapid CD process. So to speed up the process, and because the UED is most essential for large system design, we do not cover the UED—return to the original Contextual Design book for a discussion of this technique.

Paper prototypes and mock-up interviews. User interfaces are designed on paper and tested with the system's actual users, first in rough form and then with more detail. This ensures that the basic system function and structure work for the users, and that the basic UI concept is sound. After several iterations on paper you are ready for final interaction and visual design and then can begin running prototype testing.

We introduce the primary concepts of paper prototyping in Chapter 13, and explain how to interpret the mock-up data in Chapter 14. This process has caught on and is covered in many other publications as well.

What is rapid about Rapid CD?

Time has become a driving force in systems design. Today teams and companies want to include users in their design processes. But how can they do this without adding significant time to the process? Organizations have their existing methodologies and practices—how can user-centered design techniques be included within these processes? Opposition to bringing users into the center of the design process still exists. Surveys and focus groups are deemed to be enough for the voice of the customer. Complaints about increased time and resources for including user data in a real way abound. But the drive for designing products and systems with user data is moving to the mainstream of the development process.

One goal of *Rapid Contextual Design* is to remove the arguments against getting customer data into a development process. In our experience time is less about overall clock-time and more about how user data fits into the existing habits, processes, job descriptions, and schedules of a company. So "rapid" doesn't mainly mean "Do everything in CD but do it shorter and faster." Rather, it means:

- Do I have to do all those steps? What can I skip? When can I skip it?
- How does CD fit with my existing design process? Can't I use CD techniques to get customer data and then use the steps I'm accustomed to using?

- I have only two people on the team, can I still do it?

- What can I do in a few weeks?

User-centered design will be seen as "rapid" if it can fit within the existing structures, expectations, and development processes of the organizations that deliver systems and products. This still means change, but like any organizational change process, the change comes in steps. Chapter 16 discusses organizational adoption issues.

Any requirements gathering and design process takes time. For Contextual Design, the real speed (clock-time) of the process depends on the:

- Number of customer visits that you choose to perform

- Number of people who can work simultaneously on the project, or the helpers you can get at key points

- Dedication of the people assigned to the project, and whether they can work full-time

- Size of the problem, the more complex the business process, the more complex the product (therefore the longer it will take to define or redesign)

- Number of stakeholders that have to be satisfied, coordinated with, and communicated to (the more buy-in you need the longer it will take)

With a small enough project and focused, trained, dedicated resources you can do each of the major steps of the full Contextual Design process within five to seven weeks, particularly if you reduce the number of work models that you use (see the box, **Karen and Ingrid's story: a five-week Contextual Design project**, for an example).

At InContext, we routinely do two-person projects covering every step of the process but use only the affinity diagram and sequence model to characterize the users' work practice. Lapsed time for requirements gathering when the number of users is small (about 10 users) can be reduced to as little as two to three weeks, depending on the dedication of the team and the formality required for communicating findings. Even in one week you can collect data, build an affinity, and vision a solution after interviewing six users.

The LANDesk project is an example of a three-week project we ran to help them start to characterize their user population and drive data into their XP process. In many cases, CD is used only to gather and organize customer data and then other methods are used for the design phase. Any of these variants of CD will be considered to be more rapid by an organization rather than using all the steps of the full CD process and collecting data on a large number of users.

In Chapter 2, we lay out several ways to organize your design process to support a more rapid or limited CD process. We offer several variations of how two-person teams can use customer data in projects ranging from one to ten weeks of work. Depending on the steps you choose to do, the number of people on your team, the number of helpers you can get, and the number of users you want to talk to, you can design a variant of Contextual Design to fit your circumstances.

Our goal is to give you the hands-on examples and guidance you need to increase your productivity and help you bring user data into your requirements and design processes quickly and confidently.

Karen and Ingrid's story: a five-week Contextual Design project

Last year a small pharmaceutical research lab in our company asked for a team to design some software to run their work process. This lab was new, and many of the people we were supporting had been doing the work for only a few months. Because they did not have established ways of working, they were open to our investigating how they did their jobs and ways their work could be changed. However, the team and the lab were both on a tight schedule. We needed to deliver a working system in three months.

As two of our company's trained experts in Contextual Design, we were excited and a bit overwhelmed by this opportunity to coach and train our own team. Part of our strategy for getting the Contextual Design finished quickly was to have several team members who were already trained in CD. We had two developers who were already fully trained, two who were not previously trained in CD (and whom we only minimally trained), and a project leader who participated fully in the training. Two of our customers were also involved peripherally and received some training.

The system would have only four direct users, and we interviewed all of them. The customers learned a lot about their jobs through the interviews and consolidations. We consolidated some of the data with the users so they would understand where the data and designs came from and could participate in visioning the new system.

To reduce the time necessary for the Contextual Design process, we consolidated only three models, the affinity, the flow model, and the sequences. We then visioned and storyboarded the tasks. Based on these, we built a User Environment design for the new system. Our users got very excited about the User Environment design. They found they could see their work process in this model, and could see how the system would support the process and the different roles in the organization. In fact, the managers of the lab had a number of conversations about their work practice while walking the User Environment model.

The UI design and object modeling went forward in parallel once we had the User Environment design in place. For the UI, we built paper prototypes and did three rounds of testing (UI interviews) on them before moving to online prototypes. We used the redesigned sequences and User Environment design to develop use cases, using the focus areas on the User Environment to identify potential objects. We kept the User Environment design and use cases synchronized pretty well until we got to coding.

The customers are excited and involved, and used our data to help them see how to improve their own processes. Their new system actually eliminated a large portion of the work one person was doing. She spent a lot of time reformatting files as part of analyzing them. Now, she can do this analysis directly and spend this saved time on other projects.

For this focused project, the process took us eight weeks full-time, from initial data gathering through the object modeling and UI design. The Contextual Design portion took only five weeks.

How do I get my organization to adopt a customer centered design process?

Any introduction of user-centered techniques implies a change from existing practices. Companies already have the way that they do requirements and design—whether the process is written down or not, whether it is actually followed or not. So any change to those daily activities for developing systems means integrating contextual techniques with existing methodologies. Sometimes companies are adopting more formal methods like Rational Unified Programming (RUP) or starting to implement new methodologies like XP (Extreme Programming) neither of which have a strong user experience component. Questions arise about how Contextual Design fits with these methods.

But no matter the method, size of company, or type of system being developed introducing customer-centered design practices means organizational change—change in method, change in roles people play, change in skill sets, change in time spent with the users, and change in project management.

Chapter 2 defines the methodologies we reference throughout the book and provides an overview of how to integrate contextual techniques into these processes. Chapter 15 provides examples of how to map contextual design artifacts to those used by other methods. Chapter 16 provides strategies for organizational adoption.

Rapid Contextual Design and other methodologies. Successful adoption of CD includes making it work with other methodologies. In Chapter 15 we discuss how Contextual Design works with corporate methods, RUP or Agile techniques. We discuss how Rapid CD techniques augment these techniques. We discuss the relationship between consolidated sequences and use cases for characterizing the as-is user process. We also provide examples of how storyboards are used for developing scenarios, to-be use cases, and driving user stories.

Issues of organization adoption. Incorporating Rapid CD will require a strategy on your part as you decide on the best way to bring it into your organization. You need to think about what kind of project to start with, how to create excitement, and how to garner support. You also need to be ready to address the objections that will be raised by people who are reluctant to change. Chapter 16 gives you specific techniques to use, and the arguments you can make, in order to move forward.

Finally, one of the best means of getting support in your organization is to simply get customer data to help make decisions. However you get it—the data itself is the best technique for opening the door to customer-centered design techniques.

What is CDTools?
Along with wanting a faster process, teams have consistently requested tool support for Contextual Design to reduce the reliance on paper and to share and reuse the results. And interestingly, having a tool is another way to entice the organization to adopt a customer-centered design process. Requirements gathering is a "soft" technique and talking to users often doesn't "feel" like engineering. But using a tool suddenly makes what was "soft" feel "hard." Especially when you are working with engineers, tools like CDTools both help you manage the data and bring reluctant team members into the process.

CDTools is an integrated and modular software application that helps you organize your data and collaborate across your organization. Using this tool, you can capture your qualitative customer data in a team-based design environment. CDTools supports key aspects of the Contextual Design process, while guiding and supporting teams or individuals gathering and interpreting field data, analyzing and consolidating the data into an affinity diagram, and sharing it throughout the organization.

CDTools will help you organize your user visits, capture affinity notes, and put your affinity online. Throughout *Rapid Contextual Design* we present when to use CDTools in the context of how the tool can support the steps of the Contextual Design process.

CDTools will enable you to:

Streamline the Contextual Design process. The tool minimizes paper use and speeds up data capture, analysis, management, and maintenance. CDTools has features to help improve quality of both the data and your analysis of it.

Enable distributed teams. CDTools supports distributed interpretation and design sessions.

Share and reuse data. Views of the data can be published in a browser format for cross-project, cross-team, and vendor-sharing supporting reuse, extension, and discussion of customer data and design.

Our intent with CDTools is to provide a tool that supports your process; we do not want the tool to take over. Using Contextual Design we found that focusing on using any software tool can get in the way of focusing on the actual work, so we have taken care to ensure that CDTools lets you take the focus off the tool and supports the work you are trying to accomplish.

What project examples do we use?

Throughout the book, we will provide examples of real user data and other artifacts created in the CD process. Examples have been drawn from real projects that we or our clients have conducted. The eChalk example runs through every chapter of the book, providing a consistent context for talking about the process. eChalk develops web-based tools for schools in the United States. eChalk began using Contextual Design in 2000 to create eChalk version 3.0 and has continued to leverage and extend their initial data with Contextual Design since that time.

We also draw on examples from projects we did with Agilent, Apropos, and LANDesk Software as well as an internal project InContext did on business-to-business (B2B) purchasing. In addition to these projects, other data examples are used to illustrate particular points. Sign up to access our resource web site www.incent.com/cdtools and see more examples of data to help guide your own projects.

We have taken care to protect our clients' intellectual property and innovations. The data described in *Rapid Contextual Design* is used to illustrate how to use the CD process, and what real data and design artifacts look like. We have not tried to provide the whole process story for any example, nor do we reveal the nature of their ultimate product. Go see the final products to understand the full results of using Contextual techniques for product definition and design.

Thank you to all who supplied their examples so that others could learn.

eChalk

eChalk is the leading provider of affordable, web-based communication platforms specifically designed for K–12 schools in the United States. The eChalk product is designed to enhance collaboration between students, teachers, parents, and school administrators. It provides features such as e-mail, calendaring, digital lockers for file storage and sharing, a school directory, teacher and class web pages, and online sharing of classroom assignments and information. The eChalk team has been using Contextual Design for several years; the data reflected here was gathered for eChalk version 3.0. For version 3.0, the team primarily focused on teachers, administrators, and school paraprofessionals, but also collected data from students. The team then used the entire Contextual Design process. This allowed them to use the project data—which was collected in 2000—to drive multiple, coherent product releases that fit into their long-term vision based on customer need. In late 2003 the team went back out and collected additional, focused data for additional features that will be rolled out in 2004 in eChalk version 5.0. See www.echalk.com for more information.

Agilent

Agilent Technologies is a global company and one of the leading providers of analytical instruments. These devices are used in the chemical, petrochemical, and pharmaceutical industries to determine the content and purity of products. They also are used by government and private laboratories to test for presence of pollutants, pesticides, and drugs of abuse.

The data used for examples in *Rapid Contextual Design* come from two projects that Agilent contracted. The first project focused on understanding and documenting how analytical labs run their business. This information was used to develop a consistent software architecture to support work flow processes that are key to the success of a laboratory. In such a lab, the analytical devices are networked together. Samples are logged and run on these devices. Analysts in the lab get daily lists of samples to be analyzed. Data is stored and queried from a database. The second project built on this original work and focused on quality control laboratories in the chemical and pharmaceutical industries.

The release of Agilent's Cerity for Pharmaceutical QA/QC was the first application on the new architecture that was designed using contextual design. Customers were involved in the user interface design through the entire project. Many major pharmaceutical companies are using Cerity today in their quality control laboratories. Cerity provides security and compliance for electronic records and signatures that are now mandated by the U.S. FDA. These labs process high volumes of samples using predefined procedures.

Customers love the user interface and have purchased the product because it meets their workflow needs. Learn more about the product:

Press release: www.agilent.com/about/newsroom/features/2004jan29_cerity.html

Product page: www.chem.agilent.com/scripts/PDS.asp?lPage=272

Apropos

Apropos Technology is an industry leader in providing multichannel customer interaction management, integrating e-mail, web, and voice. This project was part of the work that led Apropos from supporting call centers—where customers called in with problems—to supporting customers consistently across all interaction media.

The project goal was to understand how to support contact centers—any kind of organization that people go to for help or services. By understanding the nature of customer interaction in call centers—primarily voice-based—we could anticipate and design for issues of supporting people with e-mail and phone. The project looked at how customers can be helped through immediate contact with the right people and information. It investigated how people in the call center with no direct customer contact could benefit from the knowledge of the customer interaction. The project looked at interactions across the call center and also at specific interactions with callers.

Purchasing project

This project was part of a larger report on business-to-business relationships across multiple industries commissioned by SAP. The goal was to understand and support the role of purchasing in large organizations, looking for opportunities to support this relationship on the Web. The team focused on understanding how purchasing does their job and how they manage their two primary relationships: with the internal groups needing items and with the external suppliers providing goods and services. The project looked at all levels of purchasing, from providing commodities such as office supplies through creating long-term business-to-business relationships that make the supplier part of the production process.

LANDesk

LANDesk Software is a leading provider of unified desktop, server, and mobile device management solutions. LANDesk Software products are proven with more than 250 million nodes shipped worldwide. The company's flagship LANDesk Management Suite is the result of over a decade of innovation in systems management processes and technologies. The LANDesk team used rapid Contextual Design processes to bring valuable contextual data into their Extreme Programming development environment, allowing them to deliver a user-focused OS deployment solution on a tight timeline. The resulting LANDesk® OS Deployment Wizard automates the costly and time-consuming process IT administrators face for planning, deploying, configuring, and maintaining Windows operating system upgrades. The team created key project story lines and a target customer persona from the affinity diagrams and sequence models. The data continues to influence product design plans.

See the product at: www.landesk.com/products/product.php?pid=6.

Terms

System. Contextual Design can be used to design desk top applications, business systems, web pages, consumer tools, scientific instruments, manufacturing processes, even home appliances and products. It can be used for products delivered to a market or for systems created internally to support business. In this book we use the terms products, systems, and web sites interchangeably. By these terms we simply mean "that which you are designing."

Customer. When developing for a market your user population is the customers in your market. But when developing for internal users your user population is your business users. We use the term customer and user interchangeably to mean the people who directly use the system you are designing, consume its information, or direct work to be done in the system. Users or customers are the people whose work your tool will be supporting directly or indirectly. We do not mean the person who spends the money to purchase. So we are using customer in the same way as quality professionals do—that person whom you need to service.

Similarly, we use the term market and user population interchangeably.

Work. Throughout the book we talk about work, work practice, and work models. By this we mean whatever the activities the user is engaged in that we are interested in supporting. Work is a good term for business applications or business web sites. But consumers engage in life, life activities, and life tasks. Although sometimes we refer to life tasks, we primarily use the word work to mean any user activity.

Similarly a **work model** is a diagramming technique or drawing to represent the human activity observed in the field. Any of the five work models may be representing real work activities or simple life activities.

Customer-centered design. Whether we are talking about user-centered design or customer-centered design we are talking about the tools and techniques described in this book and others who seek to include user data and the voice of the customer into their design process.

Mock-up interview. Whether we use the term mock-up or paper prototype we are talking about a representation of the user interface of a potential product built from paper and taken out into the field to test it and extend the functional requirements.

Endnotes

[1] H. Beyer and K. Holtzblatt, *Contextual Design: Defining Customer-Centered Systems*, San Francisco: Morgan Kaufmann, 1998.

[2] InContext Enterprises is a design firm offering a wide range of customer-centered design services. Karen Holtzblatt and Hugh Beyer, InContext's founders, have been key figures in moving the industry away from product-driven, and toward customer-driven, design solutions based on in-depth study of people's work and life practice. They brought the Contextual Design methodology, which draws on proven techniques from a number of fields, to business. Contextual Design techniques are used by companies and at universities all over the world.

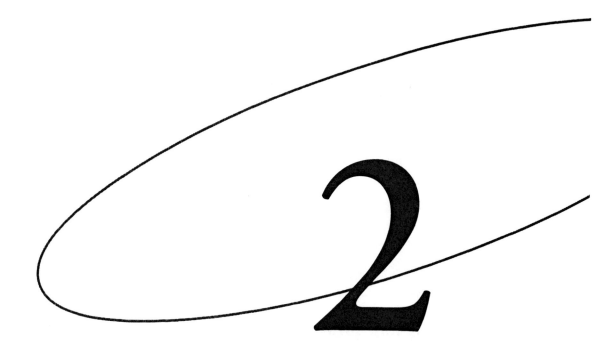

Planning Your Rapid CD Project

If we analyze the "right" way to do customer-centered design for any project we may be dismayed at the time and resources it takes. Today companies want to infuse more user data into their processes. And companies are also resistant to changing their own development processes. So what to do?

Rapid Contextual Design presents our strategies for getting user data into projects. Rapid CD design processes pull together sets of techniques from Contextual Design to help you address your project problems. We present several viable Rapid CD design processes to guide you in choosing what CD techniques to use for your project:

Lightning Fast. Characterize your user population and vision a solution in one to four weeks.

Lightning Fast +. Characterize your user population, vision a solution, mock it up in paper, and test it in four to eight weeks.

Focused Rapid CD. Characterize your user population, collect and consolidate sequences for a task analysis, vision a solution, work out the details by storyboarding, mock it up in paper, and test it in six to ten weeks.

Choose the Rapid CD process best for your problem and organization. Sometimes you will choose a Rapid CD process to go all the way from collecting user data through developing the user interface. Other times you will choose a Rapid CD process just to get some user data into the project. Some Rapid CD techniques better support your corporate methodologies like Agile Programming, Rational Unified Programming (RUP), or your own internal methodologies. Sometimes your choice of Rapid CD techniques will be based on their fit to the time or the resources within which you have to operate.

But no matter the project—even if all you have is a week—you can use a variant of CD techniques. Any user data infused into a project is always better than no user data—it gives you a basis for design and for making informed decisions.

In this chapter we help you walk through planning your Rapid CD project. Once you have a plan you can execute it. Remember that project leading to a clear plan is probably the most important variable for its success.

See Chapter 20, "Putting It into Practice," in *Contextual Design: Defining Customer-Centered Systems.*

Is your project a good candidate for Rapid CD?

Rapid CD techniques can be used on any project to gather customer data. But some projects are well suited for Rapid CD with no trade-offs in quality or extent of the data used and collected. Depending on the scope of your project you may be a good candidate. The basic rule of thumb is to have a small, tight project scope targeting a few clearly defined job roles. (See Chapter 3 to learn how to identify job roles.) Following are some example projects that work well for Rapid CD:

Usability fixes, low-hanging fruit, quick fixes. Sometimes a project or system is just looking for the top fixes to take a significant step to improve the product or system. The central challenge of this project is to observe a cross-section of users, or a subset of the key users, interacting with the existing product, system, or web site. From this data top recommendations can easily be generated.

Market or population characterization for new system concepts. The goal of this kind of project is to understand the users and generate ideas for new system directions. For example, you want to understand the needs of your existing population or of a new user population, you have identified the target users you want to characterize, and there are no more than four job roles. Perhaps you are investigating the viability of entering a new market or you want to determine the new product possibilities for your current market. Or, you need to prioritize directions for in-house system development and so you need to understand the real pain points of your current population. This data may also be the first step in a more complete system development process. Rapid CD can work very well for market characterization projects if you have one to four target job roles.

Web site evaluation and redesign. You realize that your web site is moving from a marketing web site to a work-support web site and you need to provide your users access to information and transactions. Or, you have targeted the homepage for redesign to bring more information up to the top of the site and make the possible transactions visible. In either instance, you know your target user population—the ones that are trying to get to the information—and they cover one to three major job roles.

Rapid CD can evaluate how people currently are using your web site and other related sites as long as the number of your target job roles is small.

Next generation system. You have an existing product (not a product suite) and you have identified your target users for this project. You want to identify what new function to add, how to grow the product, and how to improve the user experience. You are looking for short-term fixes but also new significant features and enhancements. You are interested in better understanding the work and needs of your users. In a Rapid CD process for next generation systems you can get in-depth data for one to two target job roles or reliable but shallower data for up to four job roles.

Supporting a coherent task. You want to build a system to support a coherent task. The task may be accomplished by one to four job roles in collaboration or through a series of hand-offs. You may be integrating support of this task into an existing system, an ERP environment, a portal, a product, or a web site. Your job is to understand how the task is performed, how automation can increase productivity, and how to seamlessly integrate support of this task into a larger tool or system. As long as the number of job roles needed to support this task is not greater than four, Rapid CD can do a good job.

Reporting. You have a system or product that produces a lot of data but it's hard to get the data out in any usable form. You have identified the target users who consume that data and you know the subset of data that you are going to try to provide. The target consumers of the information fall into no more than four job roles including only one job role that is tasked with customizing the reporting software. Rapid CD can do a good job because the interviews with report consumers are short, making coverage possible.

If your project falls into one of these categories, see the recommended project plans in Table 2-1.

Rapid CD Process	Contextual Interviews with Interpretation	Sequence Model with Consolidation	Affinity Diagrams	Wall Walk and Visioning	Story-boarding	Paper Mock-up Interviews with Interpretation
Lightning Fast 1-4 weeks	4-12 users					
Lightning Fast + 4-8 weeks	6-12 users					4-9 users
Focused Rapid CD 6-10 weeks	8-12 users					6-12 users

Table 2-1: A comparison of Rapid CD processes. If you are time or resource constrained, use this table to select the process you want to start with for your project.

What if your project has a larger scope?

Is it worth it to use Rapid CD even if your project doesn't fit into one of the profiles in Table 2-1? If you are trading off getting some user data against getting none, it is always better to get some user data. The problem is that if you have too many job roles you simply have to collect more data, and the more data you collect the longer it takes. If you are covering a very large process, you have a lot of steps, procedures, and people in the process. If you want to collect both local and international data you need to interview more people, which takes more time.

One solution is simply to take the time. You can use the full Contextual Design process so that you can better represent a complex population and system. Or you can use the more simplified Rapid CD techniques to limit the number of work models used but extend the time to accommodate more users overall. You can also start with a *broad and shallow study* covering a few interviews with all the key job roles or in all geographic locations. Then use the results of that study to define subsequent shorter projects that go into detail.

But if you can't take the time or if you don't have the resources, use the following suggestions to chunk the work into shorter sequential steps appropriate for Rapid CD. This philosophy breaks up projects into coherent chunks and works on them one at a time, delivering value at each step.

A long process. Most business processes can be chunked into coherent activities from the beginning to the end. Each activity is supported by a set of people communicating and coordinating with each other (a work group). Use Rapid CD to support a work group at each step of the process. Then move to the next logical work group and activity in the process. Continue until all parts of the process are covered.

Parallel departments. You have a number of departments that do the same or similar work. One example is a claims department in an insurance company; many adjusters for different kinds of claims. Each department does similar tasks but the exact task, the data, and the collaboration changes. Yet you suspect that the same system—the same architecture, the same databases, the same user interaction framework—can support them all. Start with one department that is core to the business and design for it. Move to the next most important department. By the time you get to the last department you'll probably be taking initial paper prototype mock-ups out to users because the work is so similar across departments.

Geographic differences. You want to ensure your web site or system will work for people around the world, but to do that you have to collect data from many, many people worldwide. If you suspect that the work practice is similar around the world (how they use your tool or structure their work) then Rapid CD can help. Choose a part of the world to start in—most companies choose their own country and develop there. Then pick the part of the world you suspect is most different, and do a market characterization there looking for real differences. Also pick the part of the world you suspect is most similar; do a project to check your designs with them adding changes. Combine your findings, normalize your designs, and now iterate in the other parts of the world to finalize the system.

The key to success for all these projects is how you chunk and define the projects. Planning ensures that the process, the work, and the design remains coherent as you move from chunk to chunk. If you use the same team for the whole project the system will end up coherent; if you try to work in parallel you may inappropriately break up the work or fracture the design. This is bad for the user and for system maintenance.

So if you want to work in parallel, create an overseer design group that has power and is deeply involved with the details of all the groups. This group should be composed of a work practice designer, a user interface (UI) designer, and a technologist. This team oversees the work of all the teams and maintains coherence of the design and the work.

What type of Rapid CD should you use?

Although there are many ways to choose between Contextual Design techniques, we have outlined several typical paths through the process that can support the type of projects just outlined. Table 2-1 provided a high-level overview of tasks, Table 2-2 lists resource expectations, and Table 2-3 provides a brief description of each step and how it would be used in each Rapid CD process. Here we also map the project types to the processes. Start with this plan and alter it for your own project design.

Rapid CD Process	Contextual Interviews with Interpretation	Sequence Model with Consolidation	Affinity Diagrams	Wall Walk and Visioning	Story-boarding	Paper Mock-up Interviews with Interpretation
Resources 2-person, full-time team	1 helper in each 2-hour interpretation for higher quality.		2-3 helpers for a day to complete the affinity in 1-2 days.	Stake-holders and developers walk the data and co-create the vision.		1 helper in each 2-hour interpretation for higher quality.

Table 2-2: CD assumes a two-person core team, but it also works for larger teams.

Note in Table 2-2 that at different points in the process Rapid CD techniques benefit from additional helpers: increase data quality, gain perspective from stakeholders, speed the process, and create organizational buy-in.

In the rest of this handbook we lay out the techniques underlying these steps to guide you in their use, with references to the full description in our original book, *Contextual Design: Defining Customer-Centered Systems*.

Following are the variants of Rapid CD. These time estimates assume that you have set up the customer visits before the schedule begins. You may have a department inside your organization or you can hire an agency that will find users in two to three weeks. Or your team may need to take the time to do the visit set-up themselves. See Chapter 3 for a discussion of selecting your users.

These estimates also assume that you have identified the team members and any other helpers, located a team room, and have any tools that you need available for the project.

Lightning Fast (one to four weeks for a two-person team). Lightning Fast Contextual Design is the fastest form of CD you can conduct. Lightning Fast CD is good for a project that is interested primarily in identifying the key issues of a product or in a user population. If you only gather data from four to six people you can build your affinity to organize that data and use it to generate design recommendations in one week. With more users to interview and a more extensive deliverable like a vision or simple personas, your team might take up to four weeks. With more than a two-person team, a larger project can go faster.

Lightning Fast CD will not produce a task analysis (sequence model consolidation) because it does not require capturing any work models. And it does not develop or test any design; you are left to do that using your normal processes. Lightning Fast CD gets customer data up front to drive your design thinking. Any project can probably take a week or two to hear the voice of the users.

See Tables 2-4 and 2-5 for example schedules for Lightning Fast CD.

Lightning Fast + (four to eight weeks for a two-person team). Lightning Fast + CD is the second fastest form of CD you can conduct. Lightning Fast + extends the preceding process to include building a paper prototype of the proposed system and testing it with users. Lightning Fast + is good for projects that are straightforward and not highly task-based; simple fixes, web pages, and reporting interfaces all can be developed more easily without storyboarding.

Simple UI fixes can be generated, represented in a paper mock-up and tested with users. Web pages and reporting UIs that are dominated by visual scanning of information and not explicit tasks and steps also can be designed without formal storyboarding. For such a project moving from vision to interface is reasonable, and it gets in the much-needed user testing to validate the design.

See Tables 2-6 and 2-7 for example schedules for Lightning Fast +.

Focused Rapid CD (six to ten weeks for a two-person team). Focused CD takes more time because it includes consolidating the sequence model to provide a real task analysis and working out the design with storyboards. Focused CD, therefore, is the best process for producing the user stories required by XP and RUP techniques discussed later, as well as in-depth data to drive rich persona development. Focused CD is the best rapid method for developing significant new features, new products, and systems supporting processes or procedures.

A focused project can be extended for more extensive data collection if the process or work group you are trying to support is larger. You can finish within similar time frames as outlined here if you add people to the core team, or you will extend the overall time schedule if you stay with a two-person team.

See Tables 2-8 and 2-9 for example schedules for Focused Rapid CD.

Table 2-3 contains the steps of the Rapid CD processes. Use this to guide your thinking and tailor them to the needs of your projects. Remember that if you add users to any step you need to either add more team members or extend the time of the overall schedule.

Process Step	Description	Lightning Fast	Lightning Fast +	Focused Rapid CD
Recommended Project Types		Quick fixes. Marketcharacterization. Web site evaluation.	Market characterization. Web site redesign. Next-generation system. Reporting.	Web site redesign for transactions. Next-generation system. Supporting a coherent task. Long process.
Problem Analysis	Initial investigation of the market space. Investigate best practices, market expectations, business expectations, and competition. Collect known product or system issues, preliminary design ideas, and stakeholder concerns.	Use information to set focus for interviews. Decide if you want to generate any notes for the affinity from this preliminary research. Interview stakeholders to understand their issues and create buy-in.	Same as Lightning Fast.	Same as Lightning Fast, but for in-house projects add any process reengineering expectations for productivity enhancement.
Contextual Inquiry Interviews	1-on-1 field interviews with key users in their workplace observing and talking about how they do the tasks the project is going to support.	4-12 interviews covering 1-4 job roles in 4-6 businesses or business contexts.	4-12 interviews covering 1-4 job roles in 4-6 businesses, business contexts, or stages of a process.	8-12 interviews covering 2-4 job roles in 4-6 businesses, business contexts, or stages of a process. Focus on observing key tasks to be supported.
Interpret and Model Data	Group analysis of interview findings capturing key issues and sequence models. Invite interested parties and stakeholders to give them a flavor of the data.	Two-person core team interprets the data, capturing notes only.	Two-person core team interprets the data, capturing notes only.	Two-person core team interprets the data capturing notes and sequences with physical and artifact models to provide context. It helps to have a third person on the team or helpers rotating in and out.
Consolidation	Bring individual data together showing issues across the market or user population.	Build affinity only.	Build affinity only.	Build affinity and consolidate sequence models.

Table 2-3:
Brief description of the tasks in each Rapid CD process.

Table 2-3
continued:
Brief description of
the tasks in each
Rapid CD process.

Process Step	Description	Lightning Fast	Lightning Fast +	Focused Rapid CD
Consolidation (continued)	Affinity diagramming creates a hierarchical view of cross-user issues. Get helpers to complete in 1-2 days. Sequence consolidation to generate as-is state tasks.			
Visioning	Walk the consolidated data defining key issues and tasks to support. Create a high-level view of how people will work in the future with the new system.	Walk affinity generating design ideas and fixes. Brain-storm a list of quick recommendations grouped by impact on user. Or vision new product concepts and significant system redesign.	Walk affinity generating design ideas and fixes. Vision new product concepts and significant system redesign.	Vision the new work practice focusing on core task support and integrating with existing systems and manual processes.
Storyboarding	Work out detailed stories of use in the new system guided by the consolidated data and the vision.	Use recommendations and data within your existing processes.	Use vision with your existing processes to generate UI for mock-up interviews.	Build storyboards based on consolidated data. Flesh out redesigned tasks and activities. Clarify automation and business rules.
UI Design and Paper Prototyping	Mock up design in paper and iterate with users to test structure, function, and initial user interface layout. Two to three rounds of mock-up interviews with key users to be supported.	Use recommendations and data within your existing processes.	Mock-up interviews focused on prototype testing and redesign. Two or three rounds of iteration.	Mock-up interviews focused on prototype and process testing and redesign. Three rounds of iteration for process redesign.

The Rapid CD team

Rapid CD projects assume a two-person cross-functional core team: this could be any combination of UI designer, developer, and work practice professional. The designer is knowledgeable in interaction design and visual design. The work practice professional is knowledgeable in user data collection, analysis, work practice redesign, and system design. The developer is knowledgeable about the technology. A cross-functional team ensures that people with different perspectives will pay attention to different aspects of the data and the design. However your two-person team is configured, try to include the missing role as helper or introduce the right skills into the process as needed. For example, involve the UI designer in storyboarding and paper prototyping.

Time projections presented in this book for Rapid CD projects assume that these two people will be full time on the project. At different points in the project, helpers are recommended to shorten the process, or to infuse their expertise. If you have a larger team you can collect more data in the same time frame. Or you can identify a core team of two and then augment the team at key times with others.

All the Rapid CD processes benefit from stakeholders, interested parties, developers who will be coding the project, and others participating at different points in the project to incorporate their perspective and to create buy-in. To improve the data invite people to the interpretation sessions. Every project will go faster if you have helpers participating in the affinity building; they get to know the data and to lend a hand. To enhance the design thinking and create shared ownership of the design invite stakeholders and those who will build the product to the visioning sessions. Although any Rapid CD process can be performed by two people, all will benefit in quality and the work will speed up with the introduction of helpers.

You may not have two resources who can be dedicated full time. Or you may want to involve your marketing professionals or analysts more heavily in the first part of the process and your interaction designers and technologists in the second half of the project. You can do this if you dedicate one person to the project throughout for continuity and overlap others' participation. For example, if you want to roll in interaction designers later, have them attend one or two interpretation sessions, include them in affinity building, and start them full time with the vision. Careful planning can make these transitions work.

But be careful of your expectations; two people can't redesign a whole business process supporting multiple job roles in two weeks, no matter what method is used! With unreasonable expectations like this you need to focus on educating your community (See Chapter 16 for a discussion of organizational change issues). In that case just get whatever data you can in the time available, use it, share it, and talk about how it impacted the design and decision-making. Next time you may get to take another step toward a more complete user-centered design process.

Finally, more and more companies are expecting their teams to be distributed. Throughout this handbook we make reference to how to use Rapid CD in this way. We do recommend, however, that you plan enough face-to-face time to create a shared understanding of the user and the system. It is always better for communication and design coherence to work as a co-located team. But if you can't do that, look for the tips throughout the book.

Who are your stakeholders?

Any project in any organization has to manage its stakeholders and interested parties. Managers, related projects, people who will build the product all care about the data and need to be brought into the design.

When you start your project, identify who these people are and how you are going to involve and communicate with them. Don't disappear into your design process, develop great ideas, then wonder why no one is listening. Following are some suggestions:

Gather their goals, worries, and entering ideas. For key stakeholders and influencers, do some informational interviews at the beginning of your project. Use this to help set project and interview focus. Know their plans for the product and any design ideas they are attached to, then watch out for whether it looks like the idea will be supported by user data or not. Be prepared to talk with them about your findings.

Involve them. Take them out on one field visit with you so they can hear the data directly and understand its value. Include them in interpretation sessions to get their perspective and technical or business expertise. Invite them to share sessions as part of checkpoint meetings to keep them informed. Hold a group visioning session to share the data and solicit their design input. Take them out on mock-up interviews so they can see how the design is being received. Involvement breeds buy-in. This is especially important for product managers, marketers, and developers who will take the product forward after you define it.

Plan formal times to communicate progress. Some teams just use their team room as a continuous place to hold bag lunches and open sessions to share their data and designs. Other teams created checkpoint meetings with more formal presentations of user stories and insights from the interpretation sessions. Once you have an affinity you can walk people through selected parts of the wall. With friendly stakeholders the natural share meetings for user data and storyboards become a forum for a checkpoint meeting. Finally, plan one or two formal presentations midway and at the end of the project.

Communicate their way. Different people can understand information in different ways. Some people will love walking the affinity because it gets them close to the data. Others will like storyboards because they can envision how a process might unfold. But most people and all managers want slide shows; we find this to be the usual form of communication within companies. The affinity diagram lends itself to slide show format—you can use the labels as content and the Post-it® notes as talking points. Create a slide show deliverable after you collect the data to introduce it and your design recommendations. Then when you have a completed and tested design, create a slide show sharing the final design and the user quotes supporting it.

Communicate the design. In addition to slide shows, user interfaces are the language of design communication. Show your paper mock-ups and walk people through them at checkpoint meetings. When you start putting your mock-ups online, share these wire frames. Finally, to bring the results of your mock-up interviews alive you may need to communicate the design via a working demo or

HTML version of the visual interface. These are all effective ways of helping people visualize your design ideas.

Do you have a predefined software methodology?

Some companies have software methodologies within which any user-centered design process must fit. CD, in general, and Rapid CD, specifically, can fit into any software or system development methodology. Most methodologies define a series of stages, each with deliverables and milestones. Few define specific ways of gathering requirements so CD easily fits the bill. Methodologies differ in the deliverables they require for their milestones. The natural data and design artifacts of CD easily can be used as inputs into any methodology's format. But sometimes a methodology will require the collection of certain types of data and the production of certain design artifacts. If this is the case, you must plan your Rapid CD process to ensure that you get the necessary deliverables.

Following are some typical methods or requirements that affect your project planning.

General corporate methodologies

Most corporate methodologies are broken into four main segments:

Business case. Define the marketing or work improvement rationale for building a new or revised product or system.

Requirements gathering. Gather user needs and overall business needs to guide building the product or system.

Design. Detailed design of the product or system, both the user interface and underlying technology, making sure it can be implemented.

Implementation. Build and test the user interface and the overall system.

Contextual Design can support all these steps like this:

Business case. This is the same as the Rapid CD market characterization. Understand the needs and generate product concepts with business intelligence to support investing time and money into development.

Requirements Gathering. This is the same as the Rapid CD project for next-generation system, coherent task, or new product or system. This means get the detailed data on issues and tasks needed to develop a system and generate system requirements at the level of the UI and the function. Some companies would be satisfied with requirements extracted from untested storyboards. We prefer that you finalize your requirements after you define and test your user interface.

Design. In this step you create the implementation structure that will support the function and UI defined through your Rapid CD process. There is usually some negotiation at this point to fit implementation into the time available. Any changes at the user-visible level need to be checked and, where necessary, tested with users.

Implementation. This is the step where you code what was designed. Here you test the system with users first with running prototypes and then with Alpha and Beta releases.

If you must comply with a corporate methodology, choose Focused Rapid CD and map the steps to your deliverables. Use the data and artifacts of the CD process to inform the documents and specifications you create for your corporate processes.

Rational Unified Process

The traditional RUP[1] approach is very similar to (indeed, is an outgrowth of) the preceding corporate process. RUP phases include business modeling, requirements, analysis and design, implementation, test, and deployment.

Use the Focused Rapid CD process to support RUP as follows.

Business modeling. Use the first half of Focused Rapid CD, up to visioning. The goal is to develop an understanding of how the business operates now. This may be captured in business process diagrams or as-is use cases. Rapid CD can be a critical tool in discovering the real, informal, and ad-hoc processes that make the system work. It gives a structured way to collect business rules when those rules are not explicit in the organization. Consolidated sequences are as-is use cases.

Requirements. Use the second half of Focused Rapid CD to collect any additional task data needed to redesign the tasks to be supported by the new system. Use cases become the key representation of user behavior in the new system. Storyboards are the to-be models and will feed use case development. (See Chapter 15 for a use case example.)

Analysis and design. Use storyboarding from the Focused Rapid CD process to feed the standard RUP process to develop object models directly from use cases. Or consider developing a User Environment Design. It can be an important way to capture the proposed system and its relationships.

Agile or Extreme Programming (XP)

XP[2] is one of several "agile programming methods"—methods that focus developing your system in a series of simple modules, each of which deliver value to the customer. Rather than spending a lot of time in up-front planning and modeling, the XP process works closely with customer stakeholders to define each module, and then builds it, ships it to the customer for feedback, iterates it, and moves on to the next piece. The system is built up quickly through rapid iteration.

XP organizes development around rapid iterations using Release Planning and Iteration Planning to decide what to build. User stories define how the user will work in the new system. We recommend Focused Rapid CD for XP, making it a more user-centered design process (see the box, **What is XP?**).

Release Planning. Rapid CD provides the detailed information to decide what should go into a release. The XP philosophy is not to plan too far ahead because things will change anyway; accordingly, use a Lightning Fast style project to raise key issues. Or use Focused Rapid CD through storyboarding to also get sequences to guide the development of user stories. Bring all data into the Release Planning meeting and work out with your customer what to implement for this release.

Iteration Planning. Use CD field interviews to track the success of each iteration with your actual users. Identify problems for each iteration as you go, providing continual refinement to your project direction. Use the Iteration Planning meetings to look at issues being raised by prior iterations, and agree with your customer on prioritizing solutions. Use paper prototyping to iterate your design with users in paper or wire frames before coding.

See Chapter 15 for discussion of Rapid CD and XP.

What is XP?

XP is one of several "agile programming methods"—methods that focus on getting useful value to the customer quickly and iterating rapidly, rather than spending a lot of time in up-front planning and modeling. The philosophy behind these methods is that the up-front planning takes a huge amount of time and is always, to some degree, wrong anyway—and that if it then takes a year to deliver the system you don't find out that you're wrong until it's far too late. Instead, XP introduces a set of practices that keep the team closely tied to the customer.

The core practices of XP include:

Work as a whole team. The team, including the customer or customer representative, makes all design and planning decisions together.

The planning game. XP plans short-turnaround releases through face-to-face meetings in which the features to be included in the next release are decided.

User stories. Features are captured as user stories, describing how a user will perform a task in the new system. User stories are simple, informal, and usually written on an index card.

Rapid iteration. XP develops a project in a series of iterations, each no more than two to three weeks. Each iteration is a working subset of the system, and can be used by the customer for evaluation or in production.

Tight customer involvement. Because user stories are high level, the details of behavior and implementation have to be worked out when the coder starts work. At this point the customer or customer representative works with the developer to flesh out the details and ensure that the design makes sense.

As these practices suggest, XP already has a customer-centered attitude. However, all the usual problems with understanding customer needs apply to XP projects also: The customer representative is only one person, and cannot accurately represent all customers' needs. The representative is usually not currently doing the work the system is to support, and may not have done it for some time. The representative is no more capable than any other customer of making their tacit work practice explicit. Without being situated in their place of work, they cannot remember all the details of what they do daily.

To overcome these problems, expand XP with Rapid CD. Use Contextual Inquiry interviews to get first-hand knowledge of the work you will support. Interpret the data as a team, and use it as fodder for release planning. Do a quick vision if you need to; summarize your design ideas in user stories. Mock up your UIs before committing them to code and use paper prototype interviews to get the design right. Then, after each iteration, do short Contextual Inquiry interviews with customers to ensure you're still on track. (See in Chapter 15, the **Rapid CD for an Agile Development Process** box.)

Personas

Many companies are interested in creating personas as part of their development process. We find personas to be a good way to communicate customer data to the people who did not participate in collecting the data. They give the development team a way to get to know their users and a story to make the user real. So the development of personas augments a good user-centered design process and a good user-centered design process ensures that you get high-quality, rich data to make your personas real.

The best Rapid CD process for producing rich personas is Focused Rapid CD because it collects not only issues from the affinity diagram but also sequences for the task analysis. Consolidated sequence models, which are called for in Focused Rapid CD, will give you a richer persona, but will take more time. If instead you choose to use either Lightning CD process you can write personas based on the issues and build your task story around one of the observed scenarios from your users. If all you want are personas, consider using the first half of Focused Rapid CD up to the vision to get this richer data quickly, then carry on with your usual development process (see Chapter 9).

Usability testing

Many companies have started to get user data into their design process through usability tests. Usability tests presume that requirements have already been gathered and that a design has been built so that it can be tested. Rapid CD and any CD process are about bringing user data into the beginning of the design process to affect the requirements, the product or system concept, and the overall usability. As such, Rapid CD would precede usability testing in the lab in any software methodology.

Managing your project

No project succeeds without a dedicated project leader. The project leader plans the project with the team and oversees its execution. The project leader creates and manages the project schedule, makes sure the customer visits are set up, and generally tracks the tasks. The project leader makes sure that supplies are available, a team room or place to work is available, and is the point person for communicating to the organization. Good project leaders can multitask because they have to do all these things and participate on the project as well! In a two-person team one person usually is designated the project leader.

Throughout the book you will see tips on managing the visits, the people, and the project. We will list supplies for different tasks and tips on logistics. To get you started, the following are some example schedules for Rapid CD projects that you can use as a model and modify.

Creating the project schedule

Scheduling your project on a day-to-day level is about making trade-offs to get the work completed. Depending on the project, the number of team members, and the project length, there are an endless number of possible schedules. The goal is to make sure that you don't overextend the team by stacking too many interviews on top of each other. For the best interpretation results, interviews should be interpreted within 48 hours.

If you have the budget and can get a group of interviews scheduled in one remote location you can also have the whole team travel out and perform interpretation sessions off site.

The following considerations will help you develop a workable schedule. Sample schedules, assuming an experienced team and that all preparation has been completed, follow.

Inexperienced team. If you have one or two untrained members, bring them up to speed in "offline" training for how to interview before the project starts. Then train them in each process as you go. Go on the first set of customer interviews shortly after the training to solidify team members' new knowledge.

Allow enough time for customer visit setup. It takes time to set up customer visits. Plan for a minimum of two to three weeks lead time if you have a group in your organization devoted to this or are using an outsourced provider. But if you are doing it yourself expect it to take three to four weeks. You will stay on track with your project if you don't assume that you can do it faster—all that happens is that you do less in a week and drag the project time out.

Start with a few interviews. Interview a few people at a time. Starting with two key interviews and interpreting them right away means that you can start to learn the users and the data. Remember that the interpretation session helps reset your interview focus—you do better interviews after you start interpreting. So don't stack up the interviews so that you have too many interpretations to do.

Create a day-by-day plan. If you plan your week well everyone will know where they are supposed to be and can plan accordingly. Day-by-day schedules structure your time and set expectations for how long things will take—you will know when you are falling behind and will be able to adjust.

Conduct weekly process checks. At the end of each week (or more often) gather the team and do pluses and minuses on your process. Say what is working well in the process, the schedule, and the team dynamics and what needs to be improved. Brainstorm fixes for the problems and try them the next week.

Respect the home/work balance. No one can work all the time; down time is important not only for family life but simply to stay sharp. Contextual Design is mentally demanding (that's what makes it fun). A Contextual Design project is intense because people are working together all the time collecting, interpreting, and thinking about the data and the design. So plan for down time, even silly time.

Getting a team room

We recommend dedicating a room to the team design effort. The team is working together continuously, and taking the time to look for space, pack up materials, and relocate continuously wastes time.

During interpretation sessions it is best to project the data capture on the wall, and flipcharts are a handy way to capture work models. The affinity diagram is built first in paper on the wall, often by a group of people. When stakeholders come to interact with the data and vision, the team needs a space to hold the event.

More important, the affinity diagram and work models represent everything the team has discovered, structured for easy understanding. Keeping the data on the wall means that the team literally is surrounded by their customer data. It is readily available to consult during storyboarding and UI design. Whether the team is working together for one week or ten, having one place to go where everything you need is at hand will speed your Rapid CD process.

Finally, the team room also acts as a living record of the design process. A team member or manager who wants to catch up can browse the walls on their own, or another team member can use the walls to tell them what has happened. One manager told us he prefers to use the room to find out how the team is doing—he found it more immediate and more real than a status report or presentation.

So, try to get a dedicated team room for the duration of your project. Most teams start out complaining that it is impossible in their organization, but all have figured out how to get dedicated space once they realized its value for moving the project forward.

Sample schedules

Depending on the project, the number of team members, and the project length, there are an endless number of possible schedules. Here are some core sample schedules for each type of Rapid CD. Preparation work to set up visits, get the team room and other resources, and staff the team occur before these schedules start. Each schedule assumes a full-time two-person team experienced in the contextual techniques. Teams new to the process need to include more time for learning.

Field interviews are one-on-one with an interviewer and the user for approximately two hours each. Interviews in the same day are scheduled at the same location for each interviewer or within reasonable driving time.

Helpers are indicated in the schedule when they are essential for completing in the time scheduled. We always suggest two to four additional helpers to complete the affinity in one day. You need 60 to 80 affinity notes per person to complete the affinity in one day. Then the core team can do any clean-up the next day.

We also recommend helpers to increase the quality of the data, to share the findings as they are happening, and to create buy-in in any interpretation session for initial contextual field interviews and for mock-up interviews. Each helper can be in one two-hour interpretation session; they do not have to be dedicated (see the box, **Managing the perception of time**). These helpers are not essential to the time frame, although one additional person in a mock-up interpretation session in Focused Rapid CD will make capturing the issues easier.

The purpose of these sample schedules is to help you think about how to structure time into weeks so that you can modify the plan based on your own needs. We also include a sample of collecting data on the road for compressed trips overseas.

Lightning Fast

Just how fast Lightning Fast is depends on how many interviews you do, and if you can bring in helpers to build the affinity. If you have a larger team you can also do more interviews in parallel in the same time frame and still build the affinity within two to three days without additional resources. These two schedules show interviews with six customers versus 12 customers.

Sample Schedule 1 (Table 2-4): Six customers, five to six days to gather, interpret, and organize the data and brainstorm solutions. Preparation for visits and presentation of findings is not included.

Monday	Tuesday	Wednesday	Thursday	Friday
AM Two parallel customer interviews. Return immediately for interpretation.	**AM** Same as Monday	**AM** Same as Monday	**ALL DAY** Build the affinity of approximately 300-400 affinity notes. Include at least 2-4 more people to help. With no helpers, two people will need Friday to finish. This will extend the schedule by one day.	**ALL DAY** Finish any clean-up of the affinity by 11:00 a.m. Walk the affinity to generate design ideas. Brainstorm recommendations as a group. Capture recommendations online during the session. Formal preparation of recommendations is not included.
PM Two back-to-back interpretation sessions. Bring in a third person for perspective and buy-in. Finish both interpretations.	**PM** Same as Monday Discuss findings and reset focus to ensure the quality of the data.	**PM** Same as Monday Finish all interpretations by end of day.		

Table 2-4: Schedule for a one week long Lightning Fast project.

Sample Schedule 2 (Table 2-5): Twelve customers, five to six days to gather, interpret, and organize the data and brainstorm solutions. Preparation for visits and presentation of findings is not included.

Monday	Tuesday	Wednesday	Thursday	Friday
Week 1: Six to eight contextual field interviews				
AM Two parallel customer interviews. Return immediately for interpretation.	**AM** Same as Monday	**AM** Same as Monday	**ALL DAY** *Option 1* Build preliminary affinity of approximately 300-400 affinity notes. Include at least 2-4 people to help. With no helpers, two people will need Friday to finish. *Option 2* Two additional customer interviews and interpretations.	**ALL DAY** *Option 1* Clean up affinity. Check affinity, identify holes for subsequent interviews. *Option 2* Do a rough affinity structure with high-level labels to look for holes in the data. *Both* Reset focus for next round. *Checkpoint* Run an informal checkpoint with stakeholders to share findings.
PM Two back-to-back interpretation sessions. Bring in a third person for perspective and buy-in. Finish both interpretations.	**PM** Same as Monday	**PM** Same as Monday Discuss findings and reset focus to ensure the quality of the data.		

Table 2-5: Sample schedule for a three-week Lightning Fast project.

49

Table 2-5
continued:
Sample schedule
for a three-week
Lightning Fast pro-
ject.

Monday	Tuesday	Wednesday	Thursday	Friday
Week 2: Four to six more contextual field interviews, build affinity				
Same as Week 1	Same as Week 1	Same as Week 1 If *Option 2*, start building the affinity.	**ALL DAY** Build the affinity of approximately 500-600 affinity notes. *Option 1* You have an existing affinity. Roll additional notes into existing structure. Include at least 2-4 people to help. *Option 2* No affinity yet. Take two days with 2-3 helpers.	**ALL DAY** Finish building the affinity. Organize visioning session.
Week 3: Vision and create recommendations				
ALL DAY Walk the affinity. Anyone who will be in the vision must walk the data. Invite key stakeholders. Generate issues and hot ideas. Vision (do at least one).	**ALL DAY** Vision all day. Do pluses and minuses after 3-4 visions. Overcome minuses with DIs or additional visions.	**ALL DAY** Continue visioning if needed or start vision consolidation.	**ALL DAY** Finalize consolidated vision. Abstract potential feature requirements from vision.	**ALL DAY** Finish requirements and start planning communication of ideas to others.

Lightning Fast +

These sample schedules extend what is done with Lightning CD to include generating a UI that is tested with customers in two or three rounds of iterative paper prototype interviews. Lightning Fast + can include four to 12 Contextual Inquiry interviews and four to nine paper prototype interviews. The two variations presented next build on the Lightning Fast schedules, including the additional steps.

Two people conduct each paper prototype interview, lasting two hours. We recommend adding a helper to each paper prototype interpretation session to speed capturing notes and adding a new perspective.

Your helper does not need to be the same person for each paper prototype interview interpretation session. This person can vary from session to session; just be sure that your helper is familiar with the prototype pieces, what is being tested, and how prototype interviews are conducted.

Managing the perception of time

Time and perception of time affects the way teams and management see the success of a project. When evaluating a process, managers tend to focus more on lapsed calendar time rather than the number of resources. Missing the market window and milestone dates is more visible than getting some extra helpers for the consolidation work.

We therefore recommend that you bring in helpers to build the affinity. If you have one person for every 50-80 Post-it® notes you can build the affinity in 1-2 days. Doing so will help you avoid the complaint received by one of our clients about the affinity being "too heavyweight" because it took two people two weeks to build it.

Time blocks are another sensitivity. Helpers can usually afford a three-hour time commitment, but days on end looks like an interruption to "real work." Bring your helpers in for half-days at a time to avoid this complaint. So always keep in mind lapsed time and requests for time blocks when scheduling.

Sample Schedule 1 (Table 2-6): Four weeks to conduct six customer field interviews; gather, interpret, and organize the data; vision a solution; build a paper prototype; and conduct two rounds of prototype interviews with six additional customers. Preparation for visits and presentation of findings is not included.

Note: With helpers for the affinity so it can be completed in one day, this schedule can accommodate eight initial field interviews.

- Week 1: Conduct six field interviews and affinity building.

- Week 2: Vision and identify UI elements.

- Week 3: Create paper mock-ups, conduct the first round of three prototype interviews.

- Week 4: Iterate the paper prototypes, conduct the second round of three prototype interviews.

Monday	Tuesday	Wednesday	Thursday	Friday
Week 1: Six contextual field interviews, build affinity				
AM Two parallel customer interviews. Return immediately for interpretation.	AM Same as Monday	AM Same as Monday	ALL DAY Build preliminary affinity of approximately 300-400 affinity notes. Include at least 2-4 people to help. With no helpers, two people will need Friday to finish.	ALL DAY Finish any clean-up of the affinity, if needed. Prepare for visioning session.
PM Two back-to-back interpretations. Bring in a third person for perspective and buy-in. Finish both interpretations.	PM Same as Monday Discuss findings and reset focus to ensure the quality of the data.	PM Same as Monday Finish all interpretations by end of day.		

Table 2-6: Schedule for a four week long Lightning Fast + project.

Table 2-6
continued:
Schedule for a four
week long Light-
ning Fast + project.

	Monday	Tuesday	Wednesday	Thursday	Friday
Week 2: Vision and identify UI elements					
	ALL DAY Walk the affinity. Anyone who will be in the vision must participate. Invite stakeholders. Generate issues and hot ideas. Vision (do at least one).	**ALL DAY** Vision all day. Do pluses and minuses after 3-4 visions. Overcome minuses with DIs or additional visions.	**ALL DAY** Continue visioning if needed or start vision consolidation.	**ALL DAY** Finalize consolidated vision. Use the consolidated vision to identify UI elements.	**ALL DAY** Finish identifying UI elements and start building the paper prototype.
Week 3: Build paper prototype and test with three users					
	ALL DAY Build paper prototypes.	**ALL DAY** Finish building paper prototypes. Make enough copies for this week's interviews.	**ALL DAY** Conduct Round 1, two prototype interviews at one location. *Option* Start interpretation or do third interview here.	**AM** Conduct Round 1 with third user. **PM** Interpret paper prototype interviews with one helper if possible.	**ALL DAY** Interpret paper prototype interviews with one helper. Discuss changes to the prototype.
Week 4: Make design changes and test new prototype with three users					
	ALL DAY Determine changes needed to UI.	**ALL DAY** Rebuild paper prototype. Make copies for this week's interviews.	**AM** Conduct Round 2, two paper prototype interviews at one location. **PM** Interpret paper prototype interviews with one helper if possible.	**AM** Finish Round 2 with third user. **PM** Finish all interpretations. Start design changes.	**ALL DAY** Discuss design changes. Finalize UI. Start preparing to share or begin visual design.

Sample Schedule 2 (Table 2-7): Six weeks to conduct 12 customer field interviews; gather, interpret, and organize the data; vision a solution; build a paper prototype; and conduct three rounds of prototype interviews with nine additional customers. Preparation for visits and presentation of findings is not included.

- Week 1: Conduct six to eight contextual field interviews, optional preliminary affinity.

- Week 2: Conduct four to six more interviews, build affinity.

- Week 3: Vision and identify UI elements.

- Week 4: Create paper mock-ups, conduct the first round of three prototype interviews.

- Week 5: Iterate the paper prototypes, conduct the second round of three prototype interviews.

- Week 6: Iterate the paper prototypes, conduct the third round of three prototype interviews.

Monday	Tuesday	Wednesday	Thursday	Friday
Week 1: Six contextual field interviews				
AM Two parallel customer interviews. Return immediately for interpretation.	**AM** Same as Monday	**AM** Same as Monday	**ALL DAY** *Option 1* Build preliminary affinity of approximately 300-400 affinity notes. Include at least 2-4 people to help.	**ALL DAY** *Option 1* Clean up the affinity. Check affinity, identify holes for subsequent interviews.
PM Two back-to-back interpreta-tion sessions. Bring in a third person for perspective and buy-in. Finish both interpretations.	**PM** Same as Monday	**PM** Same as Monday Discuss findings and reset focus to ensure the quality of the data.	With no helpers, two people will need Friday to finish. *Option 2* Two additional customer interviews and interpretations.	*Option 2* Do a rough affinity structure with high-level labels to look for holes in the data. *Both* Reset focus for next round. *Checkpoint* Run an informal checkpoint with stakeholders to share findings.
Week 2: Four to six more contextual field interviews, build affinity				
Same as Week 1	Same as Week 1	Same as Week 1 If **Option 2**, start building affinity.	**ALL DAY** Build affinity of approximately 500-600 affinity notes. *Option 1* You have an existing affinity. Roll additional notes into existing structure. Include at 2-4 people to help. *Option 2* No affinity yet. Take two days with 2-3 helpers.	**ALL DAY** Finish building the affinity. Organize visioning session.

Table 2-7: Schedule for a six week long Lightning Fast + project.

Table 2-7 continued: Schedule for a six week long Lightning Fast + project.

	Monday	Tuesday	Wednesday	Thursday	Friday
Week 3: Vision and create recommendations					
	ALL DAY Walk the affinity. Anyone who will be in the vision must walk the data. Invite key stakeholders. Generate issues and hot ideas. Vision (do at least one).	**ALL DAY** Vision all day. Do pluses and minuses after 3-4 visions. Overcome minuses with DIs or additional visions.	**ALL DAY** Vision if needed or start vision consolidation.	**ALL DAY** Finalize consolidated vision. Use the consolidated vision to identify UI elements.	**ALL DAY** Finish identifying UI elements and start building the paper prototype.
Week 4: Build paper prototype and test with three users					
	ALL DAY Build paper prototypes.	**ALL DAY** Finish building paper prototypes. Make enough copies for this week's interviews.	**ALL DAY** Conduct Round 1, two paper prototype interviews at one location. *Option* Start interpretation or do third interview.	**AM** Conduct Round 1 with third user. **PM** Interpret paper prototype interviews with one helper if possible.	**ALL DAY** Interpret paper prototype interviews with one helper. Discuss changes to the prototype.
Week 5: Make design changes and test new prototype with three users					
	ALL DAY Determine changes needed to UI.	**ALL DAY** Rebuild paper prototype. Make copies for this week's interviews.	**AM** Conduct Round 2, two paper prototype interviews at one location. **PM** Interpret prototype interviews with one helper if possible.	**AM** Finish Round 2 with third user. **PM** Finish all interpretations. Start design changes.	**ALL DAY** Discuss design changes.
Week 6: Make design changes and test new prototype with three users					
	ALL DAY Determine changes needed to UI. Start rebuilding prototype.	**AM** Rebuild paper prototype. Make copies for this week's interviews. **PM** Conduct Round 3, one prototype interview.	**AM** Conduct Round 3, two paper prototype interviews at one location. **PM** Interpret prototype interview with one helper if possible.	**AM** Interpret paper prototype interview with one helper if possible. **PM** Complete all interpretations.	**ALL DAY** Discuss design changes. Finalize UI. Start preparing to share or begin visual design.

Focused Rapid CD

These sample schedules add sequence models and storyboarding to the design process. Sequences allow the team to do a true task analysis and to guide the redesign with task steps. Storyboards work out a work practice, simple business process, or focused life activity in detail, ensuring the coherence of the work.

Sequence modeling, sequence consolidation, and storyboarding add more time to the schedule. To more easily capture sequences we recommend a third person to help in interpretation sessions as well as in prototype interpretations. Again, these helpers need not be committed to the team permanently. As usual we recommend helpers for building the affinity diagram (see the box, **Day-byday scheduling keeps you on track**).

Day-by-day scheduling keeps you on track

These schedules are typical of our planning process. We find that day-by-day schedules help the team deliver on time. Since you can predict length of time for field interviews, interpretation sessions, building the affinity, and other processes you can schedule them directly into the day. You can then reliably recruit helpers for time blocks.

You can also see when your planning is not realistic. You can tell whether or not you can really do all of your interpretations in 48 hours or if you're building evening and weekend work into your schedule. For example, knowing how long it takes to drive to and from an interview site, that 2-2.5 hours will be spent in each interview, and estimating how long it will take to travel within the customer site between interviews and to eat lunch will tell you whether or not you have the three hours you need to complete an interpretation at the end of the day. Day-by-day planning helps you get control over your daily life and win respect by delivering on time.

Following are two variations representing six or 12 Contextual Inquiry interviews, with two and three rounds of prototype interviews, respectively.

Sample Schedule 1 (Table 2-8): Six weeks to conduct six customer field interviews; gather, interpret, and organize the data including the sequence model; vision and storyboard a solution; build a paper prototype; and conduct two rounds of prototype interviews with an additional six customers. Preparation for visits and presentation of findings is not included.

Note: Here we show a different configuration for interviewing that can be used in any schedule.

- Week 1: Conduct six field interviews, affinity building, and sequence consolidation.

- Week 2: Finish consolidation and vision.

- Week 3: Storyboard.

- Week 4: Identify UI elements and create paper mock-ups.

- Week 5: Conduct the first round of three prototype interviews and iterate the paper prototypes.

- Week 6: Conduct the second round of three prototype interviews and determine the final UI.

Table 2-8:
Schedule for a six-
week focused pro-
ject.

	Monday	Tuesday	Wednesday	Thursday	Friday
Week 1: Six contextual field interviews, build affinity, consolidate sequences					
	AM Interview in parallel at two locations. **PM** Interview in parallel at two locations completing four interviews.	**ALL DAY** Complete four interpretations in back-to-back sessions. Capture sequence models. Include a third person to help if possible. Discuss findings and reset focus to ensure the quality of the data.	**AM** Two parallel customer interviews. Return immediately for interpretation. **PM** Two back-to-back interpretation sessions. Bring in a third person for perspective and buy-in. Finish both interpretations.	**ALL DAY** Build preliminary affinity of approximately 300-400 affinity notes. Include at least 2-4 people to help. With no helpers, two people will need Friday to finish.	**ALL DAY** Consolidate sequence models. This will take all day choosing the top 2-4 tasks to consolidate.
Week 2: Finish consolidation and vision					
	ALL DAY Finish all consolidation.	**ALL DAY** Walk the Affinity and consolidated sequence models. Anyone who will be in the vision must participate. Build issues lists. Generate hot ideas. Vision (do at least one).	**ALL DAY** Vision all day. Do pluses and minuses after three or four visions. Overcome minuses with DIs and additional visions.	**ALL DAY** Create consolidated vision.	**ALL DAY** Identify cases to storyboard. Start storyboarding. Complete consolidations if necessary.
Week 3: Storyboard					
	ALL DAY Storyboard all day. Add new cases to storyboard as they are identified.	**AM** Continue storyboarding. **End of day** Share storyboards. Invite other stakeholders.	**ALL DAY** Revise story-boards given sharing feedback. Continue storyboarding.	**ALL DAY** Continue storyboarding. Share and fix storyboards.	**ALL DAY** Finish storyboarding as needed or start the next step.
Week 4: Identify UI elements, create paper prototypes					
	ALL DAY Identify UI elements from storyboards.	**ALL DAY** Design UI elements.	**ALL DAY** Start UI designs for paper proto-types.	**ALL DAY** Start building paper prototypes.	**ALL DAY** Finish building paper prototypes. Make copies for first interviews.

Monday	Tuesday	Wednesday	Thursday	Friday
Week 5: Build paper prototype and test with four users				
ALL DAY Conduct Round 1, two prototype interviews at one location.	**AM** Conduct Round 1 with third user.	**AM** Conduct Round 1 with fourth user.	**ALL DAY** Determine changes to UI.	**ALL DAY** Continue redesigning UI. Begin building prototypes with changes.
	PM Interpret paper prototype interviews with one helper if possible.	**PM** Interpret paper prototype interviews with one helper if possible.		
Week 6: Make design changes and test new prototype with three users, determine final UI				
AM Finish building paper prototypes.	**AM** Conduct Round 2, two interviews at one location.	**ALL DAY** Interpret all day.	**ALL DAY** Determine changes to UI.	**ALL DAY** Design final UI.
PM Conduct Round 2, one paper prototype interview.	**PM** Interpret paper prototype interviews with one helper if possible.			

Table 2-8 continued: Schedule for a six-week focused project.

Sample Schedule 2 (Table 2-9): Eight weeks to conduct 12 customer field interviews; gather, interpret, and organize the data including the sequence model; vision and story-board a solution; build a paper prototype; and conduct three rounds of prototype interviews with an additional nine customers. Preparation for visits and presentation of findings is not included.

- Week 1: Conduct six to eight contextual field interviews, optional preliminary affinity.

- Week 2: Conduct four to six more interviews, build affinity and sequence consolidations.

- Week 3: Finish consolidation and vision.

- Week 4: Storyboard.

- Week 5: Identify UI elements and create paper mock-ups.

- Week 6: Conduct the first round of three prototype interviews and iterate the paper prototypes.

- Week 7: Conduct the second round of three prototype interviews and iterate the paper prototypes.

- Week 8: Conduct the third round of three prototype interviews and determine the final UI.

Table 2-9:
Sample schedule
for an eight-week
focused project.

	Monday	Tuesday	Wednesday	Thursday	Friday
Week 1: Six to eight contextual field interviews, optional preliminary affinity					
	AM Interview in parallel at two locations. **PM** Interview in parallel at two locations completing four interviews.	**ALL DAY** Complete four interpretations in back-to-back sessions. Capture sequence models. Include a third person to help if possible. Discuss findings and reset focus to ensure the quality of the data.	**AM** Two parallel customer interviews. Return immediately for interpretation. **PM** Two back-to-back interpretation sessions. Bring in a third person to capture sequence models faster.	**ALL DAY** *Option 1* Build affinity of approximately 300-400 affinity notes. Include at least 2-4 people to help. With no helpers, two people will need Friday to finish. *Option 2* Two additional customer interviews and interpretations.	**ALL DAY** *Option 1* Clean up affinity. Check affinity, identify holes. *Option 2* Do a rough affinity with high-level labels, look for holes. *Both* Reset focus for next round. *Checkpoint* Run an informal checkpoint with stakeholders to share findings.
Week 2: Four to six more contextual field interviews, build affinity, consolidate sequences					
	Same as Week 1	Same as Week 1	Same as Week 1 If *Option 2*, start building the affinity.	**ALL DAY** Build the affinity of approximately 500-600 affinity notes. *Option 1* You have an existing affinity. Roll in additional notes. Include at least 2-4 people to help. *Option 2* No affinity yet. Take two days with 2-3 helpers.	**ALL DAY** Finish building the affinity. Begin sequence consolidation. Choose the top 2-4 tasks to consolidate.
Week 3: Finish consolidation and vision					
	ALL DAY Finish sequence consolidation. This may continue into Tuesday.	**AM** Finish sequence models if necessary. **PM** Everyone visioning, walk data. Build issues list. Generate hot ideas. Pick first idea to vision.	**ALL DAY** Vision all day. Do pluses and minuses after three or four visions. Overcome minuses with DIs or additional visions.	**ALL DAY** Continue visioning. Create consolidated vision.	**ALL DAY** Finish consolidated vision. Identify cases to storyboard. Decide which storyboards to start with.

Monday	Tuesday	Wednesday	Thursday	Friday
Week 4: Storyboard				
ALL DAY Storyboard all day. Add new cases to storyboard as they are identified.	ALL DAY Continue storyboarding. **End of day** Share storyboards. Invite stakeholders.	ALL DAY Revise storyboards. Continue storyboarding. Share and fix storyboards.	ALL DAY Continue storyboarding. Share and fix storyboards.	ALL DAY Finish storyboarding as needed or start the next step.
Week 5: Identify UI elements, create paper prototypes				
ALL DAY Identify UI elements from storyboards.	ALL DAY Design UI elements.	ALL DAY Start UI designs for paper prototypes.	ALL DAY Start building paper prototypes.	ALL DAY Finish building paper prototypes.
Week 6: Test prototype with four users, iterate design				
ALL DAY Conduct Round 1, two paper prototype interviews at one location.	AM Conduct Round 1 with third user. PM Interpret prototype interviews with one helper if possible.	AM Conduct Round 1 with fourth user. PM Interpret prototype interviews with one helper if possible.	ALL DAY Determine changes to UI.	ALL DAY Continue redesigning UI. Begin building paper prototypes with changes.
Week 7: Make design changes and test new prototype with three users, iterate design				
AM Finish building paper prototypes. Make this week's copies. PM Conduct Round 2, one paper prototype interview.	AM Conduct Round 2, two interviews at one location. PM Interpret prototype interviews with one helper if possible.	ALL DAY Interpret all day.	ALL DAY Determine changes to UI.	ALL DAY Continue redesigning UI. Begin building paper prototypes with changes.
Week 8: Make design changes and test new prototype with three users, determine final UI				
AM Finish building paper prototypes. Make copies for this week's interviews. PM Conduct Round 3, one paper prototype interview.	AM Conduct Round 3, two interviews at one location. PM Interpret prototype interviews with one helper if possible.	ALL DAY Interpret all day.	ALL DAY Determine changes to UI.	ALL DAY Design final UI.

Table 2-9 continued: Sample schedule for an eight-week focused project.

Gathering data on the road

You can always send one or two people out on the road to gather data. These on-the-road interviews can be interpreted either while traveling, or when the travelers get home (within 48 hours of the interview). Each interviewer can reasonably conduct three interviews in a day. Because of travel time, these on-the-road weeks tend to add an extra day of work to each week either to account for an entire travel day or to recognize that the team got home very late the night before. As a result, all of our sample schedules tend to slip a day for each week of travel.

The travel location, of course, will determine actual time traveling. Table 2-10 is an example of a Lightning Fast CD schedule that starts with six remote interviews in the first week returning home to interpret.

Table 2-10:
Sample schedule
for gathering data
on the road.

Monday	Tuesday	Wednesday	Thursday	Friday	Monday
AM 9:00-11:00 Two parallel interviews.	**ALL DAY** Return to home office. **Assumption** Travel requires the whole day.	**ALL DAY** Interpret 3-4 interviews.	**AM** Interpret 2-3 interviews.	**ALL DAY** Continue working on the affinity. If no helpers, finish today. If helpers, might start walking the data or leave early.	**ALL DAY** Finish any clean-up of affinity by 11:00 a.m. Walk the affinity to generate design ideas. Brainstorm recommendations as a group. Capture recommendations online during the session. Formal preparation of recommendations is not included.
PM 12:30-2:30 Two parallel customer interviews. 3:30-5:30 Two parallel interviews. **Assumption** Travel the previous day to the interview location.			**PM** Begin building the affinity of approximately 300-400 affinity notes. Include at least 2-4 more people to help.		

Using parallel interpretation sessions to move faster

The schedules we've given you have assumed two core team members and not relied on having more than one helper per interpretation session. If you can enlist more helpers, you can start running parallel interpretations for the Contextual Inquiry interpretation sessions. This means you can interpret twice as many Contextual Inquiry interviews in the same amount of time. However, you can run parallel interpretation sessions only for Contextual Inquiry interviews; they do not work well for paper prototype interview interpretations.

Table 2-11 is an example of how parallel interpretations would work for the Lightning Fast CD schedule with eight interviews.

Monday	Tuesday	Wednesday	Thursday	Friday
ALL DAY Three parallel interviews, completing six by core team members. **Assumption** Interviewers are going to do 2-4 interviews, close enough for each to do three interviews.	**ALL DAY** Three parallel interpretation sessions. Group 1 (interviewer plus at least one helper) interprets Users 1-3. Group 2 (interviewer plus at least one helper) interprets Users 4-6.	**AM** Two parallel customer interviews, User 7 and User 8, conducted by core team members. **PM** Two parallel interpretation sessions, Users 7 and 8.	**ALL DAY** Build the affinity of approximately 300-400 affinity notes. Include at least 2-4 more people to help. If number of notes is larger, include more helpers or more time. Having no helpers will extend the schedule 1-1.5 days.	**AM** Finish any clean-up of affinity by 11:00 a.m. Walk affinity to generate design ideas. **PM** Brainstorm as a group. Capture recommendations online during the session. Formal preparation of recommendations is not included.

Table 2-11: Sample schedule for running parallel interpretations session.

Endnotes

[1] Here are some references for use case development:

> L. Constantine and L. Lockwood, "Structure and Style in Use Cases for User Interface Design," in *Object-Modeling and User Interface Design*, M. van Harmelen (ed.), Boston: Addison-Wesley, 2001.

> A. Cockburn, *Writing Effective Use Cases*, Boston: Addison-Wesley, 2001.

[2] Here are some classic references for this method:

> Manifesto for Agile Software, www.agilesoftware.org, 2001.

> K. Beck, *Extreme Programming Explained: Embrace Change*, San Francisco: Addison-Wesley, 2000.

> A. Cockburn, *Agile Software Development*, Boston: Addison-Wesley, 2002.

> J. Highsmith, *Adaptive Software Development: A Collaborative Approach to Managing Complex Systems*, New York: Dorset House, 2000.

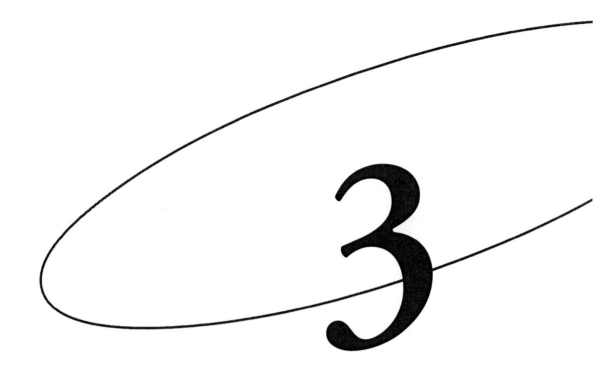

Planning Your Contextual Interviews

Your data is only as good as the people you interview. Your goal is to get a good cross-section of your target user population with a small number of participants. But you also need to get enough coverage of each type of participant. Rapid CD targets initial Contextual Interviews with four to twelve people. You can increase this population, which will increase time or the number of team members and helpers you need to complete the interviews according to schedule.

This chapter explains how to choose your initial sample of people to interview to ensure that you reveal key characteristics and issues in your population. See Chapter 14 for how to select people for paper prototyping interviews to further extend your sample of the population.

Key concepts

Target users. The people you choose to talk with in your interviews.

Job role. A person who does the target work or activity you want to study for your project. This person is performing the tasks you wish to support in your system. A job role may be played by people with different job titles.

Work group. The group of people who work together to get a job done. A work group may be a team, the people who make up a coherent part of a process, a coordinating family or social group, or an informal set of people coordinating to do a task.

Job title. The formal title a person has been given by their organization. Your goal is to collect data about people who are performing a certain set of tasks. Different related job titles may perform that job role. Don't collect data by job title, collect it by job role. For example a sales person, sales manager, and technical sales expert all may be doing the same work you are trying to study. They represent the same job role.

Who should you interview?

If you are doing the next version of a product or system or if you know what type of system you want to build, start by determining the work or life activity to be supported. Ask yourself:

- What is the work or activity you expect to support?

- How does this work fit into the customer's whole work life? To which processes is it attached?

- Who else is involved in making the work happen? With whom do they work and collaborate; who might advise them in getting the work done?

- Who provides the information needed to do the job and who uses the results? Someone may not be a direct user but they direct the work or consume the results.

- What are the key work tasks these people perform that you might want to support?

The answers to these questions will identify your current knowledge of the *work group* you are trying to support. No one works alone and no tasks are done in isolation. So no product or system supporting a task is really supporting only one person. Even if you want to target the main person, it serves you best to sample other key players in the work group. Rapid CD is effective because most work groups have no more than two to four core players.

Example: eChalk

For example, eChalk wanted to support communication within the school setting. Clearly, communication has more than one player. If we think about the work group in the school, core communication revolves around the teacher. On the student side there is the teacher-student-parent circle. On the administrative side there is the teacher-support staff-principal-colleague teacher circle. Each of these circles represents one work group. A good way for eChalk to decide on how to target a Rapid CD project is to choose one of these work groups to start with. In this case eChalk chose the teacher-support staff-principal-colleague teacher work group.

Example: Agilent

For the Agilent project, the team chose a two-person work group: the analysts working on their own projects and the senior scientist who created the testing methods. LANDesk also chose a two-person work group—the system manager and the IT manager—to get the day-to-day perspective as well as the high-level management perspective on the value of simplifying the deployment process.

Example: Apropos

For the Apropos project, the team interviewed customer service representatives while they were on the phone, the customer who called into the call center, and the escalation group members. This is also a work group.

Once you determine the work group that surrounds your target activity or process you can determine which *job roles* to interview. A job role denotes a person who does the target work. We use the term job role because we recognize that any job role may be performed by people with different job titles. When you set up visits you may list several job titles, but be sure to describe the specific job role activities you are looking to observe.

If you are doing a market characterization you may be targeting certain job roles and asking the question, "Where is there opportunity to support this person's work?" In this case start by interviewing the main person, but look for their key tasks and surrounding work group. Plan to expand the interviews to include the wider circle of players.

Our general rule of thumb is to do Contextual Interviews with three to four people performing each job role. Over the years we have found that this number of users will reveal the key issues and work structures necessary to characterize your user population. Start with this base number and then increase who you need to talk to based on the work contexts that need to be considered.

What contexts should be sampled?

Who the people are and what they do are the first criteria for choosing interviewees. You also need to consider the work and social context. You will get the best sample studying very different contexts, rather than studying people from similar contexts. You can even look at best-in-class users and worst-in-class users to see the diversity in skill set; for example, ride with best-in-class sales people to see what makes them good. Your goal is to find the underlying common work structure while considering the variation, so pick customers to sample work context diversity that impacts how people do things.

Diversity in work practice usually is not equivalent to diversity in market segment. If, for example, you are trying to redesign a traditional office desktop toolset you need not plan carefully to sample traditional market segments like finance, high-tech, and retail. Although these business practices differ, the basic requirements for writing letters, creating slide shows, and using spreadsheets will be similar. As such, these different types of companies will not give you substantially different perspectives; just choose a selection across these business types to get some variation. On the other hand, the corporate context, the school context, and the home context are substantially different in the types of tasks, levels of technical sophistication, and basic intent. You want to be sure to get enough users from each of these to see how the issues and work structures change or overlap.

Example: eChalk

So, for eChalk, demographics like married, divorced, or single parent don't really matter given their project focus.

Example: Agilent

Whereas for Agilent, different kinds of manufacturing plants testing different types of substances in the lab using different types of methods may very well affect what is needed from the instrument.

Example: LANDesk

For LANDesk, size of company or number of nodes might affect the value proposition: if a company is deploying on a few machines they may not be motivated to try something new, but if a company has to deploy to thousands of machines locally and globally the efficiency boost will be significant. So, LANDesk varied companies by number of nodes installed (5,000–30,000).

You want to determine which work contexts to sample for explicitly and when you just want to be sure to get some variation. Use your corporate knowledge about how the target users might be affected by context to determine how specific to be about contexts sampled. You want your data to reflect the contexts that represent significant differences in work practice. In this way your requirements and design solutions will be challenged to respond to a breadth of practice variation (see the box, **How can so little data characterize a whole market**).

Geographic cultural is another context. Geography matters when it affects the work itself, implies changes in law that must be conformed to, or implies preferences that influence requirements. Often business practices are unaffected by culture unless the law is different. But acceptance of web sites may vary because of aesthetic preferences and language or image sensitivities. Start by determining if task patterns, organizational structures, and laws are different from culture to culture to aid in your planning.

Local culture also affects the way people work. When you are gathering data locally try to get some variation within the country. Don't just get data from your home city. Your users and sales people soon will become saturated and resent the continuous intrusion anyway. Even businesses developing in-house applications will do best to sample from multiple sites.

Finally, if you are building products for a market, don't think of yourselves as users—your own corporate culture will permeate down to the maintenance staff! Get outside of yourselves.

For Rapid CD you are trying to keep your participant numbers small, so identify two to three contexts that matter and make sure you have at least two people representing each context. Or if context doesn't matter, just go for general variation.

Finally, when picking interviewees use your market data or for business applications your knowledge of the influencer in your company. Focus on customers from the key

How can so little data characterize a whole market?

Consolidated data is built from eight to 30 field interviews and can characterize markets of millions of people. Consolidated data from eight to 10 people can identify a large percent of the key issues that will eventually be identified in the market. For example, even on large projects we routinely consolidate after 10 interviews and then grow the models and affinity from there as more data is collected. An early affinity can show holes in the data to guide further data collection, but already represents the key areas and distinctions that will grow in detail as more data is added. Similarly, additional data adds depth and detail to all models, but the basic structure, central to the project focus, is identifiable early on. So a Rapid CD project with eight to 12 key users will reveal the vast majority of the issues that you need to consider for your project.

Early on in usability testing people were not comfortable with test results from small numbers of users. Whatever the formal arguments, years later we have learned empirically that small numbers are enough. Why? Contextual Design gets its power from designing from an understanding of work practice *structure* without losing variation.

Consolidation helps people see and find the structure in work practice, and this drives successful design. Here is a way to think about it:

We're all different, but we're all alike. Everybody looks different; humans have great variation. People are of different ethnic groups, cultures, and child rearing practices. Everyone chooses different clothes, hobbies, careers, and life styles. So at one level, we are all unique. But at the same time we are all alike, each having one head and body with two arms and two legs. For example, clothing manufacturers can make "off the rack" clothing; making a few adjustments for different body sizes is enough. Structurally, the variation between people is small and the structure of our bodies is common.

There are only so many ways to do work. Any product and system design is really a very narrow focus on the human experience. Within one kind of work, there is only so much variation possible. The roles we play, the intents and goals we have, and the way we do things is common. Variation, once you start looking for structural elements is small. We have found, for example, that there are only two to four strategies for any primary task in a work practice. And if those are the key strategies for that work practice, the question is not which we support, but how we support them all.

Designs that target a certain domain of work are created for a certain set of people doing a fixed set of work tasks, situated in the larger work culture, using the same set of tools, trying to achieve the same kind of goals. Under these constrained conditions, the work practice will have similar patterns. After you have collected data from three to six people doing the same thing, the work pattern and issues start overlapping again and again.

The reason that people get hung up on numbers is that we tend, as human beings, to focus on our variation, our differences, rather than our basic similarities. A focus on variation leads us to design products with near-infinite customizations. These either destructure a system with ever more customizable and slightly different options, or require costly upfront customizations at installation. But if people are all so different how could markets exist? Clearly there is enough similarity of practice between people for the idea of shrink-wrap software and off-the-shelf electronic products to make sense.

markets you think are most likely to spend money; include the users who work for the important manager who has to buy into an internal project.

How do you balance job roles within context?

Once you know exactly who you want to interview and the contexts you want to cover see if they fit the numbers you can cover in a Rapid CD project. If not, you may have to do a series of short projects to cover the space or enlarge your project.

Following are some examples to help you with the thinking process; don't feel like you have to fill out a spread sheet to figure it out, but this structure will help you think about how to balance your choices. Remember your goal is to get variation on the dimensions that matter and let the other variables float.

Example: eChalk

eChalk decided that for their initial releases, the core work group was the teacher circle. Consider the following examples using their problem.

Table 3-1 illustrates two contexts, two job roles, four schools. If eChalk had time for only eight interviews they could do a good sample and look at this core communication dyad.

Table 3-1:
Eight interviews spread out over two roles and contexts.

	Computer teacher	Colleague non-computer teacher	**Total Contexts**
Inner City	2	2	4
Suburb	2	2	4
Total Job Roles	4	4	

If eChalk added two to four more interviews, the 10 to 12 people interviewed could include the principal. To get just a taste of the principal's role, reduce this from two interviews to one in each context, and collect data from only 10 people (see Table 3-2).

Table 3-2:
Interviews with 12 people across three roles and two contexts.

	Computer teacher	Colleague non-computer teacher	Principal	**Total Contexts**
Inner City	2	2	2 (1)	6 (5)
Suburb	2	2	2 (1)	6 (5)
Total Job Roles	4	4	4 (2)	

If eChalk decided that location didn't matter they could cover the full work group in 12 interviews. In Table 3-3 three schools are covered.

Table 3-3:
Twelve interviews spread out across four roles with no concern for context.

	Computer teacher	Colleague non-computer teacher	Principal	Administrative office support staff
Any type of school	3	3	3	3

You don't always have to get the whole work group at each physical location either. Consider the following plan, which still samples the right number of users but from more places. This plan emphasizes the teacher as the core actor and the principal as a secondary player in the work group (see Table 3-4).

Remember, each of these target users interact with others in their related work groups. So you will get data about other job roles outside of this work group, which can drive future studies but also will influence results in this one.

	Computer teacher	Colleague non-computer teacher	Principal	Administrative office support staff	**Total Contexts**
New York 1	1	1	1		
New York 2	1		1		5
Chicago 1	1	1		1	
Chicago 2		1		1	5
Atlanta	1			1	2
Total Job Roles	4	3	2	3	

Table 3-4:
Twelve interviews across four roles and three contexts.

Try laying out your variables in this way to help balance the things you want to consider when planning your project (see the box, **Checklist for determining context**). But remember—whoever you visit, you will learn a lot and increase the quality of your product or system.

Checklist for determining context

Ask yourself some of these questions to determine what contexts matter for your project.

- What is the physical context in which the work happens? Identify the types of locations the work occurs in and determine if that affects the nature of the work.

- Do size and organizational structure of the company matter? Are you interested only in large businesses, or small- to medium-sized businesses? You may be interested only in companies that use a specific process or operate within a particular industry.

- Do income and family structure matter? If you are developing a consumer application this may affect resources and how family members interact.

- Does physical location affect values and lifestyle that will in turn affect the work or access to resources? City dwellers have different values and access to resources than country dwellers. This may matter for your consumer products.

- Do mobility or distribution matter? If your target task may be done by a mobile team or a stationary team, by a distributed team, or by a co-located team, sample these differences.

- Do organizations do the same type of work in different ways? Sample both.

- Do competitors matter? Look at organizations that are using your competitors' products.

What style of interview will you use?

Most field studies will follow the standard format of conducting the interview in the person's workplace or life context that it occurs. This assumes that the work itself is interruptible so that you can talk during the situation, and that significant parts of the target task can be observed within two hours or recounted with a retrospective account of a recent past event (see the box, **Retrospective interview**, Chapter 4).

But some interviewing situations will change how you interview, how many people have to go, and instructions you give to the user. Consider the following:

Intermittent. The work is not continuous; for example, reading documentation, ordering, or searching. Ask the user to save the tasks to do while you are there or to think about tasks they can do for you even if it is earlier than they would have done it. Also, during the interview, do retrospective accounts of tasks that happened in the last two weeks.

Uninterruptible. Some work, like meetings, classroom activity, or manufacturing line work, simply can't be interrupted. Plan instead to have a pre-meeting to get context and talk about what is about to happen, ask to have an informant (someone else who knows the work) sit with you during it if possible, and then have a post meeting to go over what was observed. Sometimes it is possible to take breaks during meetings and talk to the whole group at that time as well. If you want the perspectives of multiple roles during a group context, send more than one interviewer to shadow the two different job roles.

Extremely long. If the process being studied takes place over months or years, like drug development, pick your users to sample different stages in the process. Consider these different job roles. This kind of cross-sectional data is just as good as following the process in real-time and it's a lot shorter. Remember to go to more than one company.

Mobile. For police, traveling sales people, repair workers, and other traveling workers you need to plan to go out on a "run." You will have to be careful about what you can interrupt and what you can't. But you may have to do a longer shift because you are on their time. Collect only the data relevant to your focus, not everything you observe the user doing, or you will never be able to reasonably get through the interpretation session.

Extremely focused. Sometimes the work you are observing is so focused that if you interrupted frequently you would lose the work. Good examples of this are reading and coding. Alternate between longer observation and then discussions of what just happened. If you must see the moment-by-moment details and you can't keep up with your notes, you may want to videotape.

Environment centered interviews. Sometimes the activities you are observing are more dominated by a physical context like a museum to understand what works in interactive exhibits: a retail environment to understand the impact of displays on the buying process, a kiosk to understand how people use it, and the airport to observe mobile device usage. In these cases you are "interviewing" the environmental context by observing and talking with whomever comes to your location. Be sure to have the permission both of the organization and of the people you are talking with directly. Explain what you are doing and why, and be sure to take no for an answer. Wear your company t-shirt, or a shirt provided by the organization to assuage fear.

For a longer discussion of these interviewing situations see Chapter 4, "Contextual Inquiry in Practice," pgs. 73–76, in *Contextual Design: Defining Customer-Centered Systems*.

What logistics do you need to consider?

Planning for a smooth interviewing schedule is your goal. Remember that the idiosyncrasies of the users and their businesses will influence the best of plans. So consider the following issues when picking your users and making your plans:

Distance. The farther the user, the more expensive the cost, the more time is needed to travel back and forth. So if you are going to travel, plan at least two interviews, if not three, for one person at a site. Make the most of the time whenever you go to the customer.

Resistance. Make sure people want to participate; resistance just means they are likely to cancel or cut your time short. Find people that want to do it; remember you are looking for a good informant.

Confidentiality and security. Make sure you understand the confidentiality expectations at that site. Make sure you can go into the workplace and if you have to wear protective gear make sure you can get paper to take notes. If you need to sign a nondisclosure before going, do so. If they are going to resist talking with users in their natural environment try to find someone else.

Time commitment. You are looking for people who willingly will commit to two hours. If you can't find anyone who will do this, get what you can in one hour and know you may want to do a few more interviews.

Cultural issues. Different geographic cultures have different rituals for meetings and may be more or less comfortable with providing negative information. If you are going into someone's home there is different etiquette than if you are at the office. Familiarize yourself with these differences and make sure you behave appropriately, set appropriate expectations, and alter your interviewing process if needed.

Dress. We always recommend dressing up one level of formality than your users. So if you are in a bank, of course you will go in a suit. But if you are going to a home, suits are overkill, wear business casual. If you are going to be following someone working in muddy, construction, or other informal contexts you want to at least wear what is appropriate for the setting.

Interviewing style. Depending on the interviewing context described earlier, you need to prepare the user for what to expect while the interviewer is there. For example, if you are observing a meeting you will do a pre- and post-brief and simply observe during it.

Spacing of interviews. Even though the interview is scheduled with the customer for two hours, allow for 2.5 hours in your schedule. Interviews sometimes run over if the interviewee is willing. You also need to plan for travel time between users within a company and between physical locations.

Coordinating with interpretation sessions. You want to interpret within 48 hours and you can only do three to five interpretations in a day depending on how many people are available. So plan time between interviews for interpretation sessions including travel time back to home office if you are not interpreting on the road (see schedule examples in Chapter 2).

Lost interviews. Always set up more interviews than you need: interviews fall through, people get sick, corporate fires happen. Keep some back-up interviews in your pocket. You can always use them for your mock-up visits later.

How do you find and set up the customer visits?

Many people think that finding the interviewees to interview is the hardest task of user-centered design. Today organizations are set up to get usability test participants but fewer have separate organizations to set up field studies. Eventually when organizations start using field data they will want to set up groups to get these users. We also recommend creating partnerships with customers who agree to be visited to support design work.

We are often asked, "Why would anyone participate? What do we need to do to motivate them?" People participate for many reasons—sometimes because they get paid, or they get free software from a company they value; other "rewards" may be packages to theater or restaurants, or simple gifts. But the people who ultimately volunteer, even when paid, do it because they want to help out the companies that produce their software or hardware—and they get to have their opinion and needs directly affect the product.

Inside of businesses, IT professionals and business analysts have to convince the businesses that field data is the best way to understand and improve the business processes. Sometimes this means going up against the usual practice of having a "user advocate" assigned to speak for the users. But user advocates do not help you characterize your population or ensure that the organization that will be impacted will have a "voice" in the system design. Working directly with users is the best way to create buy-in and increase user adoption. And this is a great argument to management for why you want to have end-user involvement (see the box, **A user advocate isn't the user**).

Without formal organizational support mechanisms to help get customers, we suggest the following strategies:

Work through vendors. Focus group vendors and others in the business of getting users for market studies are a good source for setting up visits that are in the field instead of in a focus group setting. Ethnographic studies are being conducted more and more for marketing and product design so venders are familiar with the process. But if the vender is not used to field studies, work with them closely so they understand the expectations. Expect to pay a fee for each participant. Find a set of these services to call upon. This is the easiest solution to setting up visits.

Work through Sales. Sales often likes to know what is going on in their accounts, and some companies insist you go through the sales department. But you have to motivate Sales to do the work. Give them a presentation of what you are doing and why. Be clear about which of their companies you are looking for and exactly who you want to interview. Expect to nag them a lot. Look for people who get enthusiastic and work through them. Let them come on the interview to see what is going on—this often gets them excited.

A user advocate isn't the user

The core to your success is to get to the real users of your proposed system. Some organizations resist letting teams go to the user because they think they have in-house expertise. Some companies hire business analysts who used to be users in the hope that they will provide the requirements knowledge needed. And some methods like XP advocate that a customer representative is all you need to iterate the design.

But a "representative" user is not the same as a set of current actual users.

A representative user never is. No one person can embody all the users of a real enterprise system. Although interviewing several users reveals a common work practice, no *one* user ever represents that work practice in its entirety. Other stakeholders in the system—secondary users, management, upstream and downstream roles in the process—also must be considered. Furthermore, the more that person becomes part of the engineering organization, the less useful they are as a user surrogate. They learn too much about the technology and they become invested in the team's thinking. They become more empathic to the engineer's challenges and less connected to the challenges they faced in their previous job. We found that our own user representatives are just too nice to us.

Even users cannot articulate their own work practice. We go to the field to collect data while it is happening because even the real users are unaware of their own activities. Users know everything about their work but when they are experts it becomes a habit. And no one watches the details of their own work practice! So if users themselves are unaware of what they do, a user representative who has not done the work for many months or years is also unclear about the real user needs.

So involve the user advocate in your process, put them on the team, or take them with you on interviews but don't use them for a user substitute.

Get to inside support or Sales support. Many companies assign people to work with key customers. These contacts really know the users and are the best source in the sales organization for finding users. Treat them the same as Sales to get them on board.

Work through management. Setting up visits for an internal project is the easiest. You will, however, need to go to the management of the department and explain what you are doing and why. They need to be convinced because you will be "slowing down" their workers. So involve them, don't over use the same sites, and they will help you.

Work through the user advocate. Many IT organizations have to work through a business person who is supposed to represent the user needs. This person can get in the way of getting to the real end user. Explain to them why you need to see a number of people and not just depend on their personal experience (see the box, **A user advocate isn't the user**). Then get them to help pick out the right people, take them on visits, or invite them to be on the team.

Work off a list of who bought the product or service. Most companies track who recently bought products or uses their web services. Use these lists and call down the user lists trying to qualify potential interviewees.

Advertise for volunteers. If you are redesigning a web site or if there are online user communities, consider advertising for users to be in your study. Several of our clients have had good success with craigslist.org and similar resources. If you are doing consumer products, hang up signs in neighborhoods, go through your religious and social groups asking for volunteers. We find that when you are part of the community volunteers always happen.

When you make first contact with an interview site explain who you are and what you are trying to accomplish. You will also need to set their expectations and inform them about the Contextual Design process and their part in it.

See the sample introduction to set the users' expectations properly (see the box, **Sample script for soliciting interviews**). Make sure they understand this is a one-on-one interview, which will happen in their workplace (or home) while they are working. Explain that you are not presenting product information. They should not clean up their office (or home) to prepare for the interview.

Sample script for soliciting interviewees

We are developing the next version of our product (describe it briefly, or describe the kind of work you want to support).

We would like to come and work with some of your people to understand how they currently work and what they might need in our product. We believe we cannot design it effectively unless we understand our customers and how they work in detail.

Based on the information you give us, we can develop products that fit the way people actually work. This is your opportunity to change the product we build by shaping our understanding of your work.

To find out how people really work, we need to observe people doing their actual jobs. While they work, we ask questions about what they are doing and why. The person we observe will get some work done, but will also be telling us about their job while they do it.

Your people will be talking one-on-one to a member of the design team with the task of doing this design. Therefore, you have an opportunity to tell us and show us exactly what you need. All the interviewers are trained in this requirements gathering technique.

We'd like to observe and talk with people, in their offices or wherever they do their work. We would take about two hours of each person's time. We also ask that no one clean up their office in advance of the interview.

We keep anything we find out confidential to our team. We'd like to audio record the sessions—we don't have to, if it's against company policy or if any of the individuals object. It just gives us a backup to our handwritten notes.

(Explain what a typical interview experience is like.)

Before the interview, we will call to remind the people we are interviewing that we are coming to (1) make sure they know who's coming and what our expectations are and (2) make sure they set aside some real work associated with the project focus to do when we get there.

If necessary, we will meet with all the interviewees and whomever in management we set up the interviews with before we start the interviews. We will do this to introduce the plan for the morning and pair up interviewers with interviewees. This lasts about 15 minutes.

Then the interviewers go off with their interviewees for about two hours.

When we are finished we will meet up with each other and if appropriate will meet with our contact person to thank him and wrap up.

We will provide gifts to participants (describe them) but your greatest reward will be the new system we will be able to produce for you.

If your contact person is interested ask for the names of the people he or she thinks will fit your interview criteria and ask for permission to talk to them directly. If you can't talk to the interview candidates directly you will have to qualify them through your contact person.

Note: Someone should send a thank you note to the interviewees after the interview.

Compose a project/interview summary sheet

Prior to contacting people to set up interviews, write up a project/interview summary sheet. This sheet will include information about your company and describe what takes place in a Contextual Inquiry interview (see the box, **Points from our project summary sheet**). It will also describe the type of user you are looking to interview. The purpose of this sheet is two-fold. First, it gives the person setting up the interview talking points. Second, it can be sent out to potential interviewees to supplement the phone conversation and help them understand what you are asking them to do for you.

Warning: Often this sheet is not enough or it never makes it past the manager who set up the interviews. You might arrive at an interview site and sit down with a person who has no idea what you're doing or why you are there. Get specific contact information for each interview you set up so that you can call and confirm with the users as well as make sure they understand what they are being asked to do.

Points from our project summary sheet

- We will set up two-hour interviews with participating employees in their own offices. Because we want to learn about their daily work practice, we will talk with them about their work while they do it. Interviews combine a review of past events with watching ongoing work related to the role of the interviewee. This "shadowing" will be with participants in the workplaces so all their natural work activities, tools, and objects are available to stimulate memory. No one should clean up his or her workspace for the visit.

- While users work, we ask questions about what they are doing and why. The person we observe will get some work done, but will also be telling us about his or her job while he or she does it. We are not presenting product information.

- Trained personnel conduct interviews.

- Every interview is entirely confidential. Company-specific information will not be shared with anyone.

- Interviews will be audio recorded when possible. These recordings are entirely confidential and will be destroyed at the end of the study.

- We are looking for these types of people to interview: (fill in description of job roles and activities they would be performing).

Qualify interview candidates

Once you have identified potential organizations and interview candidates, verify that you are talking to the right person within that organization and that you are actually lining up interviews with the right people. If an agency or an administrator is doing the actual calling, you will need to give them a qualification checklist to be sure you get the right people (see the box, **Qualification questions for a web site redesign project**).

Qualification questions for a web site redesign project

The following list of questions would be appropriate for a web site redesign project for a company trying to provide support and product information to users. Use the web site to get basic company information if you can.

These questions focused on finding the right kind of developer who used the web site the team was redesigning.

1. What is the primary business of your company (i.e., commercial tool or web development, application or business development to support business processes)?

2. How large is your company?

3. Is it a start-up business or otherwise going through a period of fast growth?

4. What is your job title?

5. How long have you been a developer?

6. Do you primarily develop commercial software, or do you perform a mix of IT duties and software development?

7. Do you:

   - Work full time as a regular employee for your company?

   - Telecommute; and if so, how often?

   - Run your own business?

   - Work as a consultant?

8. Do you use the (company name) web site in the course of doing your work?

9. What is your primary development tool(s) (i.e., list company tools)?

10. How long have you been using this tool?

11. Are you currently learning or getting used to any new (company) tools, or new versions of a tool you have used before?

12. Are you involved in purchase decisions?

Once you have talked to each potential interview candidate you may be able to determine that he or she is right for your project right away and commit to an interview. However, you may find that you really have to think about it.

Making trade-offs is not an easy task. You need to look at your interview requirements and the user's qualifications and decide whether to set up the interview. When in doubt about whether or not to schedule an interview, consider your schedule and the rest of your user population. If you have a good user set and you think you might get a new perspective from this user, take the risk and do the interview. Or if you are having trouble setting up visits, take the users you have. Often you get better data than you might think. Some interviews will always be better than others. And you may want to set up one or two substitute interviews anyway.

Track interviews set up

Once you schedule an interview keep track of your interview counts and contexts. You may want to use a tracking sheet like the one in Figure 3-1 to keep track of the types of interviews you have set up. Or set up your users in CDTools and track them there.

User number	Industry	Company	Job title	Role	Tasks	Context
User 1						
User 2						
User ...						

Figure 3.1:
Example of a user
tracking sheet.

Figure 3-2 shows the CDTools screen for tracking your mix of users and organizations. The project window also shows you the progress of your interviews, interpretation sessions, and affinity building.

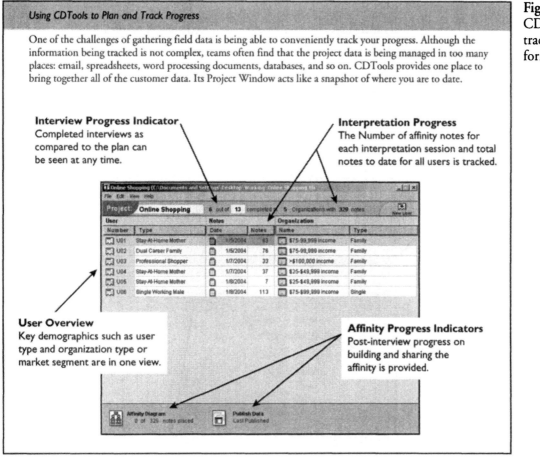

Figure 3.2:
CDTools screen for
tracking project in-
formation.

As you schedule interviews, confirm the user's contact information, location, and directions to their location. You will need to share this with the team member conducting the interview.

Prepare the team for their interviews

Once each interview is set up make sure the team knows what is going on. You will want to provide the team with the following information:

- Contact information
  - Name

- Title
- Company name
- Division/business unit/etc.
- Address
- Phone number
- E-mail
- Interview details
  - Interview date
  - Interview time
  - Interview location
  - Directions to interview site (include estimated driving time)
  - Recommended hotels

You can do this via e-mail or other communication or you can direct each interviewer to his or her user's information in CDTools. Figure 3-3 shows the user information screen in CDTools, here you can capture the user's contact information, user and organization profiles, as well as job and organization types.

Figure 3.3:
CDTools screen for capturing user information.

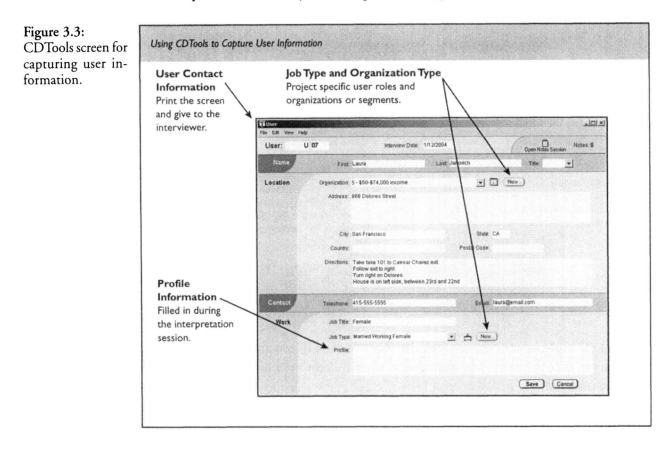

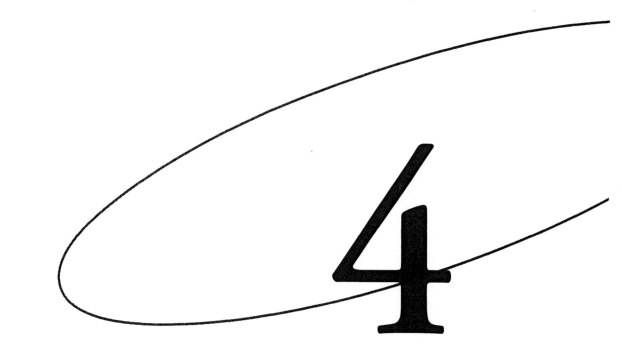

The Contextual
Inquiry Interview

Rapid CD Process	Lightning Fast	Lightning Fast +	Focused Rapid CD
Contextual Interviews and Interpretation	✓	✓	✓

If your planning up until now has been thorough and complete, your interview schedule should run smoothly. Now you need to conduct your Contextual Interviews (CI) and get the data you have outlined in your plan.

This chapter will prepare you for the data-gathering phase of your project. It covers how to run the Contextual Interview, the types of information you should look for, and how to approach users and let them know what you plan to accomplish while you are with them. Even with the best planning, when you arrive in the field things may not go the way you thought they would. And, as events unfold you will need to respond and act accordingly. This chapter also provides guidance on how to handle the various situations you may encounter while out in the field.

In order to design a product that meets customers' real needs, designers must understand the customers and their work practice. Yet designers are not usually familiar with or experienced in the work they are supporting. If they operate from their gut feel, they rely on their own experience as a user. But designers generally are more tolerant of technology than average users, so they are not representative of end users.

Yet you cannot simply ask people for design requirements, in part because they do not understand what technology is capable of, but more because they are not aware of what they really do. Because the things people do everyday become habitual and unconscious, people usually are unable to articulate their work practice. People are conscious of general directions, such as identifying critical problems, and they can say what makes them angry at the system. However, they cannot provide the day-to-day detail about what they are doing to ground designers in what the practice entails and how it might be augmented with technology.

The challenge of getting design data is being able to get that level of detail about work that is unconscious and tacit. The first step of Contextual Design is Contextual Inquiry, our field data gathering technique that allows designers to go out into the field and talk with people about their work or lives while they are observing them. If designers watch people while they work, the people do not have to articulate their own work practice. If they do blow-by-blow retrospective accounts of things that happened in the recent past, people can stick with the details of a case using artifacts and reenactment to remind them of what happened. Field data overcomes the difficulties of discovering tacit information.

See "Part 1, Understanding the Customer," in *Contextual Design: Defining Customer-Centered Systems*.

Definition

Contextual Interviews are one-on-one interviews conducted in the user's workspace that focus on observations of ongoing work (see the box, **How many interviewers: one or two?**). Conducting a thorough Contextual Inquiry interview is more than observing and recording the user's current tasks. You want and need to discuss what is happening in the moment with the user.

Key concepts

Context. Understand user needs in the context of their work by collecting data from users doing real tasks at the site of real work.

Partnership. Work with users as partners in the inquiry, operating like an apprentice, letting the users lead you through their actual activities while you make observations and ask questions about what is going on in the work. Together you will identify the explicit and implicit aspects of their work.

Interpretation. Create a shared understanding of what is going on to uncover the meaning and implications behind user action and language by sharing your hypotheses with the user.

Focus. Steer the conversation by listening and probing from a clearly defined project focus, while always challenging your entering assumptions. Do not use a set of predefined questions; instead, know the areas of concern to your project so you will know what to ask more about and what to ignore when you are observing the work.

CI process checklist

☐ Preparation:

☐ Confirm the interview

☐ During the field interview:

    ☐ (Optional) Give introductory group talk to multiple participants at a work site

    ☐ Deal with unexpected organizational issues

    ☐ Go to workspace

    ☐ Run the interview

☐ After the interview, get ready to interpret

Confirm the interview

The day before the interview, call the user to confirm. Make sure you have the correct contact information and directions to the site. You may also want to ask about building security; that can often take several minutes that you'll need to factor into your arrival time.

Be sure that the user does not clean up. People naturally feel like they are getting visitors and will clean up unless you tell them not to. When they clean up, they are accidentally hiding work practice and work environment details that you need to see.

You should have dealt with confidentiality issues during the initial interview set up. However, if you haven't, you need to be prepared for handling any emergent issues about accessing proprietary information or places now. Find out if you need to sign a nondisclosure agreement (nda). Let the user know that you will black out any sensitive information on artifacts you collect and that they can black out information before they show you artifacts (see the box, **Dealing with confidentiality at the customer site**).

How many interviewers: one or two?

A CI interview is one-on-one, the interviewer and the user. Some teams want to send two people, one to interview and one to act as the notetaker. If you want to do this because you think you will get more detailed data, our experience shows that to be unnecessary. A well-run interpretation session will extract all the data needed out of a single interviewer. Indeed, one of our consulting clients was thrilled when we coached them away from a practice of sending two people. After convincing them to try one person they examined the resulting data and agreed that they produced no greater detail with two people. The manager called to thank us because now they could save significant money in travel, time, and cost to their clients.

We also don't recommend two people because of its effect on the interview itself. To establish an intimate relationship you want the user to focus on relating to one person. When one person drives the conversation he follows his focus and the conversation has a coherent thread that the user can engage with. But if two people talk, then the necessary jumping back and forth makes the conversation more disconnected, creates less intimacy, and produces competing threads of conversation. This can confuse the users and frustrate the interviewers. Also, the dynamic becomes more of a traditional interview. And when both people start talking, inevitably no one is taking notes.

So if you do send two people, the rules are to separate the roles of the interviewer and notetaker. This means the interviewer leads the discussion and the notetaker cannot ask questions. You and your partner can switch roles during the interview—just make the switch explicit and tell the user what you are doing. And at the end of the interview allow your partner to ask their questions as part of the wrap-up.

Repeat again that you will be talking with them about their actual work while they are doing it in their real workplace. Listen to ensure that they understand that this is a "shadowing" experience and not a survey or training in your product.

If you haven't discussed recording the interview during set-up you should do so now. Explain that the tape is a personal backup to your notes and will be destroyed at the end of the project. Even if someone is worried about it, politely push to make a recording—it is your only backup.

Note: If you can't tape record, just be sure you interpret the interview as soon as possible. Don't wait more than a day.

Dealing with confidentiality at the customer site

Sometimes client work is so sensitive that even a nondisclosure isn't sufficient for them. In one project, the work studied was about mergers and acquisitions. The users didn't want to share those details. Several approaches got us the details of the structure of the work anyway:

- They used code names for the merger candidates and for the industry so the interviewers couldn't figure out which company was being acquired.

- Artifacts first were printed out, and then sensitive information was blacked out before we looked at it together.

- That same artifact was then resketched with the user so the interviewer could capture the details without taking the sensitive document.

- Any time a sensitive matter was discussed the interviewer turned off the tape recorder, or just didn't record if the user had security concerns.

Give an introductory group talk

When you get to the interview site you may find it useful to brief the users, management, and your sales team. This is particularly useful if you are interviewing more than two people at this physical site. It is an easy way to verify that your users are people you want to interview. This introduction lets you educate everyone about the process and what you are going to be doing while on site at their company.

If your interviews are in homes you can use the same type of introduction for the family if you are planning on interviewing more than one of them. If you are alone, just start with one person and move to the next. If two of you interview, you can do it in parallel. Families like to know what is going on in the home the same way that businesses like to know what is going on in their business.

Keep this talk to less than 20 minutes, which includes the time it takes to assemble everyone. This meeting is attended by the users, their managers, sales people who may want to be there because they set up the visit, and the interviewers who will be conducting the visit.

A typical presentation is a quick, informal discussion and includes the following:

- Introduce everyone who is going to be interviewed and who will be doing the interviewing.

- Introduce the project focus and what you are trying to find out at a high level. Express your appreciation for how valuable this information is, and remind them how it will benefit them.

- Introduce the Contextual Inquiry process and explain that you will do one-on-one, two-hour interviews so that you can really understand what they are doing at a low level of detail (see the box, **Why is a CI interview scheduled for two hours?**).

- Tell them that you will tape record and of your confidentiality policy. Assure them that their activities will be shared only with the design team and not with management. Tell them that even their names will not be used; they will get code names. Find out if anyone objects personally.

- Pair off the interviewer and customer and go do your interviews.

Even if you don't have more than one interview at a site, organizational politics sometimes require that you spend time with managers or others who are not the people who do the work you really want to see. Assess the situation carefully. Does the manager really want to talk to you, or are they doing that because every other time someone has come in to do interviews they've wanted to spend time with management? They may be delighted not to have to spend time with you. Otherwise, schedule a short interview with them before you start the interviews. If you did not do a group introduction, provide the same overview outlined earlier. Discuss with whom you will be talking, and ensure that they are the right people. With management's support you may be able to do a last-minute substitution if one of the users is not a correct match.

This is also the time to collect the manager's views on the product or system you are building. You need management's support and they need to express their views. Their

Why is a CI interview scheduled for two hours?

We often get questioned about why we tell people to schedule the Contextual Inquiry for two hours. They wonder how that can possibly be long enough to really find out what the user does. First, the two-hour time length is not a hard and fast rule. However, in our 16 years of experience, it is usually the right amount of time for the user, the interviewer, and the quality of the data.

In two hours you can observe a set of key tasks as they unfold and do retrospective accounts of tasks that occur at different times in the process. Through a series of interviews with people at different stages of a long process like drug discovery you can sample activities across roles and time, and reconstruct the full process. So two hours is enough for the data.

It is also enough for the interviewer because they are working the whole time and incorporating more and more detailed data. This is difficult and tiring work, which is why we tell people to do no more than three interviews in a day. By the end of two hours the interviewer is tired. And the user is ready to get back to fully self-directed activities.

Finally, two hours with two people is better than four hours with the same person because you get a broader scope of data. One exception to this rule is when the work is so intermittent that you must spend half a day. For example, going with emergency workers on the road to study the use of one piece of equipment may take longer to see it in use.

An interview may also be shorter when the work itself is intermittent or very focused. For example, understanding how managers use reports generated from software will be a shorter interview since you are not interested in their whole job.

data can give you a perspective on buying decisions and cultural factors. Interpretation of this data will simply add some issues to the affinity diagram.

Sometimes the sales force has set up the interviews. They may want to be at this management interview to ensure that their clients are well managed. They may also wish to come along to observe an interview for a short period of time. If they do, explain the rules: not to interrupt during the interview. Remember Sales is your entrée to other interviews. Like management, they need to feel good about the process.

Deal with the unexpected issues

When you arrive on site you may encounter one or more unexpected situations. Here are some typical situations and some suggestions of how to handle them:

Interview in a conference room. You arrive to conduct a field interview and you're told you are meeting in a conference room. No matter how well you explain this in advance, some people have a preconceived idea that interviews are in meeting rooms. Be polite, be deferential, but explain why you need the interview to be in the office. Reassure the user that it's ok if it is small, messy, or noisy—we need to be sure our system works in the normal work environment.

Confidentiality issues. You arrive and even though you discussed confidentiality and tape recording you discover that the facility does not allow recorders and the user's management doesn't want anyone in the offices. They suggest interviewing in a conference room. Suggest that you forgo recording and that you will not take away any artifacts. If they insist that you can do the interview only in a conference room, ask the user to bring their computer if possible into the room or use a computer that is already in the conference room to connect to his materials or the web as relevant. Ask them to bring examples of acceptable materials or blank artifacts. Then conduct the interview as a retrospective account using the materials as props to walk the cases. Also draw pictures to represent where the user went and how other artifacts were used. If you are exploring software have them walk through the software replaying their last usage cases. Although this is not the optimum way to collect data, this method will yield some high-level issues, which is better than a wasted trip. Remember to work through real cases and not settle for a demo of complaints and high-level descriptions of tasks. If you see that you aren't getting any kind of quality data after half an hour end the interview and thank the user.

Only one hour. You arrive expecting a two-hour interview and the user tells you she can give you only an hour. Explain why you are there and what you want to do, emphasizing why two hours would be helpful. Often times the user will go longer once she understands how interested you are in her work. Or start with one hour, but at the end of that time, ask if you might go a bit longer to complete a key task. If you do have only an hour, focus your interview on work practice tasks that are key to your focus.

Wrong person. You've started the interview and realize part way through that you are not talking to the right person. Although it may feel rude to cut the interview short, it is far ruder to keep talking to the person when you are not going to be able to use his or her information. Talk with them for about 30 minutes, focusing on the aspects of their work that touch your problem or product support. Thank them for their help. In the discussion with them you may have identified another person who might be more relevant, ask if you might speak to that other person while you are there, especially since you aren't likely to have the luxury of rescheduling for another day.

Additional interview. During any interview you may discover another role that is important to your project. If you have the time you may want to try to do an additional interview. Ask the current user or the manager if it would be possible to talk to that person, even if it is only for a short time.

No-show user. You confirmed the interview the day before, but when you arrive the user is not there: they called in sick, had a personal or business emergency, or simply aren't available. Be careful that you don't get angry or upset, and see if you can find a manager to talk with to identify a substitute. Sometimes there simply is no one else who really does the work you care about, but you won't know unless you ask.

Go to the workspace

On your way make the most use out of your time. This is your preliminary contact with the user and their cultural environment. Ask questions about their job. Talk about your focus. You may be able to do the majority of your introduction while you are walking to the user's desk. You also will be sensing the culture and the physical layout. Be sure to walk with an open notebook so you can jot down notes.

Run the interview

Contextual Interviews (CI) follow a defined process. Working within this process enables you to stay on focus and capture quality data. This section outlines the parts of the CI interview. You will also find examples and tips for structuring a successful CI. For information on what to bring see the box, **What to bring**.

> **What to bring**
> Make sure everyone participating in the interview process who will be involved in the interviewing knows what's happening.
>
> Every interviewer will need:
> - A portable tape recorder
> - Two 90-minute tapes
> - Fresh batteries
> - A full-size spiral-bound notebook
> - Two pens

The introduction

The introduction should take no more than the first 10 to 15 minutes of the interview. You'll want to cover what a CI is in your introduction, and you should expect to reinforce it through your actions throughout the interview. After all, the user's only experience will be with traditional question and answer interviews.

Introduce yourself, your project focus, and the interviewing method. Make sure the user understands what you are trying to learn. Often, even though the user has been told about how the interview will be conducted, they don't understand what that means.

Reinforce your focus by restating it throughout the introduction and the rest of the interview. Mention the focus several times to plant the idea that although the user's job entails a lot of things, you are concerned with only a small part that you want to focus on for the interview.

Set expectations for the length of the interview. Tell the user that you plan to be with them for the next two hours. If, prior to the interview, the user agreed to only an hour or one and a half hours use this time to find out if you can run longer—the goal is to try and get a full two-hour interview.

Set up the user as the expert and your role as understanding what they do (see the box, **Do you need to be an expert?**). Get an overview of the user's background and role as it pertains to your focus, as well as any demographic information about the user or the organization that is relevant to you.

Do you need to be an expert?

No. The expert in the situation is the user. In the apprenticeship model of interviewing (see page 42 in *Contextual Design: Defining Customer-Centered Systems*) the user is the expert and you are the apprentice, learning about the work practice by observing and talking with the expert. When you don't know a particular field of work the first few interviews will teach you the process and the issues, and show you all the low-level detail about a process or application that you need to know. Your understanding should be shaped by the user and not by a book, a class, or someone who, although expert, is not the user. You want your understanding of the user to represent the real work practice, not the espoused practice. You want your application to support what people are really doing, not what they say they are doing. If the business wants to introduce new practices, you need to understand how to take the users from where they really are to where the business wants them to be—using software and business rules appropriately to get there.

So what personal preparation is reasonable? If you are going to be studying a business process, ask for an overview of the process at a high level just to orient you to the roles and goals. This is part of your initial analysis of business goals, where you learn what the business plans and cares about. Don't worry about the low-level detail of how the user works or their jargon, however; they will teach you that.

If you are studying a web site or application, walk through the application or site to get oriented, and to understand any technical constraints. Ask the team, management, and marketing for typical complaints and requests. All this helps you set focus for the interviews.

But remember, your most important teacher is the user, not the application manual or business process document. Your job in the beginning is to understand processes, system, business goals, and entering concerns to let the existing knowledge shape your entering focus. Then your Contextual Interviews will change that entering focus to better reflect reality.

If you are an expert, watch out! Your pre-existing assumptions and expectations can get in the way of seeing what is really happening for the user. Your task will be to challenge every expectation and every idea you have of the right way to do the work. And often that is much harder than just letting the user shape what you understand from scratch.

Describe your confidentiality policy. Reassure the user that everything that is said in the interview is confidential. Tell them that their identity will be replaced with a user number and that they are free to say anything.

Get permission to audio record. Ask the user if it is all right for you to record the interview. If need be, explain that the recording is for your benefit only. It is a backup to the notes that you take in the interview and will be destroyed at the end of your project. Don't forget to start recording. Make sure you don't place it near a fan or the keyboard.

Deal with opinions about tools. The user may have opinions they want to express right at the start of the interview about your tool or company. Listen politely and write them down so the user feels heard from the start. But do not follow up on the opinions now. If you do, the Contextual Inquiry portion of the interview will get sidetracked, or even derailed, before you start. During the interview, look for circumstances that might have given rise to the opinion and explore it in the context of the work.

Deal with natural interruptions and movement. Tell the user that you are interested in observing every facet of her work. Let her know that she should answer the telephone and coworker's questions. Encourage her to do so when the situation arises. Otherwise, the user might be reluctant to do so for fear it will seem rude. To the contrary, it is data you want to collect. If the phone call or question sounds relevant to your focus, ask the user to tell you about it. During your introduction, let the user know that she should also move around the office like she normally would. And when she moves, you will go with her. But do respect privacy when the user clearly needs to deal with something alone.

Look for cases to start the CI part of the interview. While talking with the user about her job and responsibilities, look for references to work that fall within your focus. When you find several tasks that fit, use one to move into the transition phase of the interview.

Example script: eChalk

Let me start by telling you a bit about this project and what we are trying to do. Our team is developing a web application to support communication between students, teachers, parents, and school administrators. We want to understand your work so that we can provide technology to enhance that communication. We also are interested in how you communicate now with your colleagues, and how you use technology. We also are interested in your classroom activities. Specifically, we would like to focus on lesson plan creation, homework assignment, attendance taking, and the creation of progress reports.

We gather this data in a field interview because we know that people know everything about what they do but they can't tell us. Work becomes so habitual that it is unconscious. You know everything about how you work but you don't spend time watching yourself work! So you are unaware of many of the details of your collaboration and coordination that we need to understand to properly support you. So to get the detailed data that we need we simply watch what you are doing and talk with you about it as you do it. This won't be a traditional interview with questions and answers—see, I don't even have any questions with me!

So, let's start by getting a bit of an overview of what you do that involves communicating with colleagues, students, and parents. Then please do any of the collaboration and coordination tasks you have to do. Check your messages, call people, take attendance, communicate with parents and students, create lessons, assign homework, and your other classroom-related tasks. I'll be observing you and when it won't disrupt the class I'll stop you when I see something interesting and ask questions. Or, I'll wait until there is a break or talk to you between classes. I'll also share my observations so you can tell me if I really understand what you do.

To help me later with my notes I'd like to tape record. I will be the only person to listen to this. You will be given a code when your data is shared with the team. Recording is just a backup to my notes. Are you okay with using the tape? Thanks.

So let's get started.

The transition

The transition phase is a brief (two minute), but explicit part of the interview process. During the introduction you are not merely getting acquainted, you are also looking for relevant tasks or work the user performs that you can ask him or her to do or re-create for you. The transition is a critical piece of the interview. During the transition you move out of the question and answer mode of the introduction and into the observation behavior of the Contextual Inquiry.

The transition is clearly a shift from traditional interview mode to CI mode. Make the transition as soon as you have enough background information about what the user does as it is relevant to your focus. Once you have found several "hooks" between their work and your focus, transition them to performing real work tasks.

Use the example that follows as a starting place for your interview transition.

Example script: eChalk
I think you've given me a good overview of the work that you do. What I'd like now is for you to start doing your real work. You mentioned that you need to communicate with parents about a variety of different things: their child's progress in class, discipline problems, upcoming school events, and so on. Is there a parent you need to communicate with now? Can you show me now how you do this? I'll interrupt if I have any questions.

The field interview

The full Contextual Interview should take approximately two hours; about 1.5 hours of this should be the field interview portion. During this time observe the user performing his or her work and talk about what you observe. Although a CI is not the standard ask-and-answer interview situation, you do want to stop the user and ask them directed questions about what you have observed, share your observations, and offer hypotheses about why they are engaged in various behaviors.

Observe and discuss. You set the tone and rules of the interview session. Follow your focus, observe and discuss the tasks in your focus, and conduct relevant retrospective accounts using artifacts and re-creation (see the box, **Look beyond the task**). If you ask an off-topic question the user will think this is relevant and talk more about it. Stick to your focus.

Look beyond the task

- Identify tasks in context with the rest of the process. Task is only one part of the larger story.

- A task fits into a larger story; focus on the overall process that the task is a part of.

- Understand how informal collaboration with others fits inside of the formal process.

- Look for the larger picture, probe to ask where your user's task fits in the larger workflow of the organization. Look for alternate ways of performing tasks. Look for instances where the user deviates from the norm or company recommended processes.

- Focus on the user's job role, not their job title to understand what they really are doing. Many users wear multiple hats and participate in multiple processes within an organization or family, and contribute to their work and life context in many ways. Look for what they do, not what they are called or expected to do formally.

Identify work groups:

- Work groups are core to any kind of work.

- No one works alone; all products are part of collaboration.

- Distributed work is about a distributed work group.

- Communities are just big, loose work groups.

- Ask your user from whom they are getting tasks and information. Identify to whom the user's work product is being passed. Probe the flow of information throughout the group, department, and business.

- Remember that work groups are both formal and informal. Formal work groups participate in organizational processes that are recognized by the organization. Informal work groups are the relationships a user has inside and outside of their organization that help get the formal work done.

Be nosy. Ask about the work you are observing. Asking questions allows you to get to the low-level details you are looking for. Capture each step in her processes. Ask questions if you observe something unexpected. Look for UI level details while the user is doing her work if that is in your focus.

Take notes. Capture your notes in longhand in a spiral-bound notebook (spiral-bound so you don't lose any pages or drop them and get them out of order). You are the only one who is going to see these notes so they don't have to be neat, only neat enough for you to be able to decipher them during the interpretation session and clear enough for you to remember exactly what happened during the interview. A good rule of thumb, depending on your handwriting, is 10 to 20 pages of notes for a two-hour interview.

Do not use a computer to take notes. It is a barrier between you and the user. No matter how second nature the computer is to you, it is a layer between you and the user that can get in the way of you paying attention to the user. Besides, what if the user needs to walk to the printer, go down the hall, or otherwise move around. You need to be able to keep on the move with him or her.

Everyone complains about note taking. But note taking gets easier (not necessarily easy) over time, especially when you have done a couple of interviews and know from experience how much you need to write down in order to do a good job reporting back to the team in the interpretation session.

Know what to capture. Identify types of information that you should be looking for while you are in the interviews. Even if you are not formally capturing any work models you should be on the lookout for the following:

- The roles the user is playing in his or her organization.

- The user's responsibilities within the roles he or she plays and within the business organization.

- The types of communication the user engages in.

- Evidence of the corporate culture—not only what the official culture is, but also how it is manifest informally.

- How the user organizes her physical space.

- Any artifact the user uses or refers to. Ask for and annotate a copy of the artifact or draw it in your notebook.

- The user's key tasks, work strategies, and intents. What are they trying to do and how? Why?

- Breakdowns in the user's work—what doesn't work for the user, not which functions in your product that simply aren't used.

- What works and doesn't work in the tools that the user uses.

Collect artifacts. During the course of the interview you may notice the user accessing different pieces of paper, online forms, or reference sheets. Ask if you can have a copy of the form/sheet or a printout from an online reference. If you can't get a physical copy of the artifact, draw a sketch of it in your interview notebook. If your user prints out artifacts for you, don't forget them on the printer. You don't want to get to the interpretation session and realize that you left everything at the client site.

After you ask for artifacts, walk through them. Try to answer the following questions:

- Where did the information come from?

- How is the artifact created?

- How is it used?

- Who will get it next?

Share design ideas stimulated by events. Share your design ideas with the user as you have them during the interview. Sharing provides you with immediate feedback on your idea and how well you understood the work that generated it. Sharing also will prevent you from being distracted by thinking about it instead of paying attention to what the user is now doing.

Draw the physical workspace. Drawing the physical workspace is important for two reasons: one, it helps you in the interpretation. Two, the user's workspace may prove important to your design.

For more on the physical model see Chapter 6, "Work Modeling."

The role of digital photos. Digital photos have made capturing key aspects of the physical environment easy. If you can't take an artifact away, you might be able to take a photo. To provide the team back home with a feel for the person's environment, take a photo. If you are designing hardware, appliances, or machinery you may want to zero in on particular areas to illustrate your observations. Or you may want to show placement of books, sticky notes, piles, and other aspects of the individual's workflow that will inform your focus. If you are using CDTools, you can include the digital photos in your interpretation session notes (see Chapter 5). See the box, **Videotaping the interview**, for information on the role of videotape in the interview.

If you are going to take photos be sure to get permission before you start. Note what photos you want to take in your notebook as you go along. At the end of the interview you can snap them all to avoid disrupting the flow of the session.

Videotaping the interview

We generally don't recommend videotaping the field interview for the purpose of getting detailed data. People often say, "We are trying to capture so much detail; I'm worried about losing some of it in my notes." But videotaping comes with a set of costs that, over the years, we have not found to be worth the effort for typical application design.

Videotaping requires a second person or a stationary videotape player. In the first case, you use an extra resource, which costs time and travel accommodations. More importantly the presence of a second person more dramatically disrupts the workplace than one person with a tape recorder. It is easy to have an "apprentice" sit next to the user and observe and talk—this is much like training a new employee. But coming with equipment and two people into the workplace is significantly more disruptive. The camera is more "present" than the audiotape, tending to inhibit interaction. Even a stationary video heightens the abnormality of the situation, creates more user discomfort, and may get more confidentiality push-back.

The worry is that you won't get the detail you need. We find that for a backup to get details, the audiotape does the job. And if you interpret the data within 48 hours, even from your notes, you will get all the detail you need or could want. Interpreting within 48 hours also will produce higher quality data than analyzing the videotape days or weeks later. The tape captures only one view of the interview; much is not taped and therefore is forgotten over time. Videotape interpretation is very, very time consuming compared to the interpretation session. Finally, we have never met an engineer willing to engage in videotape analysis, even though they like seeing video clips produced by someone else. Our goal is to engage the actual team members in interpreting the details of the user's life and work.

So although videotaping seems like a good idea—indeed, we tried it early on in the history of Contextual Inquiry—we found that it cost too much time and interfered with developing a shared understanding among the team. So we recommend audiotape instead and augment key aspects of the physical environment with digital photos.

However, there are exceptions:

- If it is critical to the design that you see *exactly* how people are moving, which hand (or even fingers) they are using, how they position their body, or any time detailed physical movements and very small steps matter, then videotaping may be worthwhile. For example, if you are designing a medical device that a surgeon is precisely using with the patient's anatomy, you might need to videotape, or if you are designing an appliance and you need to capture how a person manipulates angles and dishes to load a dishwasher.

→

- If you are designing a mobile application and want to see the manipulations of the buttons as it relates to navigation and scanning, a video camera attached to the device may be useful. If you are so mobile that you can't take any notes having a second person shadowing the whole experience may be useful.

In any of these cases, however, don't stop taking notes; this is still your first level of recording and will produce the fastest, most direct results. If you do videotape, decide exactly what sequences of action you want to capture permanently and extract only those. Try not to put yourself in the position of feeling that you must use everything that happens to be on the tape.

Finally, you may want to videotape to make a highlight tape to make the problems and issues of users real for management and developers. Or you may want to get clips of testimonials on products. In this case you are videotaping for the purpose of internal marketing. So run your interview first in the standard way, watching for special quotes and breakdowns that you want to show. Then at the end of the session, do a series of video clips targeted at what you want to show. In this way you won't be burdened by extra tape nor will you need a second person to go out on the interview.

Collect retrospective accounts. In an ideal situation your user will be doing the exact piece of work that you are looking to observe. But if they aren't, you can pursue a respective account of the work. When you collect retrospective data you want the user to recollect activity that is no more than two weeks old. After two weeks the data starts to get abstract.

One format for a retrospective account is the replaying of the event. The user walks to the places they did in the real event, uses the software repeating their actions in the real event, and generally reconstructs the event in order while being probed by the interviewer.

Another format is to use artifacts to facilitate a retelling of the story. Most activities leave artifact trails; walking these can help the user remember the details between or referenced by the artifacts.

Example script: eChalk

In this portion of a re-created eChalk retrospective account notice how the user is eager to tell the story of something that happened several months ago. The interviewer gently and repeatedly probes for a more recent case. The interviewer is also careful not to follow up right now on interesting points that might derail this user from staying focused on this story. The interviewer makes a note to come back to those points later. Lastly, the user spots an opportunity to use artifacts to drive out key details—this technique is not just relevant to retrospective accounts.

Interviewer: You mentioned that you had to coordinate parent/teacher events. Have you done that recently?

User: Sure, I do it all the time. It is a really important part of the teacher's job. I've got a lot of great ideas. But, it also takes a lot of time to do right.

Interviewer: Tell me about the last time you had to coordinate an event.

User: Let me tell you, the biggest hassle was the First Week Back event.

Interviewer: (Knows that this was several months ago, doesn't follow up on that story.) Since that was six months ago, anything more recent, or something you have to work on now for the future?

User: Well, we could talk about how I'm going to schedule First Week Back when we do it again next year.

Interviewer: (Doesn't want to do "pretend" work where the user has to predict the future.) Since you mentioned you do this all the time, is there anything you had to coordinate this month?

User: As a matter of fact, yes, we had an event last week for the entire families of the fourth, fifth, and sixth graders.

Interviewer: That sounds good. Tell me about it.

User: I got this idea to have a family event instead of just inviting the parents. So, I sent invitations to all the parents.

Interviewer: (Realizes that a few steps got skipped, and that eChalk needs to understand the genesis of events to better support their coordination and planning around them.) How did you get the idea? Had the school done this before?

User: No, this was the first time; it was my idea.

Interviewer: (Offers a hypothesis about where the idea came from so the user will give details.) Did you read an article about having family events?

User: No, I attended a workshop sponsored by the school district on how to increase parent and family involvement in the school.

User: (Digs into a file folder.) Here's the invitation we sent out to the parents.

Interviewer: (Decides that she would come back and explore how the teacher found out about the workshop after she finished finding out the details of how the event was coordinated and communicated.) How was the invitation created?

User: I did it in my word processor.

Interviewer: (Realizes she wasn't specific enough and doesn't want to skip ahead to the mechanics of creating an invitation.) Before we get to that, did you have to talk to the other teachers?

User: About how to do the event, no. That's between the principal and me.

Interviewer: So you had a conversation with the principal. Did you just go into his office and talk about it?

User: Sure, along with my plan.

Interviewer: You created a plan? Do you have a copy of it we can look at?

User: Sure. (Digs it out of the file folder.)

Interviewer: Is that folder where you keep everything about this family night?

User: Yes.

Interviewer: Can I look in it?

User: (Hands the folder to the interviewer.)

Interviewer: (Sees that the folder has copies of the plan, the invitation, a follow-up survey sent to the parents, notes to the homeroom teachers who distributed the invitation to the students. The interviewer realizes that she can run the retrospective account by walking through each of these artifacts.) Can we pause for a second while I make copies of these? I'd like to talk about each one and makes notes on them as we go along.

They walk together to the photocopy machine in the administrative office. The interviewer decided to go along to see if there was anything interesting. But, she doesn't follow up on it right now because she'll accidentally sidetrack the user if she does.

Interviewer: So let's reconstruct what you talked to the principal about to get permission, using the plan to remind us what you specifically talked about.

The interview continues....

The Wrap-up

When you come to the end of the interview you will want to wrap up. Your wrap-up does not need to be more than 10 to 15 minutes. A wrap-up is not: "Thank you very much, I appreciate your time. Goodbye." It is also not a complete retelling of what you now understand about the user's work within your project focus.

Create a large interpretation of your learning about their role. The wrap-up is your opportunity to summarize what you learned about the user's role and work. It is a way for you to check your high-level understanding with the user.

Ask about pet issues. This is also your time to ask any marketing or business questions that did not come up naturally while observing the work practice, but that you or others in your company want to take the opportunity to ask while you are with the user.

Give tips on system use. If the user had questions about the tool while you were in the middle of the interview, now is the time to answer them. Also, if you know something that would make the user's work easier you can tell them at this point in the interview. But note their responses. If the user has tried those features before, you can collect data on why it worked or did not. Asking about a particular feature may also trigger the user to walk through a recent retrospective account of its use. Be sure to leave enough time to allow for this discussion.

Thank the user and give the gift if you have one. Before you leave, be sure to thank the user for her time. Get her card if you are going to send a thank-you note or wish to follow-up by phone. This would also be the time to give her any gift or token of your appreciation that you have brought with you.

Example script: eChalk

The following is a re-creation from a portion of the wrap-up of one of the eChalk interviews. Notice how the user is confirming the key points and fine tuning them. The wrap-up is a last chance for you to confirm that you really understood the big picture for the user.

Interviewer: I really appreciate all the time you've given me. As we wrap up, let me summarize some of the key points I've learned about your role here. It's really important to you that you stay in touch with parents about their child's progress, but that's difficult to do because you have so little time and so many students. So, you have to balance being in touch and being available to the parents on one hand against a concern that if each parent has a really easy way to contact you for every little thing that you'll constantly be interrupted and potentially overwhelmed.

User: I really do want the parents to stay involved and I don't want to do anything to discourage that, but I also have to manage my time.

Interviewer: So for you, improving parent and teacher communication means both encouraging but also making it time efficient.

User: That's correct.

Interviewer: Another important role for you is being the advisor to the debate team. You spend a lot of time scheduling meetings, getting permissions for trips, and coordinating competitions. (Continues on with the wrap-up and finishes)

Interviewer: Before I leave, I noticed that you weren't using a couple of eChalk's calendar features that I think would really help you schedule the debate team meetings. If you have a couple of extra minutes, can I show them to you?

Get ready to interpret after the interview

After you have finished the interview don't talk about the data before the interpretation session. Every time you tell someone about what happened, your brain is subconsciously condensing the story. It's like those times when you say to someone, "Have I already told you this?" The brain thinks it has told the story, so it leaves out details. You need all the details fresh for the interpretation session. See Chapter 5 for how to run the interpretation session.

Schedule the interpretation within a 48-hour window. If you do this you do not need to prepare any material for the interpretation session. If you have to go past the two days, you will need to listen to the tape and annotate your notes with additional content.

Don't wait too long or your data will no longer be easy to recall or capture. It is much better to spread out your interviews, interpreting between them. In this way you can shift your focus between interviews and ensure high quality data with no preparation overhead for the interpretation session.

Tips

In this section you will find examples and tips for conducting a successful Contextual Interview.

Context

Context means getting as close to the real work as possible by going to the users wherever they do work and interviewing them while they are doing it. No focus groups, no user conferences, no tradeshow floors, and no conference rooms at the workplace instead of the user's desk. Our eChalk team will be in the classroom, the school's computer lab, the teacher's lounge, the administrative offices, and the principal's office. As you recall, their project focus was the school. However, if they expand their focus in their future, they would be at the home, workplace, or wherever parents and students have Internet access.

Context also means conducting the interview by observing the real work practice or talking about the detail of real cases that the user experienced within the last two weeks.

The interviewing technique requires guiding the user away from abstract general discussion and toward their ongoing work or a real retrospective case.

Dos and don'ts

In Table 4-1, you will find tips to stay connected to concrete data rather than abstract data. These tips will help you stay grounded in the work.

Table 4-1: Tips for staying connected to concrete data during a contextual interview.

Dos and don'ts for staying connected to concrete data and grounded in the work	
Don't	**Do**
Let the user talk in the air or talk in abstractions.	Make talk concrete: Follow the actual work and specific cases from the recent past. Get or draw artifacts; annotate with intent and structure.
Allow the user to summarize a story.	Reconstruct a situation: Back the user up when he skips a step. Hypothesize steps to prompt the user.
Take on the expert role: Do not teach or tell users how to do their jobs. Do not give tool tips.	When asked for tool tips, ask how would she have done it without you. Give tips at the end.
Discuss feature requests out of the context of usage.	Probe to understand what actual work situation prompted the request. Follow the real work example.
Ask, "what would you have done next" when the user did not actually do it in this case.	Avoid predictions of future scenarios. Only care about what has happened or is happening now. Do a retrospective account of past work.

Table 4-2 contains common situations interviewers find themselves in when the interview is going offtrack. It also contains tips for redirecting the interview.

Partnership

The partnership principle dictates probing the user's work practice together. The Contextual Interview is based on an apprenticeship model of relationship where the user drives the direction of the discussion and tasks and you probe from your project focus uncovering the work practice issues. The principle of partnership emphasizes the balanced power relationship between you and the user, unlike in a traditional interview where the interviewer controls all the discussion.

The core of partnership is the alternation between periods of watching work unfold interspersed with discussions of how work is structured. Watching reveals work patterns; stopping to talk about them uncovers the structure and meaning of the work to

Trigger	What it means	Your action
User says: "Typically I" "Normally I" "In general" "We usually" "In our company"	The user is talking about abstractions, not a concrete experience.	Redirect to actual work, a specific instance, or a particular artifact. What to say: "When was the last time you did that?" "Can you show me what you did then?" "Let's look at the report/document/screen/etc. you used."
Interview falls into question/response pattern that feels like "I ask/you answer"	The relationship has reverted to a questionnaire.	Return to ongoing work. What to say: "You were working before and I interrupted you. Please go ahead and go back to it." "When was the last time you did that? Can you show me what you did then?"
The user has lots of questions for help on the tool.	You turned into the expert.	What to say: "What would you do if I weren't here?" "I can give you some tips later, but I'll never learn how to improve the product if I don't understand how you work now."
The user requests specific features.	You have a proposed solution but you don't yet understand the underlying problem.	Probe to understand what work situation prompted the request. Try to get to an actual situation with an artifact. What to say: "I want to understand what you need. Please show me what you were doing the last time you wanted that feature."
You just nod while watching or listening, not asking any questions or requesting a specific example.	You are assuming an understanding of the work situation without probing. You've seen or heard this before and think you already know why the user is doing the same thing.	Check your understanding with the user. What to say: "Let me see if I understand. I think you are doing that because ..." "I don't want to make any assump-tions, even if it seems obvious. So, let me check what I'm thinking with you."
You think to yourself, "No one else would do that. This is person is one user in a thousand."	You are throwing away unexpected data. After all, what are the odds you are actually seeing one user in a thousand?	Find out more about the situation and why. What to say: "Let's stop and talk about more about why you do that."
You have no idea what's going on so you decide to write it all down and then ask someone back in the office to explain it to you.	You're not finding out what's really going on by asking the only person who can really tell you, the user.	Ask the user. You're not the expert about his or her work, and neither is anyone back at the office. What to say: "Can you stop a minute? I'm not sure I really understand what you are doing. Please explain it to me."

Table 4-2:
Tips for staying on task during an interview.

the users. Delving into the user's work helps the user become more aware. So partnership means that you and the user are engaged in exploring and discovering the user's work and are working as a team.

Dos and don'ts

The tips in Table 4-3 will help you engage the user in a collaborative relationship. These tips will help you draw the user into a working partnership with you throughout the interview.

Table 4-3:
Tips for creating a solid, productive relationship with the interviewee.

Dos and don'ts for engaging the user in a collaborative relationship	
Don't	Do
Hide your focus.	Share your focus. The interviewee can help find relevant cases and issues.
Create a distant relationship: Sit back, have a reserved attitude. Be apologetic or timid. Be overbearing.	Create an intimate relationship: Lean forward, be fascinated. Be confiding and genuine.
Create a formal relationship.	Be nosy, overcome formality.
Interview by rote: I ask/You answer. Questions not related to action.	Respond to non-verbal cues: If the user is self-doubting, nervous, or withdrawn gently draw him out by asking him to show you how he does a particular task. If the user is talkative or distracted from the task at hand, draw her attention back to the concrete. Ask her to re-create the exact steps she took the last time she performed a task. Recognize that you may need to do this several times for some users.
Sit on the "visitor" side of the desk while the user is talking.	Pull up a chair next to the user and her computer screen. Make sure that you can see what is happening.
Be the expert.	Invite users to educate you in their work.

You don't need to be an expert to do the interview. The user is the expert; you are the expert in probing and understanding their world. So don't worry about asking questions—you won't "look stupid" or embarrass your company. You will look interested in the user and gain respect for listening and caring.

Interpretation

Determine meaning together with the user. Don't just collect facts and make up what they mean. Facts are not data that matters for design, you need the meaning or the "why."

Only the user can tell you why they do what they do. But if you ask why directly, they might make something up because they aren't aware of why they are doing it. Instead, share your own hypothesis of what you are observing and let the user tune your interpretation.

You may think you know, but can't be sure that the user is doing something for the reason you assume they are doing it. So share it and let the user "fix" your understanding. Fixing is easier and more accurate than asking why directly. Be honest and listen for the no hidden in the user's words, indirect language, and nonverbal behavior. Then let your wrong interpretation go.

Dos and don'ts

Throughout the interview you need to verify that you understand the work you are observing. You do this by offering your interpretation of the work for your user's comments. The tips in Table 4-4 provide you with ways to verify your interpretation within the context of the interview.

Dos and don'ts for interpreting during an interview	
Don't	Do
Just watch what happens and record it.	Look for patterns, intents, issues, and the role people play in the work and share them with the user.
Just ask yes or no questions.	Offer hypotheses that invite elaboration.
Just ask why or use open ended questions.	Use metaphors to explain what the work is like and ask the user if you got it right.
Nod without asking, to verify everything you think you understand.	Share your interpretation of their words and work even if it is obvious.
Just replay what happened with no synthesis at the end of the interview.	Give a coherent wrap up: User's work strategy. Role in organization.

Table 4-4: Tips for verifying and capturing interpretations during an interview.

Focus

Your project focus tells you what kind of task and experiences to observe and probe. Your personal experience makes some things more interesting to you than others. But both of these are limiting and may obscure what really matters to the work.

The principle of focus calls upon you to challenge your assumptions to expand focus and see more data. Pay attention to things that don't seem to fit into your existing assumptions. The internal triggers described later will help you know when that is happening. And avoid veering off focus during the interview or you will waste time getting information that you don't care about.

Dos and don'ts

Throughout the interview you need to make sure that you are staying on track and that you are not veering off focus. Use your focus as a guide; write it on the top of each page of your interview notebook. Table 4-5 contains tips to help you direct the interview without taking complete control.

Table 4-5:
Tips for staying on
focus during an in-
terview.

Do and don'ts for staying on focus	
Don't	Do
Focus on the software, configuration or hardware.	Focus on work; identify cases in the focus to pursue.
Pursue issues or events outside your focus.	Expand focus based on what you see the user do. Gloss over irrelevant events introduced by the user. It is NOT rude to NOT engage the user in conversation about things that are not in focus. You don't want to teach the user that you are interested in irrelevant information.
Dismiss issues because you don't understand them yet.	Probe things you don't understand or are surprised by.
Ask marketing related questions if not in a buying situation.	
Talk from an implicit list of questions you want answered.	Follow the work, discuss how the work is structured, not topics in your head.

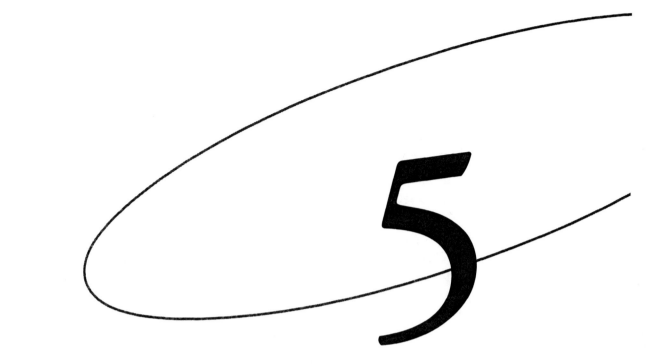

Contextual Interview Interpretation Session

Rapid CD Process	Lightning Fast	Lightning Fast +	Focused Rapid CD
Contextual Interviews and Interpretation	✓	✓	✓

Once you have completed an interview your next step is to share it with the rest of your team in an interpretation session. Contextual Interviews produce large amounts of customer data, all of which must be shared among the core design team and potentially with other stakeholders: user interface designers, engineers, documentation people, internal business users, and marketers. Traditional methods of sharing by presentations, in reports, or by e-mail do not allow the people tasked with building the system to truly process the information or bring their perspectives into a shared understanding. Contextual Design overcomes this by involving the team in interactive sessions to review, analyze, and capture key issues revealed by the customer data.

An interpretation session occurs within 48 hours after the field interview and is best conducted by a cross-functional team chartered with designing the system. During the session the team hears the story of the field interview and "captures" key issues online, which later will be built into an affinity diagram (see Chapter 8). All forms of Rapid CD will perform interpretation sessions. If you are using Focused Rapid CD you also will be capturing your sequence model (see Chapter 6).

No preparation of the data is necessary before the interpretation session if you interpret within 48 hours. Remember, don't talk about the details of the interview before the interpretation session to keep the detail and your enthusiasm fresh.

This chapter defines the interpretation session and guides you through running the meeting.

Definition

We refer to this session as an interpretation, but your organization may call it a download, brain dump, or debrief. During the interpretation session, you will share your interview experience with the rest of the team and interpret the data, capturing the key issues and doing any work models you have chosen to capture. As a rule, plan on your interpretation session lasting approximately the same amount of time as the Contextual Interview.

Key concepts

Interpretation session or affinity notes. The team takes notes during the interpretation session that capture the key issues they want to record about the data. These notes will be built into an affinity diagram, so they are often called affinity notes. Affinity notes are captured online and displayed during the interpretation session via CDTools or a word processor.

"Capture that." We refer to the process of recording the data, whether an affinity note, a work model, or an insight, as "capturing" the data. This means that it is written down and recorded in a form that can be reused later. So teams often will say "capture that" when they want to be sure that a particular point is recorded appropriately.

Session role. Defined roles that each participant plays during the interpretation session. Operating within the session roles enables the team to stay focused and on track throughout the interpretation.

Design ideas, holes, and questions. Method of capturing people's issues during the interpretation session. Capturing design ideas (DIs), holes, and questions (Qs) as affinity notes allows participants to capture their issues without derailing the interpretation session.

Rat hole. Any conversation that takes the focus of the interpretation meeting away from the interview. Calling a rat hole is a signal to the team that the conversation has digressed from the main focus—the interview with the user.

Insight. An insight is a major work observation or lesson about the users' work practice and application experience that has significant implications for the design of the system. Insights are captured at the end of each interpretation session, giving the team a moment to step back and record more holistic learnings.

Interpretation

- ☐ Preparation:
  - ☐ Locate and prepare a team room
  - ☐ Identify the interpretation team
- ☐ During the interpretation session:
  - ☐ Identify who will play each interpretation session role
  - ☐ Capture the user and organization profiles

□ Capture affinity notes and work models

□ Capture insights

□ (Optional) After the interpretation session conduct a share session

Prepare a team room

In order to function as efficiently as possible, try to find a dedicated team room to keep your supplies, affinity wall, and other project materials for the duration of your project. Finding a room that you can reserve for several weeks in your company may be difficult, but having a permanent place makes it easier for people to work together. It is also good to have a room that is not off the beaten path; part of your communication strategy is inviting people into your team room to see your data. Encourage people to drop in and ask about what you are doing.

If you are unable to stay in the room for the duration of your project, you will need to pack everything and carry it with you from room to room. Once your affinity is built you can tape down your affinity notes and roll the sections up in order to move them. Or get your data online and print it out to hang on the wall.

Your team room should have the following supplies:

- A computer with CDTools or a word processor loaded onto it (this can be any team member's laptop). Some people also capture their affinity notes in a spreadsheet, however we find this makes it nearly impossible to print them easily for affinity building.

- A projector or a large monitor with a display big enough that the team can view the affinity notes as they are captured. Seeing the affinity notes helps pace the meeting. If you are using CDTools, you can use its features to adjust the display so everyone can read what's on-screen.

- One flipchart to capture work models or team discussions. Flipcharts are generally useful as a place to draw aspects of the user's work for clarification during the interpretation session. But for Focused Rapid CD you need a flipchart to capture the sequence model.

- Red, blue, and green Sharpie® Fine Tip pens for capturing models. Blue is the default color, red is for breakdowns, green is for holes, questions, or high-level summary data. (Note: If someone is color blind, use black instead of green.)

If you are running more than one interpretation session at a time, provide the same supplies in your second room.

Identify the interpretation team

Interpretation sessions bring multiple perspectives to bear on each user interview. An interpretation team delivers the best results when its members represent a range of job functions and viewpoints. A two-person team can run all the Rapid CD interpretation sessions (see the box, **Don't interpret by yourself**). However we recommend that you

103

take the opportunity to find helpers from among the stakeholders who will build the system and involve them in the interpretation sessions as well to increase buy-in and to get their perspectives on the data. You can have one helper at each session but don't bring too many or it will be hard to manage—a total of four people is a good size.

A minimum interpretation session team consists of the interviewer and one other team member, preferably with an alternative perspective. So if the interviewer is a developer, the other person could be marketing, business, or user experience. You can mix your interpretation team compositions if you include stakeholders as additional people for an interpretation session to ensure that different perspectives are included. Participating in an interpretation session is only a two-hour commitment so it is often easy to get stakeholders involved.

If your team is bigger than two you can include four to six people in one interpretation session and still manage it. You also can do parallel interpretation sessions with a larger team and thereby increase the amount of data you can collect in a short period of time. Or you can take turns participating in sessions to use resources more efficiently. But then conduct share sessions to share high-level findings with team members who missed the interpretation session.

Don't interpret by yourself

Why interpret in a team? We recommend a minimum of two people for an interpretation session. When you are the interviewer you have your point of view on the data. You implicitly picked out what you think matters—what matters from your perspective. Everything that doesn't matter to you is invisible to you.

But if you have to tell your story from beginning to end to others and together capture the key issues, you will find many more insights and design implications than you can working alone. Why? Because each person listening will hear from their own experience and business expertise. They will see in your data what you can't see; you will see in their data what they miss. They will probe you for details you forgot or thought irrelevant. Together you will get the most out of your data—all the while you are sharing what happened with the team. The team working together in this way will start to have a shared understanding on the data without even trying.

And because you hear each other's issues you will pick them up as your own. In future interviews you, too, can start to see things from a wider perspective. So always interpret with at least one other person.

If you are operating on a schedule that requires you to gather a lot of data in a week you can run parallel interpretation sessions by soliciting helpers from your stakeholder community to ensure you can run two sessions at once. If your team members are spread out across multiple locations you can also run a distributed interpretation session (see the box, **How do we interpret with a distributed team?**).

Your interpretation session is a good way to communicate early findings informally. Consider including a manager, business people, decision-makers, developers not on the core team, someone from the business side like marketing or an analyst, or other stakeholders in the project. This provides a broader perspective and gives them a stake in the outcome of the project. Not only will you encourage their acceptance of the project, but you will also gain valuable insight into the work and larger business implications of the data. Having an "outsider" in the interpretation session can bring a much-needed perspective to the user's data.

Any time a helper is included, make sure they are aware of your focus and the intent of your data gathering endeavors. Coach any newcomers in the roles and process of an interpretation session meeting. Interested parties or others not on the team shouldn't outnumber those who are. If they do you run the risk of the meeting reverting to standard meeting behavior instead of interpretation session behavior. This will cause the interpretation session to become bogged down and run longer.

How do we interpret with a distributed team?

If you are part of a distributed team you will need to figure out how you are going to share information across locations for interpretation and share sessions. If you have collaboration or virtual meeting software, you can use that to run a distributed meeting. Simply display CDTools or your word processor in a collaboration space so all can see and comment on what the applications actually do.

Simply get everyone on the phone and then display CDTools or your word processor so the application is shared in all meeting locations. This will let everyone see and comment on the affinity notes as they are captured.

If you have a video conferencing system, you may wish to use that to show the work models as they are being captured on flipcharts. However, using a video conferencing system is often logistically more trouble than it is worth. If you are capturing only sequence models, you may want to consider capturing those online in a word processing, spreadsheet, or drawing application, switching the shared display from the affinity notes to the work model as needed. Periodically stopping to check the work models will add to your interpretation session time, but is a critical step to be sure that the data is being captured correctly.

Tips:

Running distributed interpretation sessions requires a bit more logistical planning before the meeting, and additional ongoing communication throughout the meeting. Think about things like:

- Can the interviewer readily see the affinity notes and the models? In a distributed session you may want to have the work modeler in the same location as the notetaker. The notetaker can then see the affinity notes on the shared displayed, and the models in the same room. But then you will need to show the models to the interviewer for a proper quality check if they are at the other end of the display.

- Can everyone easily hear? People will become frustrated if they cannot hear the data as it unfolds, or if they cannot get airtime because their teammates don't realize they are trying to add their thoughts.

- Does the video conferencing phone have too much lag? If there's a delay between when you start speaking and the others hear you, everyone will be talking over each other and it will be very frustrating. In this situation, turn off the sound on the video conferencing and use teleconferencing on the telephone in parallel.

- Is everyone staying engaged? Be sure that everyone has a role and is actively participating. If someone has been quiet for a period of time, check in with him or her. Consider having both sides responsible for some type of data capture to keep everyone engaged.

An interpretation session lasts about as long as the interview if it is well managed. Your first interpretation will be longer as you get used to the data and the process. But thereafter they should be about two hours. We have found that when interpretation sessions drag out past two hours people find it hard to focus and experience the process as "too heavy." To stay within this metric, plan your interpretation team as follows:

- If you are capturing affinity notes only you need two people, the interviewer and one other.

- If you are capturing affinity notes and sequence models you need three people, the interviewer and two others.

Multiple people in an interpretation session not only ensure that you get multiple perspectives on the data and can easily share the findings, they also speed up the process. The interviewer is looking at his or her paper notes while talking and should not be expected to record the data on a computer. The notetaker is working on a computer and so can capture affinity notes as the interviewer talks. A third person simultaneously can capture the sequence model online or on a flipchart. Each person has one job and doesn't need to switch tools or contexts.

With multiple people in an interpretation session the overall time taken to capture the necessary data is reduced. And the quality of the data is increased because others are probing the interviewer and providing their insights on the data. For this reason the interpretation session process necessarily creates a shared understanding of the user population within the team.

But involvement has its limits: the more people you have in an interpretation session the harder it is to manage. Four people is the optimum number for involvement, and you should not have more than six. Even if you want "everyone" to hear the data, more than six people limits the air time and results in too many people who are not actively playing a role in the session. Attention wanders and impatience increases. Idle people tend to drag the focus from the main conversation. It is better to have a small, fast, tight interpretation team and share the data later in the share session.

Identify who will play each interpretation session role

A successful work meeting requires each person to know what they are doing in the meeting and to be clear on the goals and process of the meeting. In other words, each person needs to know what the mainline conversation (the primary topic of the meeting) is and what role they are to play in meeting the goals of the meeting. The mainline conversation in an interpretation session is "What happened in this interview and what do we make of it?"

Depending on the number of people in your interpretation session, people may end up playing one or more of these roles. Following are the roles and responsibilities for a basic interpretation session.

Interviewer

The interviewer needs to do no preparation for the interpretation session. The goal is to share what happened in the interview and to let the team help identify the key issues and work practices to capture. If it has been more than two days since the interview, the interviewer should review the audio recording of the interview prior to the interpretation session.

The interviewer introduces the user to the interpretation team starting with the user and organization profiles. Then he or she recounts the interview guided by paper notes. Go through your paper notes in order, don't summarize or edit out things you don't think are important. Yours is only one perspective on the data, you are in the interpretation session as an informant to the team recounting everything you saw, heard, or said so they can identify the issues that matter from their perspective and raise issues you never thought of during the interview.

But the interviewer is not passive. He or she also:

- Takes part in the discussion

- Offers insights, interpretations, and design ideas that occur to him or her

- Ensures ideas are captured by saying, "capture that!" and checking what gets captured

- Validates that an interpretation made by a team member is indeed true to the user's experience

The interviewer is the last word on the "truth" about the user and their experience. If the interviewer says that an interpretation made by another team member is valid, it is valid and an affinity note is captured. If the interviewer says an interpretation is not true to the user's experience, it is not valid and should not be captured as an affinity note. The interviewer is the quality check on any data captured in the interpretation session.

Notetaker

The notetaker writes concise, informative affinity notes, which are displayed with a projector or a large monitor for the entire group to see. The notetaker needs to be able to listen, type, and process information simultaneously; he or she sets the pace for the interpretation session.

In addition to participating as a general team member, the notetaker:

- Records, in CDTools or in a document, the participant roles team members are playing in the interpretation session so that if anyone has any questions about the data captured they know who to talk to later

- Writes affinity notes to capture observations, issues, breakdowns in the work, questions, holes, insights, and design ideas as requested by session participants

- Adds any new demographic data to the profile as it is identified throughout the interpretation session since it may not be complete at the start of the session

- Asks clarifying questions to determine the best way to phrase an affinity note

- For online sequence capture: flips between the affinity notes screen and the sequence document as needed

The notetaker is not a gatekeeper. Any affinity note that a team member wants to capture is acceptable as long as it does not break the rules of the process. You will not know at the time you are capturing any one affinity note how it might impact the design. Only when you look across all the data will the importance of an observation become clear. Discussing the goodness of one affinity note simply slows down the meeting and creates friction within the team. Adding multiple affinity notes is always faster than discussion.

Work modeler for Focused Rapid CD

The work modeler is responsible for any work models being created on flipchart paper for all to see. Work models are captured real-time writing steps and data as they are heard. See Chapter 6 for how to capture work models during the interpretation session.

In addition the work modeler participates as a general team member.

General interpretation team member

Every member of the interpretation team listens to the interviewer and determines what to record as affinity notes. A general team member:

- Listens to the interviewer and probe to discover work practice

- Ensures ideas are captured by saying, "capture that" and checking what gets captured

- Offers insights, interpretations, and design ideas that occur to them

- Asks questions of the interviewer if they feel that the interviewer may be skipping something or summarizing pieces of the interview

- Reviews the affinity notes and models as they are captured for accuracy

- Keeps the conversation on track by declaring rat holes

Every team member must also remember to stay on the mainline conversation and avoid sharing about any other user with similar experience that they may have interviewed but whose data has not been interpreted yet. General discussion of personal experience and attitudes are also discouraged as off-topic rat holes. (This just slows down the session. See the box, **What is a rat hole?**)

Moderator

The moderator is responsible for keeping the interpretation session on track. In a two-person team both team members need to have an attitude of moderation, stopping every so often to ask how they are doing.

But if you are managing a three- to six-person team, moderation is important to keep the interpretation session running smoothly, ensures quality data is captured, and keeps the conversation focused (see the box, **Guidelines for a good interpretation session**).

In addition to being a general team member the moderator also:

- Keeps the meeting focused on the main conversation

- Ensures everyone is involved in the conversation

- Ensures that the notetaker and work modelers are not falling behind

- Helps the interviewer stay in the order of their notes, not skipping ahead in response to questions

What is a rat hole?

During an interpretation session your goal is to identify and record the key issues and data from a single user visit. All other topics are "rat holes" to be avoided. So to keep the meeting on track we create a fun role that all can play: the rat hole watcher. Some examples of rat holes are discussions about:

- What happened in a different interview or contact with a different user

- What you, your friends, or your relatives do in this situation

- The pluses or minuses of a design idea

- How to implement a design idea

- What you do, like, or believe (as opposed to the data coming from this user)

For fun the team might want to make a few rat hole signs. These signs can be as simple as a piece of paper with the words "rat hole" written on it or a red flag. When the conversation goes off focus, whoever notices it first should raise the flag, call the rat hole, and redirect the conversation back to the interview.

To move back to the mainline conversation it may be necessary to capture a question or design idea implied by the rat hole discussion. The important thing to do in these situations is to make sure each participant's issues are heard and documented while moving forward through the interview interpretation session.

- Ensures that the notetaker is not overly controlling what goes in the affinity notes, capturing the ideas that only he or she likes

- Ensures that everyone keeps up the pace

- Makes the final decision on process

- Watches out for "steam rolling" by team and nonteam members

The moderator is the authoritative voice in the meeting, ensuring that it is running according to the rules of an interpretation session. If so, your interpretation session will be focused, on time, and a good environment to produce and share user data.

Capture the user and organization profiles

At the start of the interpretation session, after assigning roles, capture the user and organizational profile. This is the way the interviewer introduces the user to the team, starting the main body of the interpretation session.

Teams like to be able to characterize the users they talked to and their organizations by traditional demographics: years of experience, age, software used, size of organization, and so on. These demographics help others to understand the scope of the user population sampled. But demographic observations rarely yield insight into the work practice. So capturing this information as affinity notes is not recommended unless it has direct bearing on the project focus.

What you include in the user and organizational profiles depends on your project and what kind of background and demographic information you want to know about. If you want you can bring a short survey to the interview and formally capture any important demographics.

Guidelines for a good interpretation session

Any good meeting has a clear focus, clear roles that people have to play to make the meeting work, and a set of cultural expectations that ensure that the meeting progresses successfully for both the tangible outcome and the people involved. Here are the rules of the interpretation session that make it a highly productive meeting.

- Create a safe environment for everyone to take part. This includes:
  - Encouraging the quiet folks to speak their "silly" ideas.
  - Helping those who talk too much to manage themselves by keeping a pack of Post-it® notes to write down their ideas. Then they can check to see if no one else brought up the topic or point and bring it up after others get a chance. Often they can learn that the same issues will be raised and that they can control their own participation by writing down the idea so they won't forget instead of sharing it right away.

- Watch for chaos:
  - Signs include rising noise and rising tension.
  - Stop the meeting to sort out the issues clearly for the team instead of bulldozing ahead.

- Make sure you are still following the mainline conversation—what happened with this one user and nothing else.

- Don't allow the meeting to veer into design conversations. This is not the time to develop design ideas. Just state the design idea so it is captured as an affinity note, and then move on.

- Make sure everyone is heard.
  - If someone does not feel heard, they will repeat their point frequently.
  - Handle this by writing the point down, either in the affinity notes or as an issue for one of the models.

- Watch the pace of the meeting.
  - Slow meetings are boring, less creative, and harder to track.
  - Keep the pace moving by moving the team from issue to issue quickly.
  - Have the goal of finishing each interpretation session in two hours; pace yourself.
  - A slow notetaker slows the entire meeting; if someone is agonizing over words or struggling to keep up, move them off that role. (Remember, it's not a statement of personal worth, simply an inborn skill.)

- Arguing is never productive.
  - Decisions should be based in user data. Arguments often arise when you simply need more data.
  - Sometimes people want to know what happens next in the process but you don't have the data; avoid hypothesizing the future.
  - Sometimes interviewers just don't know why something happened; make it a question and avoid hypothesizing what might have happened.
  - Arguments often result when people are concerned about two different issues. Clarifying the issues can help people see how their issues are different and compatible. Alternatively, write down both issues so you can move on.
  - Don't argue over word definitions and choices. Write what you mean (see examples) in plain English. If it persists, give yourself seven minutes to discuss a definition then move on.

Because of your promise of confidentiality you want to associate the user code and number (for example U01) with the user profile, not the user's real name and organization. Maintain a separate document matching the user's actual name and company to the user code to protect confidentiality.

Using a user code encourages the team to maintain the confidentiality of the user whenever they are talking about them to others. And it also gives you a way to track different market segments or user contexts if you want to see how this data clusters. So if you are studying urban and rural environments you may have U01 for urban and R02 for rural; the letter code represents the context and the number code represents each user interviewed.

User profile

The user profile includes demographic information about the user's job and the roles that she plays. For instance, you may want to capture the user's job title, responsibilities, and other demographic information. Depending on your project, you may also want to capture training levels, system use, and knowledge.

Example: eChalk

Here you see one of eChalk's user profiles. You can see that it was important to this team to know what kind of teacher the user is, how long he has been teaching, the kinds of classes taught, and the software and hardware available and used. This team decided to capture teachers' ages to be sure their interview spread covered people in different age groups to see if there was any relationship between that and comfort with technology.

U09 Profile

- Works at Org 4
- Current Position: Computer Teacher in a middle school. Teaching for 3 years; teaches music and computers.
- Number of Students: 8 core students (computer club—informal/kids drift in during free periods (subs in class go to the computer club) creating flash, help him with special projects
- Teaches 4 computer classes, 5 music courses, computer tech class, and Vanguard class (high achiever's class); Computer class = web page design
- Only uses MSIE—web pages look better in IE than in Netscape
- Best guess of age: thirty-something (35?)
- Lab: 32 computers in the room—partial T1 line used in the classroom for connectivity
- Applications: MS Office (used at beginning of semester—mostly interested in designing web pages)
- Fiber optic cable is used for the telephone system
- Software: MS Office (Excel), MS Works (easier), MS Access, Flash, Hyperstudio (Kids PowerPoint app), Compton's, Encarta, Groliers (CD-ROM), Web games (Pac Man, Space Invaders, Pong, Solitaire), Photo Image Ready, Photoshop

User profiles can be captured in the User Information window of CDTools. If you are not using CDTools, user profiles should be captured in a word processor. Capture the profiles in a separate document from the affinity notes. Usually it is easier to have one document that has all user profiles. (See Chapter 3 for a description of CDTools' User Information window.)

Example: Agilent user profiles

Note that in this project, the team was interested in the difference between their two primary markets: chemical labs (often petrochemical) and pharmaceutical labs. To track these differences, their user codes start with C or P, respectively. Commercial analytical labs, doing tests for others, are flagged with U.

U02: Has been at Org7 for over two years. Does analyses of in-testing support of stability samples. Writes SOP, IQ (In-process Qualification), and OQ (Operational Qualification). U32 calibrates and maintains instruments. Has a BS in Chemistry with some graduate work.

U03: Has worked at Org7 for two years. Has a BS in Biochemistry, MS in Biotechnology. He has the title of R&D Chemist. He came from Ireland and both degrees are from Ireland. He came here for an apprenticeship and decided to stay because job market is bad in Ireland.

Example: Apropos user profiles

U04: Part of the Advanced Group support team, U04 handles help and support calls for one of Org01's products. Her goal is to solve problems without sending them to the Escalation Group. She also monitors a chat room where Level 1 technicians can ask questions about problems they cannot answer. She provides answers and solutions to these reps via the chat.

U05: Part of the Escalation Group, supporting one of Org01's products. He will not take ownership of issues until the Advanced Group has tried everything they can. He is the last direct contact with the customer, although he will discuss issues with engineering, and push bugs to them.

Example: Purchasing user profiles

U4: Female, in her 30s, working in Germany. She is an operations purchaser—the person who sets up and manages the relationships between an automotive OEM (the auto manufacturer) and suppliers. She has worked at this OEM for three years, but is still considered a new hire. She is a power user of SAP; she trains other users and is first-line help.

Organization profile

The organization profile includes a generalized description of the organization's business and its industry. You may want to include the number of employees, locations the organization operates, the number and kind of products they use, or the services they contract for. Recording an organization profile is not required, but it is a good way to keep track of the types of organizations from which you collected data.

Example: eChalk

Here's the profile for User 09's organization. You can see that some school-wide technology was captured here.

- Public school in New York City

- 1750 students grades 6–8; one of the top 40 schools in the city; 2,500 different countries represented by student population—heavy Russian, Chinese, Spanish population; Russian is the biggest challenge in the school (lots of students have Russian as a first language)

- 45 special needs kids in the school; students from outside of the school can apply

- Altaris is their network mgmt. tool; Using NetZero as their ISP

- Hardware: Dell Power Edge 4300 network server

Organization profiles should be captured in the Organization Information box of CDTools. (See Chapter 3 for a description of CDTools' User Information window.) If you are not using CDTools, organization profiles should be captured in your word processor. Capture the organizational profiles in the same document as the user profiles. You can then use this document as a reference during the affinity building described in Chapter 7.

Tip: It is a good practice to also include the interpretation session participants' names and roles played in the document that holds the users' and organizations' profiles. This information can come in handy during affinity building. In CDTools, capture session participants in the Notes Session window.

> **Example: Agilent organization profiles**
>
> **Org7:** The company produces pharmaceutical and nutritional products and performs R&D development for larger pharmaceutical companies. The focus for their own products is in development rather than research. They were acquired six years ago by a Japanese company. Their consumer products are sold by multilevel marketing. They follow GLP/cGMP procedures. They are building an additional plant. When it is complete, they will be in two buildings—one pilot and the other development. The new buildings will be pharmaceutical only. They do small scale production at one location but the scaled-up work is in another location.
>
> The types of drugs that they work on include antihypertensive, Alzheimer's, cardiac maintenance drugs, hypnotic sedatives, and calcium blockers. Some methods come from the client, but they would like to have the latitude to change them. There were at least ten chemists during the shift. Management trusts the chemists because they are professionals. They went GMP three to four years ago. They separated the pharmaceutical and nutrition product, because nutritional products do not need GMP. Equipment in the lab includes a lot of Shimadzu LC and HP Vectras.
>
> **Example: Apropos organization profiles**
>
> **Org 01:** A software company specializing in storage and backup tools. The call center handles sales and support calls. One of their goals is to avoid putting callers through a telephone menu system, so they employ "dispatch" agents who send the calls to the appropriate queue with sales or support. Within support, their levels are: 1, Dispatch; 2, Level 1; 3, Advanced Group; and 4, Escalation Group. The escalation technicians are the last level that talks to the customer—they will discuss problems and bugs with engineering, but engineers rarely talk to customers.
>
> **Example: Purchasing organization profiles**
>
> **Org 2:** A maker of small, high-priced, prestigious sports cars. This company works with many suppliers to provide all the different parts of a car, but is working to reduce the number of suppliers they have to work with. They maintain tight control over all parts made by their suppliers. They have suppliers they work with regularly, but will add new suppliers to serve special needs. Suppliers must manufacture parts to Org 2's schedule and quantities.

Capture affinity notes and work models

Once you have finished capturing profile information, begin the interpretation session proper. Capture affinity notes in CDTools (see Figure 5-1) or in a word processor. Project the affinity notes on the wall so all can see what is being recorded.

The interviewer starts by walking the group through the interview without summarizing or skipping anything. If you took photos of the physical environment show them now or draw a simple physical model (see Chapter 6), sketching the physical context in which the interview occurred.

Figure 5-1:
CDTools interpretation screen used for capturing notes which will be used to build the affinity diagram.

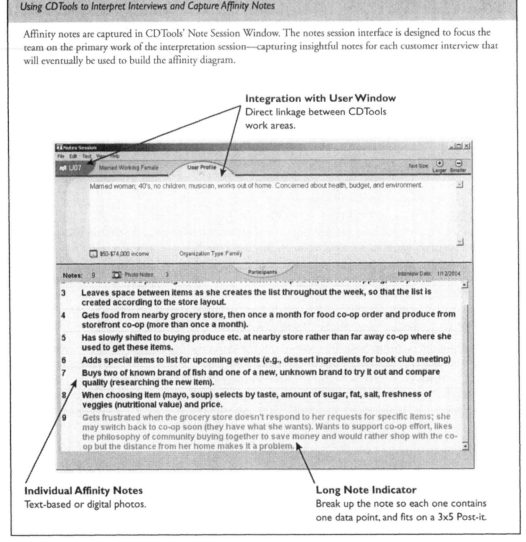

The interpretation team interrupts and asks questions about what is happening at each stage of the interview, but not about what is going to happen next. Interviewers will remember more accurately if they do not skip around in their notes.

The goal of the interaction between the interviewer and the rest of the group is to maintain the right level of tension between letting the interviewer tell the story and probing into what happened. The interviewer shares what happened in order, the group pushes to get to the detailed "what" and "why" behind the user's actions. Doing so leads to effective interpretation and high quality affinity notes.

During this process the notetaker's role is to capture the key ideas emerging from this discussion. When the interviewer emphasizes a certain point it implies that it is worth capturing. When the participants probe for a point or offer an interpretation that is confirmed, it again implies an affinity note to be captured. The notetaker is the central listener, capturing both implied affinity notes and those the team directs him or her to take (see the box, **What to record in the affinity notes**).

What to record in the affinity notes

Do record:
- Interpretations of events, use of artifacts, problems, and opportunities
- Important characteristics of the work
- Breakdowns in the work
- Cultural influences
- Design ideas (flag with DI:)
- Questions for future interviews (flag with a Q:)
- Insightful customer quotes

Don't record:
- Demographics; put them on the profile as part of the user description
- Other information represented on work models

Periodically the notetaker will stop and remind the team to look at the affinity notes and make sure they are correct. Each affinity note should contain only one thought or point with clear references to who said or did what (see the box, **Grammar does matter when capturing affinity notes (sort of)**). Each note eventually must stand alone during affinity building. (See the note examples on pages 117 and 118.)

Grammar does matter when capturing affinity notes (sort of)

It is not necessary to be a professional writer to write affinity notes, but you do have to write them well or as well as possible. Remember, these affinity notes represent your data and your team; other people are going to be reading them. Bad grammar and poorly written text gets in the way of understanding and interpretation. It also wastes time when you are building the affinity. A good notetaker can write succinct affinity notes with enough description to stand alone. A good practice, particularly if you are going to present your affinity to your customers, is to edit the affinity notes for clarity before you build the affinity. You can use CDTools' spell checker and other editing features for cleaning up the notes.

In addition to general affinity notes, the notetaker also captures notes describing user issues and behavior. Other notes captured during the interpretation session are:

Questions. When the team gets bogged down over a question that the interviewer can't answer, the notetaker captures it in the affinity notes and encourages the group to move on. The act of capturing the question raises it as something that everyone needs to pay attention to in the next interviews.

Design ideas. Ideas for solutions that team members come up with are captured both to ensure they are preserved and again to encourage the team to move on and remain focused on extracting the relevant data not working out a design idea.

Good user quotes. Capture these as "quotes" to use later when you are communicating to the rest of your organization.

Interpretations. The team will hear the data and draw interpretations of how it represents a work pattern, or implies an inner experience. These also are captured as long as they ring true for the interviewer.

Table 5-1 contains Dos and Don'ts for capturing affinity notes. Try to avoid the Don'ts during a session, but remember you can always go back and edit the notes to clean them up after the session if you want to.

Table 5-1: Tips for note capturing during the interpretation session.

Dos and don'ts for capturing notes	
Don't	**Do**
Be vague or use non-specific pronouns.	Be clear, make sure you identify who you are talking about in each note, watch your pronouns e.g., she told her that he said to …, A few days after you capture a note like this you aren't going to remember who she, her, and he are. Use user numbers, job titles, or some other identifiers so that you will be able to sort out the players late.
Use jargon that is familiar only to your team.	Use common terms to describe the work. Business people, marketing, etc. may not be familiar with your shorthand. Be careful not to exclude them from gaining the most value from your data.
Refer to the user or organization by name.	Remember, your users and their organizations are supposed to be anonymous.
Overload a note with too much information.	Keep different points separate or you will have to go back and create new notes when building your affinity. You also do not want to lose nuances by putting too much in a note.
Write sequential notes.	Write notes that stand by themselves. Notes you capture in an interpretation session will be sorted and printed for the affinity. Each note needs to stand on its own.
Capture sequence model steps.	The steps are captured in the sequence model itself. If there is a distinction that the step reveals, capture that in the notes.
Capture demographic information.	The user or organizational profile is the place for demographic information.
Spend time speculating on the answer to a question when the interviewer doesn't know.	Capture the question as a note starting with "Q:".
Capture facts only.	The note will have facts, but the more important data is why a fact matters. Capture your interpretation and the fact.
Wordsmith a note or argue over definitions.	Don't waste time arguing over a specific word. Sometimes capturing multiple words which are similar with slash marks between them is faster than picking one. If you find yourselves arguing over core definitions, hold a separate definition session to define the key concepts you will use and what they mean.

As a general rule of thumb, 50 to 100 affinity notes should be captured for each two-hour interview. If you are getting fewer, check that the interviewers are recording all their observations. If you get too many, check whether you are capturing every step in a task or trying to describe things in notes that are better captured in work models.

eChalk notes	Analysis
U01-04 He is the network administrator for the school (sets up systems in the school, and connects them to the network.)	This note may look like demographic information, but it is important that eChalk capture in their affinity the different roles that teacher's have to play around technology.
U01-11 He can't answer questions verbally, teachers want him to come and show them. Verbal exchange can quickly lead to breakdown if the teacher is not technically savvy.	This note is o.k., but could be even better because it contains two points that could be in two separate notes. The first point is about how teachers need to be shown what to do, not just told. The second point is that when teachers are not technically savvy, they don't have a frame of reference to understand what they are told.
U01-49 He is frustrated by Board of Ed. filtering i.e. can't get to NASA.	This is a good example of a note capturing a cultural influence.
Q: Does U1 use computer at home for work because not getting what he needs at school (connectivity, filter)?	This is an example of Question note. The interviewer couldn't answer this question about U01, but now the entire team will be watching out for similar data in subsequent interviews.
U01-67 Sends surveys home to parents to learn what technology they have at home.	This is a good note that stands alone on its own. The team did more than capture the fact that surveys were sent home; they also captured what the survey was used for.
U01-68 DI: Templates for surveys of all kinds for school/teachers to use. Targeted for internal use by type or general public use.	This is an example of a Design Idea note, generated in response to the data in the U01-67 note.
U01-90 He likes At Ease.	This note will not work well in the affinity. Why does he like At Ease? In reality, the team captured several specific notes about U01's use of At Ease; this specific note doesn't add any new insight.
U2-01 Elementary students have to learn computer skills—principal dictates how far these standards have to go (list of topics by major curriculum areas—topics that have to be completed by the end of the year—each state has tests to test whether the teacher/class has met the standards).	This note could be broken into three notes since it contains several important points. Note: Elementary students have to learn computer skills. Note: The principal dictates how standards will be met (list of topics, topics that have to be completed). Note: Each state has tests to test whether the teacher/class has met the standards.
U02-4 Uses log book (print matter/hand written). Teaches 27 classes so this book keeps track of where each class is and where she left off.	This is a good note. The team didn't stop at capturing the fact that a log book was used; the important point is that the teacher has to track where each class is and where she left off.
U02-26 Is focused on making technology a part of the school's existing curriculum (math, English, etc), not a subject unto itself.	This is a good note, and potentially very important to the team's design. If this data is found with other users, the team will want to take advantage of the integrating technology in any lessons, not just computer class.

Example: Agilent affinity notes

C2-05 Her life is like a waitress trying to keep up with all her 'tables' (tests) in progress. This is memory intensive—things are easy to forget.

C2-07 She uses an alarm clock to remind her of when the pH analysis will be done.

C12-21 Samples tend to come in waves: "we just had a tidal wave this morning."

P4-23 Had to sneak up on someone with notebook and SAT to get another chemist to verify his results and calculations.

P10-25 Has his own organization system for lining up samples on the bench to be worked on.

C15-08 Charts on the wall represents each analysis; that's why there are so many of them. Each one is one instrument, one column, one method. Charts are graphed.

U3-23 "If I had to run back to the LIMS terminal every time I get a result it would drive me crazy."

U5-16 They used to have a validation process for LIMS entries before sending to control room, but don't anymore because they don't have time.

Example: Apropos affinity notes

K08-21 K08 gets calls from field reps who call her to get transferred to their sales rep. They can't access their sales rep's contact information from the web site.

K02-11 Says that his supervisor watches his activity and if he is not grabbing calls quick enough he will push calls to him.

K02-32 Discusses priority options with the customer and the customer decides the priority of the case.

K02-33 Q: How does self rating of problem affect the queues? Can the agent try to talk the customer down to a lower priority?

K04-78 DI: Automatic text paging to the responsible person. System extracts the information and automatically sends the page based on the priority of the interaction.

K07-94 Before sending the caller to sales K07 brings up Apropos and enters identifying information about the customer. He then sends the call to sales. Doing so provides sales with information about the caller before they pick up the phone.

Example: Purchasing affinity notes

M02-33 An RFP is about a 100-page document with multiple sections.

M06-34 It is an open-ended agreement; it's not a purchase requisition. It will lay out terms and costs, not quantities and other details.

M06-35 Different members of the team are responsible for different sections.

M08-46 She doesn't want to eliminate losing vendors, because they could partner with other vendors to meet her team's needs.

M08-48 DI: Outside aggregators could put competing vendors together to make deals, by knowing their technology.

A03-5 Says that if they have already worked with the supplier, they will keep a checklist of how the deal went.

A03-46 Sends suppliers a questionnaire asking for information on their financial condition, the likeliness that they will be bought (the OEM fears losing their sole source supplier), what other OEM's they work with, and their technical skills.

A03-47 The OEM has a fear of losing a supplier if they go out of business because 90 percent of their supplies are from single sources.

A03-58 It is easy to end a relationship with a supplier if you do not like them—the end of the production run provides a natural end to the relationship.

Capturing work models

As we have said, after capturing the profile, the interviewer starts by drawing the physical model and showing any photos of the environment. Even if you do not plan to consolidate the physical work model, draw a picture of the workplace to help situate people in the interpretation session. This lets the team visualize the user's environment.

To draw the physical model the interviewer simply sketches a diagram of the user's workspace and talks the team through it.

For Focused Rapid CD, during the body of the interpretation session, the work modeler captures the sequence model showing the steps of the user tasks (see Chapter 6).

Work models and affinity notes are recorded concurrently, as the interviewer recounts what happened during the interview.

Capture insights

When the interviewer has finished going through the affinity notes, your last step is to capture team insights. An insight is not a design idea. Insights describe patterns, situations, and needs, not solutions. Insights are people's reactions to and thoughts about the interview they just heard.

The insight list is a way to step back from the detail of the data and think about patterns in the work, key issues that must be addressed, and overall implications for your project. You may already have been capturing insights all along. This last step is a reflective moment to gather learnings into one place.

Insights will be shared with other team members who were not in the interpretation session, as well as any other interested parties in the share session. Insights are the team's opportunity to highlight key findings so that anyone who wasn't in the interpretation session can read them and get a feel for the user and the interview.

Capture your insights on a separate flipchart, including any points that have already been captured in the affinity notes. Capture any new insights as new affinity notes. This flipchart becomes your first results, which you can show to management to give them insight about what you are doing.

Example: eChalk

Here are the insights from one eChalk interview:

- Creates lesson plans together with other teachers to integrate their curriculum into the computer class schedule

- Creates and disseminates guides to help teachers set up a lesson plan and integrate their subject areas with technology

- Recording attendance takes three people and involves many different and redundant data entry steps

- He is focused on making technology a part of the school's existing curriculum (math, English, etc.), not a subject unto itself

- Technology has to be easy to use, used by all, and relevant and interesting to have value

- School is always looking for alternate ways to promote the school and raise money
- The Administration office is the central place to find out what's going on in the school

Example: Agilent insights
- They have raised not wasting motion to an art.
- There is no formal training process (e.g., operator becoming technician). Most training is by the buddy system.
- All these places test for iron because it is corroding their equipment.
- Their analysts need the right attitude: "We've had people come to us from clinical labs, but they are no good for us because they can't multitask well."
- Sample names are made up of certain ordered pieces of info—e.g., sequential number, C/V, sample point, date, time.
- The arrival of samples is not smooth—they tend to arrive all at once.
- Always assumes something other than process is wrong. More consequences if the process is wrong than if the test is wrong (so retest first).
- The computer and instruments must maintain the rhythm of the dance.
- They don't take their gloves off to use computers.
- Constantly use cues and tricks throughout their process to remember their place.

Example: Apropos insights
- There is a lot of parallel activity the agent has to handle while on the phone with the customer. Related data needs to come up quickly.
- Support notes are critical to the agent's choices in the work flow.
- They know where to find all the information they need quickly even though it is not all linked or easy to get to.
- Every person keeps a small cache of information by hand during each phone interaction. The notepad is a key tool.
- An agent needs to know when other agents are available. They might know availability, but not what they are doing. They use IM to identify individual people who might actually be able to take a call rather than put it in a queue.
- Getting multiple parties on the same line is great for the customer; makes them feel supported.

Conduct a share session

A share session is used if you have team members who did not participate in all interpretation sessions, or if you want to get your stakeholders in the loop (see the box, **Communicating out: use your team room to share your progress**). Share sessions are held after several interviews have been interpreted. If you are running parallel interpretation sessions or not all the team members were able to attend the interpretation session, you can have a weekly share session. These shares allow all team members the opportunity to process interviews that others have interpreted.

The share session is an opportunity to share the key findings and models with anyone who was not in the interpretation session. It is also an opportunity to add missing information to the models and affinity notes. It serves as a quality check.

To create a shared understanding across the larger team, everyone should attend the share session. The sharing process is relatively straightforward and the goal is not to reinterpret, but to share the data. If everyone can't be there, the interviewer is the key person to share the findings with others.

Don't share more than four or five interviews per share session; more than this makes the meeting feel too long. It should take 15 to 20 minutes for each interview being shared.

Share session roles

Prior to beginning the first interpretation share session, the following roles are assigned.

Presenter

The presenter is the interviewer. He or she:

- Provides a brief overview of the user and his or her work

- Shares the insights from the original interpretation session

- Walks the models if they were captured

  - The interviewer should present each of the models captured in the interpretation session, highlighting key points and significant findings. Don't walk through each step of the sequence model; just highlight key activities significant to the project focus.

Participants

The participants in the interpretation listen to the presenter asking questions and raising any new issues, design ideas, or questions to be captured. The team will tell them if an idea already has been captured. If you aren't sure capture it again to save time looking.

Helper for work model review

When the presenter tells the story of the sequence model they may add new steps, or intents that were not originally captured as the participants probe. The helper captures any new data on the sequence model. If there were no models, you do not need a helper.

Notetaker

The notetaker updates the affinity notes with any new observations, design ideas, questions, and insights. Just add these notes to the bottom of the session.

Share session tips

- Summarize; this is not a rebroadcast of the entire interpretation session.

- Don't search to see if an affinity note point is there, just add it again if someone is insistent after the team has told them they captured the point.

- Keep your focus on sharing the interview data and insights. Separate refocusing discussions from sharing. Schedule another meeting to discuss how you may wish to approach future interviews. Similarly, don't turn the share into a discussion of the design itself. This is also another meeting. By staying focused on sharing you can manage your team's time well.

• Consider scheduling your share session every week at the same time. Many teams prefer a working lunch because it feels like it cuts into their day less.

Communicating out: use your team room to share your progress

You need an ongoing strategy for informing others about your process and your findings as they unfold. You can share with stakeholders and managers in regular share sessions. But if you focus on a message exclusively for them, or if you want to invite teams with related problems, try these ideas in your team room:

• Invite people to tour your data. Put insights from your users and models from two to three users on the walls of the design room. Visitors now have something to look at and get involved with when they are visiting your team room. Informally talk to them about the data and how it addresses your project focus.

• Create a checkpoint meeting in your room. Plan a more formal share session walking through representative users and their data and insights. Tell stories of the interview itself. Or share personas you have created on each user. Talk about the implications of the data for the design. This is a way to bring the users alive. In this context you probably will not capture additional affinity notes since the goal of this meeting is communication.

• Plan who to invite and how to manage communication to key stakeholders and influencers. Start getting their interest by dropping some exciting findings into your discussions at lunch and meetings and let the interest grow from there.

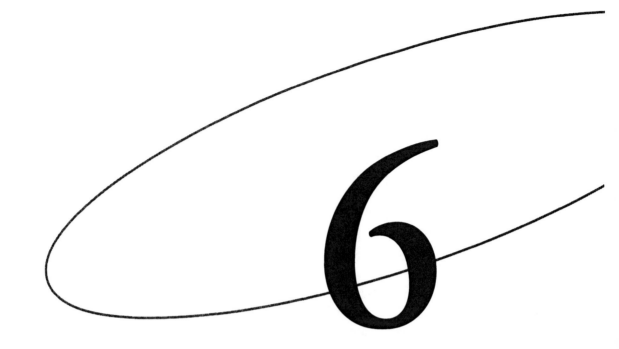

Work Modeling

Rapid CD Process	Lightning Fast	Lightning Fast +	Focused Rapid CD
Sequence Models			✓

Work models provide a language for seeing work and they help reveal important distinctions. They provide a clear way of capturing complex qualitative data and help the team see the work structure by representing it in physical diagrams.

Focused Rapid CD allows you to capture the tasks that users do in the sequence model. Most teams who start modeling work practice start with some representation of the steps a user takes to perform a task. User experience professionals talk of task analysis; personas try to characterize a day in the life task as a story; process modelers look for as-is models of the process and produce to-be models of how the process will be changed; use case modelers such as those using RUP create as-is and to-be use cases; and XP practitioners eventually want user stories, which are the steps of how a task will be performed in the system. All these approaches need the actual steps that users take when doing the activities that are targeted for support by the project.

The sequence model captures these activities, the steps a user performs during an actual task. Once consolidated (see Chapter 7) the sequence model will show all the different steps that users in the population use to accomplish the task. The consolidated sequence model is the task analysis, the as-is user process model, and the day in the life story of the user. It will guide storyboarding (see Chapter 12), which will produce the new way that users will do that task once it is redesigned with technology. The storyboard is the future scenario, the to-be use case or user process model, and the source for XP's user stories (see Chapter 15).

The sequence is the key model used for Rapid CD. See the box, **The five CD work models**, for an overview of the other Contextual Design models. Because most people who start modeling user work start with a task representation, we recommend using the sequence model for Focused Rapid CD.

We recommend that you capture the physical model for context during the interview on any projects. You should also collect the artifacts used in key tasks, giving you an artifact model, to give you examples of the things your users use during their work. We do not recommend consolidating the physical and artifact models for Rapid CD, but simply drawing and annotating them may give you new insights and as a result generate additional affinity notes.

Work modeling occurs during the interpretation session. The physical model is drawn at the beginning of the session to provide context. When the interviewer starts to recount a series of steps—usually many steps—that a user took during a task, the sequence model is captured. The artifact model is captured any time an artifact is discussed during the interview. So models are captured at any time they occur during the story of the user's interview. If additional information relevant to a model is brought up over the course of the interview, data is added to the model.

This chapter describes the sequence, physical, and artifact models and gives you examples of what they look like. It also gives examples of the affinity notes that might be generated from each model, and provides tips for capturing them in the interpretation session.

See Chapter 5, "A Language of Work," pgs. 81-87 and Chapter 6, "Work Models," in *Contextual Design: Defining Customer-Centered Systems*.

Definition

A work model is a diagram that captures the structure of the users' work or activity. We're going to cover three main types: physical models, sequence models, and artifact models. Each work model focuses on one aspect of user practice, revealing its structure and distinctions. This gives the team an external, concrete form to record and communicate what they saw on customer visits, and a way to manage complex qualitative data. When consolidated, work models along with the affinity diagram provide the team a physical representation of the characteristics of the user population they are trying to support.

Key concepts

Physical model. Represents the user's physical environment as it affects work.

Sequence model. A step-by-step recording of the tasks observed or retrospective accounts recorded during the Contextual Interview. Consolidated sequences represent the key strategies and activities that users engage in to get the work done.

Artifact model. Copies or representations of physical or electronic "things" the user creates, passes, or references to do a task. The artifact model reveals the distinction in the structure and content of an artifact.

Breakdowns. Something that gets in the way of the user accomplishing their task or intent from the user's point of view. A breakdown is not a failure to use available function in a tool or to use the tool in the prescribed way. A breakdown represents the user's experience, not the project team's expectations of proper work practice.

Trigger. The situation(s) that prompts a user to start a new task or a particular step.

Intent. The "why" behind any user activity or structuring of a physical workplace or artifact. An intent is the reason, explicit or implicit, conscious or unconscious, planned or habitual, that the user is doing something.

Work modeling during an interpretation session

☐ The sequence model

☐ The physical model

☐ The artifact model

☐ Using models during an interpretation session

The five CD work models: Why choose only some models for Rapid CD?

The five work models of Contextual Design help the team represent the complexities of the users' work practice in an orderly way. In addition to the **physical**, **sequence**, and **artifact** models described in this chapter, Contextual Design also uses the **flow** and **cultural** models to characterize the user population. These models and their uses are described here.

The **flow model** depicts people's responsibilities and the communication and coordination required to do a job. When consolidated, the flow model reveals roles people play, key work groups, information needs, core activities, communication patterns, and process work flow. The flow model is your war map, representing the players in the market or user population to target and support.

The flow model is instrumental in the design of collaboration applications, role-based portals, information and activity support web sites, work flow applications, and drives new product concepts for an existing or new market or user group. The flow model also helps characterize target personas.

The **cultural model** reveals influences on a person, whether external to the company (such as dependence on a vendor) or internal company policies. The cultural model provides insight into people's feelings about their work and the tools that they use as well as the cultural issues that exist within the organization, home, or geographic location.

When consolidated the cultural model reveals the value proposition to be supported by the application. It collects and shows the influences, constraints, interpersonal friction, policies, standards, and law that people work under. Products that support positive values or remove irritations will provide a good value proposition. And because cultural differences, policy, and law are also revealed the cultural model shows the design team what they must consider within the design to ensure user adoption.

Together with the affinity diagram all five work models concretize the practices of users and create a set of diagrams that characterize the structure of the work practice of the target population. Each work model represents a different point of view on the users' work practice, enabling the team to engage in coherent conversations focused on different aspects of the work. Each conversation then drives the generation of different design concepts, with some models forcing detailed thinking and others encouraging wide and broad design.

Rapid CD focuses on using the detailed work models that drive focused design tasks, the sequences. The flow and cultural models along with the consolidated physical model are the big picture models.

→

These models drive new product and service concepts, process redesign, and overall market characterization. But the more models a team captures the more work the team needs to do during the interpretation session and consolidation. So for Rapid CD we skip the big picture models and focus instead on the detailed models.

The sequence diagrams recommended in Rapid CD drive focused feature changes and guide the next version of an existing product. They also form the basis for the creation of user stories to drive XP and the high-level use cases required by RUP techniques.

The sequence model

The sequence models represent the ordered steps that a user performs to complete a task. Sequence models are captured throughout the interpretation session as the interviewer comes to each new user activity. A sequence model documents the real steps a user takes to do his or her work.

When the interviewer has observed a series of steps or describes a retrospective account of their activities, the work modeler captures the detailed steps on flipchart paper in the order the steps occur. Although you can capture sequences in word processors or spreadsheets, this sometimes leads to lower levels of detail than you desire and can make consolidation take longer (see the box, **Paper capture versus online capture**).

Paper capture versus online capture

If you do not have access to flipchart paper or if you are running a distributed interpretation session you may choose to capture the sequences online in a word processing or spreadsheet program. Online capture does allow you to share the sequences more easily with your distributed team.

One location may capture the notes and the other sequences displaying them in an online meeting or collaboration environment. Even if the team is collocated you will need a way to display the sequences so that the interpretation team can see the steps as they are captured.

But you do have to be careful when capturing online that you stay at the agreed upon level of detail. We have found that online capture encourages the team to capture irrelevant information and too much detail. Remember you are not taking running notes; you are capturing the key steps, triggers, and intents.

Online capture also makes it harder to see the whole sequence and its structure for consolidation. That is why we recommend printing out the first set of sequences and cutting them into steps for manual consolidation initially. Then when you have a base consolidated structure you can more easily roll in differences and extensions dynamically within a spreadsheet application.

For each new task or instance of a task the work modeler starts a new sequence. Expect to have a set of sequences for each user. As you go from user to user you will find that many of these activities overlap in type; you will consolidate these like sequences later in the process.

A sequence is composed of the following components:

- The step: The actual thing the user did at the appropriate level of detail.

- The trigger: The situation(s) that prompts a user to start a new task or a particular step (see the box, **Capturing triggers**). A trigger always starts a sequence.

Capturing triggers

Every sequence has a trigger—the event that initiated it. Triggers may be discrete events, such as the ringing of a telephone, the arrival of an invoice, or a person arriving at the door. Triggers may be based on time, like the first of the month or first thing in the morning. Triggers may be less tangible, such as the pile in the in-box getting too large. Whatever the trigger, if the work is automated it must have an analog in the new system. The system needs a way to tell the user there's something to be done. Otherwise, the user won't take action. For example, one mail product simply gets slower the larger the in-box gets. This doesn't act as a trigger for the user to clean it out, it just makes the product more and more frustrating to use.

- The intent: The reason, known or unconscious, the user is doing the task or the step (see the box, **Focus on Intents in Sequence Models**). The more intents you can identify, the better for your future design.

Focus on intents in sequence models

Sequence models are more than just a task analysis that captures the steps people take. If you only capture the steps, you are missing a core component of the task, a component that arguably is even more important to the work than the actual steps. You need to understand why the user carried out the overall task. Why did a user take a certain step or series of steps?

Those "whys" are the intents. In many ways the individual steps people take ultimately don't matter. It's their intent that counts. The ultimate goal of the sequence model is to uncover the intents so that you can call them out and specifically support them in your design. If we can find the intents, and then design to the intent, it doesn't matter that different people take different steps. As long as our product satisfies their intent, their work will be supported. We can redesign, modify, and remove steps as long as the users can still achieve their underlying intents.

Moreover, intents are stable over time; it's the steps that change. For example, for centuries people have had the intent of communicating over a distance. It's the steps that have changed—from smoke signals to handwritten notes via a messenger to the telegraph, telephone, video conferencing, e-mail, and instant messaging. So when we model the work we want to find all of the intents, the overall intent of the tasks, and the intents of activities and steps within the task. Any system has to support all the intents concealed in the work, not just the overall intent.

Know the level of detail appropriate to your project

You and your team will need to decide how detailed you are going to get in your sequences.

Work steps. For a typical project focused on understanding the user's activities you should capture work steps, what the user is doing at the level of their action including any relevant thought steps (e.g., U01 entered the user's name into the tool).

User interface steps. If you want to look at the usability of your tool you need to capture the sequences at the level of the clicks—any time the user presses a button on a piece of hardware or he clicks and inputs something into the user interface (e.g., U01 pulled down the menu, selected user data, and opened the dialog, or put the cursor in the name field).

Process steps. If you want to see the role of a user in a process, just capture the work steps. Capturing steps at the level of the group or department without real detail will show group responsibility, flow from department to department, and possibly the flow of data from group to group, but this level of sequence is too abstract with too little work practice data to allow for reliable redesign of the process. (Accounts payable received the invoice, the invoice was approved, the invoice was passed to checking to cut the check, etc.).

Each team has to determine the right level of detail for the focus of the project or you won't be able to redesign the work at the right level. And be careful to get the detail; an abstract sequence will leave out so much data that it will not be useful later on. So choose the right level of detail for your project.

Examples: eChalk

Example 1: Capturing work steps

In this sequence model (Figure 6-1) you can see that the team opted to capture work steps, but not every physical movement. This is appropriate for their focus since the user is not using the eChalk tool and the team is not trying to capture low-level steps and every breakdown. If they are going to support publishing assignments in eChalk, they need to know when and how teachers do this.

Figure 6-1: eChalk sequence example showing steps captured at a high level of detail.

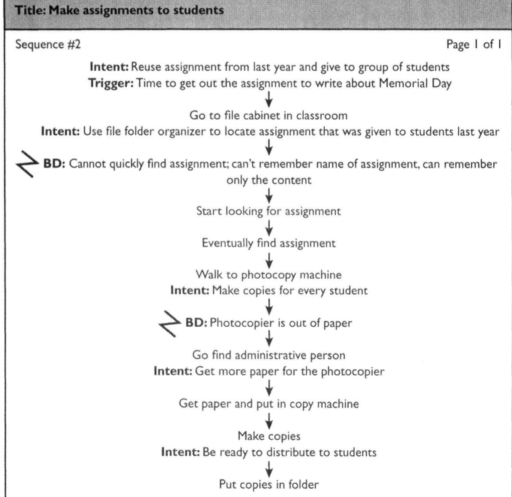

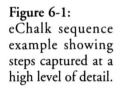

Example 2: A sequence that is too abstract

Here (Figure 6-2) the eChalk team has a sequence that is too high level. It is good that they've captured that trigger and intent; eChalk needs to know about all the different things that parents and teachers discuss to see if the structure of the work changes. However, the rest of the sequence doesn't have enough detail to really drive their design. eChalk also wants to support communication between the teachers and administrators (and other non-teaching staff). This sequence leaves too many unanswered questions. What happened during the meeting with the principal? How was the plan put together? How were the parents surveyed after the event? Fortunately eChalk has other detailed sequences for this task.

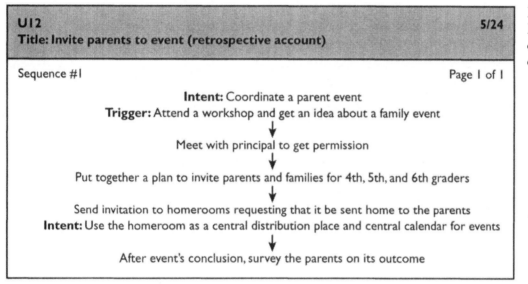

Figure 6-2: Example of a sequence that is not detailed enough.

Writing sequence models

The sequence captures what really happened. It does not include hypothetical steps that the user says he sometimes does. It does not capture branches or decision points because in any real life experience the user does only one thing. So a sequence captures life as it really occurred or as we can best reconstruct it in a retrospective account.

When you are capturing sequence models:

- Write the user code and number on the top of the flipchart page. Number each sequence (Sequence 1) and place it at the top of each page. Then number each page of that sequence.

- Start each new sequence on a new flipchart page, or a new page in a word processing document or worksheet in a spreadsheet file (see the box, **Capturing repetitive sequences**).

- Capture the trigger that started the work, at the start of the sequence. A trigger may be explicit like the phone ringing or implicit like "time of day" when the user habitually does an activity. The trigger is the event that initiates an activity.

- Write down the steps taken to accomplish the work, at the appropriate level of detail in blue ink, in the order they happened (see the box, **Why use different** colors when capturing models?). Include thought steps when you are aware of them or when you observed the user making a decision.

Capturing repetitive sequences

Sometimes during the interview the user is doing the same kind of work over and over. If you are seeing new data with each repetition, then let the user repeat several cases until it starts to repeat. The key to repetition is that each case reveals a new situation that you must take into consideration for the design.

But if you are not getting new data you need not continue to collect it. Remember that in the interview you are empowered to direct the user to the work you want to see. For example, when the eChalk interviewer already had seen the teacher communicate the assignments for the day to his students, he chose to stop watching this activity. Instead he switched to reviewing how these assignments would be communicated to absent students. After that he switched to different types of work: grading papers, creating progress reports, taking attendance, and other tasks relevant to the project.

So your goal during the interview is to collect different cases and instances of a similar task until you have seen the cases, then move on to other tasks.

If you do this during the interview, then the interpretation session will be simple. Capture the sequence that you now know will show different data. But if you do have very repetitive sequences capture the first two or three.

For the rest, have the interviewer go through his interview notes reading the steps aloud. When you hear a new distinction, capture it on a new sequence, or if it is a small differentiation annotate a step on a previous sequence. Watch out for too much annotation—in the end you will become confused about the order of events.

- Capture relevant intents for individual steps or sets of steps as you are aware of them. The user may not be aware of their intent explicitly but through discussion in the interview it will be revealed. When you know what they are write them down.

Why use different colors when capturing models?

Chapter 5 gave you a list of supplies for your interpretation session, including a specific type of marker pen and certain colors for drawing the work models. Why does the kind of pen or marker matter? Because the pen is a communication tool.

We use specific colors to communicate quality and type of data. Blue is the primary color for drawing models; blue ink means we saw it happen or saw evidence that it must have happened. Green ink is for uncertainties and red ink is for breakdowns.

Why do we care about the color? The pen color is really about team management so you can keep moving forward and avoid time-wasting conversations, which is always important, but never more so than in Rapid CD.

Don't spend time debating whether or not something happened and should be captured on your model. If you aren't sure, capture it in green ink (or type color) and move on. Green signals the team that, if this point matters for the design, you need to gather "blue data" in subsequent interviews.

You want to use a marker with a tip that writes large enough that everyone can see, but not so large that you are wasting space. Think about how to support good communication in your team; even your paper and pen "technology" can make a difference in how quickly you move because you are communicating clearly with each other.

- Document breakdowns in the work with red zigzag lines. Annotate each breakdown by writing what the problem was from the user's point of view.

- Look back over the sequence when you are finished and write an overall intent for the sequence as a whole. Write this at the top of the sequence. Remember, a sequence may have more than one overall intent as well as multiple subintents.

- Capture each step of a retrospective account as it is revealed in the interpretation, and be sure to leave space to fill in missing steps as you come across them. The interpretation team members will ask questions that will remind the interviewer of steps they forgot so space needs to be left between steps to add these in. See Table 6-1 for tips on capturing sequences during the interpretation session.

Example: eChalk retrospective account

Here (Figure 6-3) you see a retrospective account. The team remembered to capture an overall intent and the trigger, but neglected during the interpretation session to capture step level intents. They'll need those intents later when they consolidated the sequences and discuss how they can support the work.

It's better to capture the subintents during the interpretation session so the people doing the consolidation don't have to stop to figure them out, or track down the interviewer to ask. Here we have included the subintents added later to give you an example.

U0I   **5/10**
Title: Survey parents about technology available to students (retrospective account)

Sequence #4   Page I of I

Intent I: Find out if parents have technology, what they have, and how they use it to design computer courses to students
Intent 2: Communicate expectations of students in class for parents
Trigger: Class will be starting soon
↓
Give survey to homeroom teacher
Intent: Use established school structure of having the homeroom as a central distribution point to track and hold students accountable for getting information to parents
↓
Give survey to parents directly if U0I sees them at school
Intent: Opportunistically get the information directly to parent
↓
Student receives survey from homeroom teacher
↓
Parent receives survey from U0I or student
↓
Parent completes survey and gives back to student
↓
Student gives survey to homeroom teacher
↓
U0I receives survey
↓
Puts survey into folder
Intent: Keep anything having to do with parents in one place

Figure 6-3: Example of a sequence captured from a retrospective account.

Table 6-1:
Tips for sequence
capture during the
interpretation ses-
sion.

Dos and don'ts for capturing sequence models	
Don't	Do
Focus only on steps when the user touches your tool.	Capture all the steps related to the task within which a tool or process is used: actions, coordination, discussions, decision steps, reading steps (scanning the page), etc.
Summarize steps.	Capture all the detail of what happened, actual artifacts used, places walked to, tools used, conversation topics, etc.
Ignore interruptions and task switching.	Capture interruptions in the work in the place that they occur in the sequence. If the user is interweaving tasks make a note in each sequence that they switched to another one.
Forget to record intents and triggers.	Capture the trigger to start the tasks and any internal triggers that kick off a subtask. Capture intents for coherent sections of the sequence, or for individual steps.

See Figure 6-4 for an example of a sequence captured during an Agilent interpretation.

Affinity notes based on the sequence model

During the interpretation session you are capturing affinity notes and drawing work models simultaneously. Some of the aspects of the work models also should be captured as affinity notes to reveal key distinctions and issues in the work as a whole. Here are guidelines for what to capture from the sequence model. Capture:

- Breakdowns—what didn't work for the user

- Intents—why they were doing what they were doing at a particular step

- Observed strategies for working

- Triggers that are particularly important to support in the design

- Implications for collaboration, context switching, and managing interruptions

- Activities that must be supported simultaneously

- Do *not* capture the individual steps in the notes—affinity notes have no order and the structure of the task will be lost—ordered steps are captured only in the sequence

Example: eChalk notes from sequence models

U01-69 Students have to take home "Behavioral and Academic Expectations" form that the parents must sign and return to him by students.

U26-06 Breakdown: U26 had trouble with the third e-mail: used the same distribution list as previous e-mails, but this note went only to the first half of the alphabetical list of addressees.

U22-33 The school believes that the younger students are more reliable couriers for getting notes home so all communication goes through them. This is called "Family Mail."

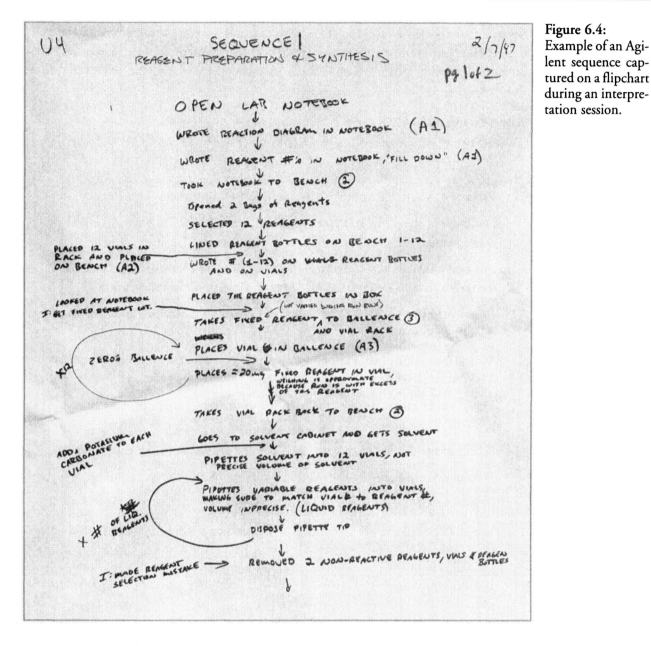

The artifact model

The artifact model captures the things people use or create when doing work. For Rapid CD we recommend that you collect artifacts and present them during the interpretation session to illustrate and clarify what the user is doing. Artifacts may be used to illustrate what the user is interacting with in sequence. For Rapid CD, hang artifacts next to their associated steps or areas of the affinity diagram (see Chapter 8) that talk about their use.

To help you articulate issues and needs associated with key artifacts you may want to create artifact models that display and annotate the artifact on a flipchart page. During the interpretation session artifacts are presented to the team as they come up in the course of the interview. The work modeler hangs up the artifacts and listens throughout the interpretation session to how they were used during the user's activities. Then the work modeler annotates the artifacts with issues, intents, breakdowns, and usage of the artifact. Important distinctions are also captured in the affinity notes. Table 6-2 includes tips for capturing artifacts and annotating them during the interpretation session.

Annotating artifact models

The interviewer or work modeler should capture the following on the artifact:

- The user code and number, and the interpretation session date

- Parts of the object that are distinct in usage and parts that are unused

- Structure of the parts, both formal and informal: how information is sectioned and grouped

- Physical characteristics important to the usage: for example, aspects of the presentation that support or impede easy scanning or communication

- Information presented by the object: data presented or input and how it is used or represented

- Work distinctions made apparent in the object: concepts implicitly or explicitly expressed in the artifact

- Usage of the artifact: what it is used for in the larger work process or task

- Intents for the artifact or a section of the artifact: why the user values that aspect of the artifact and what higher-order purpose the artifact enables

- Breakdowns in the use of the artifact, represented as red zigzag lines

Affinity notes based on the artifact model

Here are guidelines for what to capture from the artifact model. Capture:

- Breakdowns—what didn't work for the user

- Intents and usages—how the artifact was used in a process or sequence or required by law

- Concepts implied by the artifact—what key distinctions are behind any jargon used

- Implications for collaboration—does the artifact facilitate collaboration between people formally or informally?

- The types of information the artifact collects and its source

- Whether the artifact is used in more than one business or work process

- Whether data entry is in support of the user's work or another department or user within a business process

- Aspects of the presentation and structure that work and that don't work

Example: eChalk

Figure 6-5 shows a Student Progress Report, prepared by teacher and sent to parents or other schools.

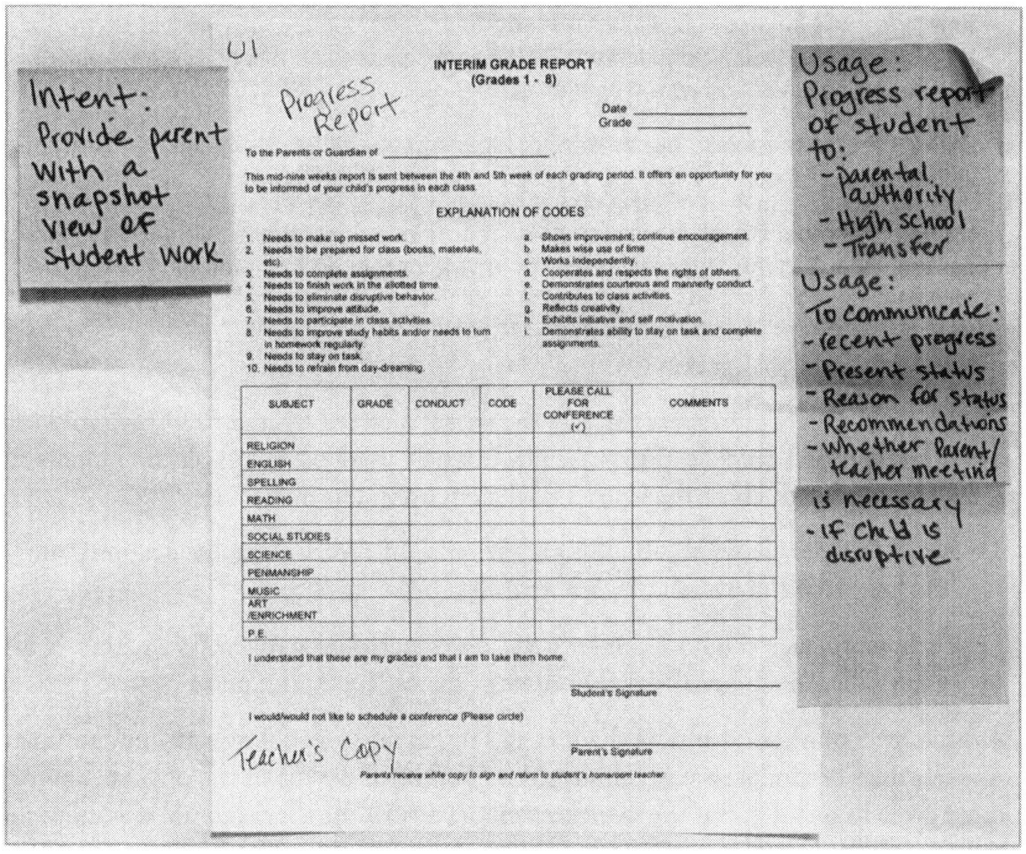

Figure 6.5:
An eChalk artifact which the team annotated by calling out intents and usages.

Dos and don'ts for capturing artifact models	
Don't	**Do**
Forget to collect key artifacts at the user site.	Collect artifacts and annotate them with intent and usage while with the user.
Hang up multiple artifacts on one flip chart for each user without annotation.	Annotate each key artifact that matters for the work on its own sheet to enable sorting and later cross-user analysis. Or if you do not plan to further analyze the artifacts simply hang them at the right step in a sequence.
Try to discuss an artifact in the interpretation session without a visual prop.	Draw a picture on the flip chart and fill in enough detail to support the story if you don't have the real artifact. It is always better to have a physical representation to help the team visualize what happened.
Collect artifacts and file them away.	Sort artifacts by type and use representative artifacts to illustrate the consolidated sequence even if you aren't consolidating them. Consider taking digital photos of key artifacts and building them into your affinity diagram.

Table 6-2:
Tips for using artifacts in your project.

135

Example: eChalk notes from artifact models
U02-04 Uses log book (handwritten). Teaches 27 classes so this book keeps track of where each class is and where she left off.

U06-21 Progress reports are broken into sections so all teachers can comment on student in one place.

U22-43 Homeroom teacher get a progress report for each student. Fills it out and then passes it along to the other teachers—no rhyme or reason to the order in which they receive it.

The physical model

The physical model represents the way the user is affected by and uses space to do the work. The physical model captures the places where work occurs. A physical model can represent varying levels of the impact of the environment on the user.

- A site model shows the buildings, structure of rooms, distant locations, and challenges of the overall physical space.

- The workplace model represents the user's personal workspace whether it is their office, a lab bench, or the trunk of the car for a sales person.

At each level of physical model the user has increasing control over the environment. As such the site model reveals opportunities and breakdowns in the physical environment given to the user. But the work area model reveals the user's natural work flow and self-organization patterns.

At the beginning of any interpretation session we recommend that the interviewer draw the workplace model on a flipchart to help situate the interpretation team in the user's work experience. If you like, digital pictures of the space can be hung on the model to augment visualization.

What kind of physical model or models you capture depends on your project focus and what you are designing. Most projects capture the user's workplace in a single physical model: an office, a work cubicle, a room in the house, a vehicle, a station on an assembly line, a sales counter—any place where the user is doing the work supported by your product. Other times the work you care about is carried out in multiple places.

In their initial project the eChalk team captured physical models for the classroom, the computer lab, and the teacher's lounge. As they expanded their product, they also captured physical models in district administrative offices. The Agilent team captured the lab for their physical model because there was no individual workplace—everyone moved from device to device in the lab.

Drawing the physical model

You will draw the initial physical model at the beginning of the interpretation session for context. Over the course of the interpretation session more elements of the model or new physical spaces may be discussed. Add to the drawings over the course of the interpretation session as needed. See Figure 6-6 for an example of a physical model that was captured during an interpretation session.

When you are drawing the physical model:

- Write the user code and number on the top of the flipchart page.

- Capture the physical structures that define the space like walls, cubicles, or hallways, and natural gathering spaces.

- Document tools, both electronic and physical, that the user uses to complete tasks you care about: hardware, software packages, online resources, fax machines, phones, PDAs.

- Capture the layout of the workplace and document access between areas that matter for your design.

  For example, if the user needs to get up and walk 100 feet to get to the copier, printer, or fax machine, and your product is trying to better support this work practice draw them on your model.

- Draw lines on the model to represent the user's movement through the space, emphasizing patterns like aisle walking in shopping or wasted steps like going back and forth between the clean glassware and the secure lab in an analytical lab setting.

- Identify any work objects, tools, books, piles, or other sectioning that the user has set up.

  For example, easily accessed books, binders the user has created to organize documents, a contact list hanging on the wall, sticky notes with reminders on computers or refrigerators, a calendar with appointments. Capture what they are and how they are used.

- Capture any breakdowns related to the use of the workspace. Represent a breakdown as red zigzags on the model—be sure to label the breakdowns. The 100-foot walk to the copier just mentioned would be a good breakdown to capture.

- Capture usage intent of spaces and setup. Annotate the model with how spaces are used and the intent of the user's organization of their workplace and area.

  For example we labeled the bakery and the liquor section of the grocery store as a "temptation place" because they served to either pull the user into them for purchases or repel them away for fear of being tempted.

Affinity notes based on the physical model

The following are guidelines for what to capture from the physical model. Capture:

- Breakdowns caused by the physical environment or how the user uses it

- Workplace features like distance, security, piles, or anything that affects the work

- Implications of how space is used to organize work

- Implications of how artifacts and objects are positioned in support of the work

- Content that the user needs access to as indicated by what they put in their immediate workspace

Example: eChalk notes related to the physical model

U01-01 Computer tips and computer policy documents are available for students to pick up at the back of the classroom.

U06-24 She has four computers in her class that are shared among all her students (nice thought to include computers in the classroom but if there aren't enough terminals for each student they go to waste)

U05-06 Multimedia presentations about the school are shown in the school lobby/entrance to show that the school values technology.

Figure 6-6:
Apropos physical model drawn during the interpretation. This model shows key workspaces, the positioning of things within the spaces, and movement between them.

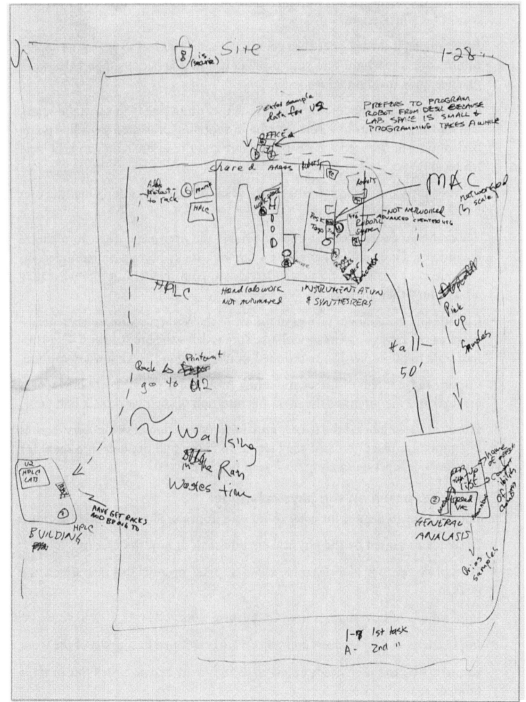

Table 6-3 includes tips for capturing the physical model during the interview and drawing it in the interpretation session.

Dos and don'ts for drawing the physical model	
Don't	**Do**
Hesitate to inquire about what is in a folder, a binder, a box, or closed cabinet during the interview.	Show the user what you are doing with your drawing and explain how it helps capture how they structure their environment to get tasks done or how the structure gets in their way.
Draw from your memory, drawing it for the first time in the interpretation session.	Capture the physical model during the contextual interview, and then redraw during the interpretation session.
Pre-draw the physical before the interpretation to save time.	Draw it from your notes at the start of the interpretation, talking as you go. This lets the interpretation team ask questions and capture notes about the key distinctions revealed in the model. Add to the physical model as appropriate throughout the interpretation session.
Draw a minimalistic sketch that doesn't tell you anything that has design significance.	Capture important work distinctions revealed by how the user uses their space. Define specific documents, books, or objects. Don't use generic titles like "papers" because you will lose the opportunity to see patterns of usage. Also pay attention to the location of the things that matter. What is near to hand? What is far away?
Put on irrelevant aspects to the work.	Focus on aspects of the physical environment that matter to the project focus. In a work oriented project, family photos, plants, and other personal things need not be included.
Try to make an exact representation of everything in users' workplace.	Draw only enough detail to situate your team in the workplace and capture important elements.

Table 6-3:
Tips for drawing the physical model.

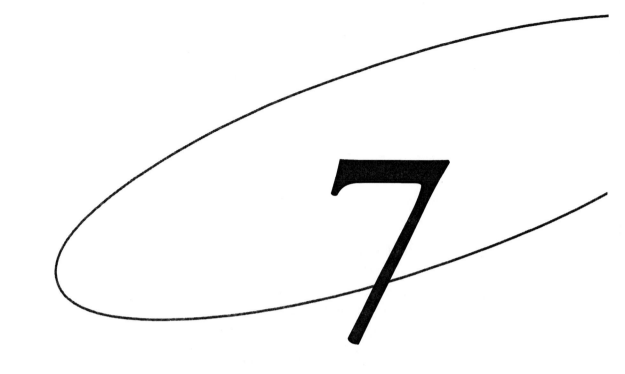

Consolidated
Sequence Models

Rapid CD Process	Lightning Fast	Lightning Fast +	Focused Rapid CD
Sequence Models			✓

Consolidating the individual work models is one of two processes in Contextual Design that help you build a single, coherent view of your customer's work practice. This chapter leads you through the process of transforming your set of individual sequence models into consolidated sequences. Chapter 8 leads you through building the affinity diagram. Together they allow you to see the issues and pattern of work across your user population.

The individual work models you have created are concrete representations of work practice and represent particular examples of how the work hangs together for one person. Consolidated work models reveal the structure of the work across users.

The consolidated sequence includes all actions you saw any user take, not just the common actions most users take—it is a superset, not a subset of user activity. We consolidate the user data, we don't condense it. As a result, the consolidated sequence reveals the structure, typical order, and different strategies of task you need to support for your project—all in one place.

A consolidated sequence is similar to traditional task analysis. It shows each step, triggers for the steps, different strategies for achieving each intent, and breakdowns in the ongoing work. Work redesign is ultimately about redesigning the steps in the sequences. Whether the redesign eliminates or changes the steps or eliminates the whole sequence, knowing the steps and intents keeps the team honest.

The goal of sequence consolidation is to produce one model for each of the primary tasks of the central roles you want to support. Focused Rapid CD includes sequence consolidation for teams who want a view of the tasks of their user population. Consolidated sequences are the basis for task analysis and as-is process models, or as-is use cases.

For Rapid CD the physical and artifact models are not consolidated and are used for context and to focus additional affinity notetaking. Consolidated sequences also can be annotated with example artifacts to provide more context for those using the sequence.

See "Consolidating Sequence Models," pgs. 171–178, in *Contextual Design: Defining Customer-Centered Systems*.

Definition

A consolidated sequence model shows the detailed work structure of the core user tasks. It collects similar sequence data across users showing a superset of the user actions: the steps performed during the task, the triggers for the task and steps, different strategies for achieving an intent, and the breakdowns observed. The planned system will need to support or replace the sequence and its steps. Sequences are consolidated on paper and not online (see the box, **Consolidating sequences online**).

Key concepts

Trigger. Event that initiates the task or its activities or steps represented in the sequence model.

Activity. Collection of abstract steps that represents a coherent piece of the work.

Abstract step. Generic step that represents the action taken by one or more users.

Intent. Reason why the user is performing a task or individual step within the task.

Strategies. There is often more than one way to complete a task. Strategies represent the variations within the user population within a consolidated sequence.

Consolidation process

☐ Choose sequences to consolidate

☐ Prepare for consolidation

☐ Create initial consolidation

☐ Roll in remaining sequences to finish the consolidation

Choose sequences to consolidate

Before you start consolidating you want to make the work manageable. Go through your sequences and collect together the sequences that concern the same task. During the interpretation session you will have written down any sequence that you observed. Now that you have all the data, you will be able to determine which sequences are central to your problem and which are peripheral. If you have peripheral sequences, you don't need to consolidate them. You may also have sequences of tasks that come from only one user—you won't consolidate these either. But you may use them to guide your design work if they are central to the project focus.

Choose a group of sequences to start with, based your choice on how central the task is to the work. Within that group choose three sequences with good detail and overlapping steps to start with. They will create a scaffold into which you can eventually roll the remaining sequences.

Example: eChalk

The eChalk team started by sorting their sequences into several groups.

- Communicating with parents, students, and other teachers
- Accessing eChalk
- Creating and teaching lessons (non-web-page creation)
- Teaching a lesson on web page creation
- Creating a school web page and calendar
- Taking attendance
- Collecting homework assignments
- Collaborating with teachers to integrate technology

Prepare for consolidation

Sequence consolidation works best when done by pairs of people. If you have more than two people in your team break up into smaller working groups to consolidate. But to establish a shared understanding, start consolidation as one large group. This will help remind everyone of the sequence consolidation process.

You need to prepare the room to consolidate your sequences. Ideally, the session will take place in your design room. If not, you will need a room large enough to hang the sequences and the butcher paper you will build consolidations on. You will also need:

- White waxless butcher paper
- Masking tape to stick butcher paper to walls
- Removable tape to hang individual sequences on the wall while you work with them
- 3x3 pink, blue, and green Post-it® notes
- Fine-tip felt pens—enough blue, red, and green for each person
- A list of who conducted each interview; if a sequence is unclear, the consolidation team may need to ask that person questions

Consolidating sequences online

We recommend, especially when you are first learning how to do them, not to try doing the consolidation in an application. Do the consolidation on paper because it is easier to visualize how the consolidation is actually working. Once the consolidated sequences are finished, you can then bring them online. The consolidated models can be put online using a variety of tools, such as word processing, spreadsheets, and diagramming software.

When you are really skilled at consolidation on paper, doing the process in a spreadsheet is possible—but watch out not to take even longer because of manipulating all the parts of every sequence. Visual scanning of sequences into a base structure after the three most detailed are consolidated is still the best way to finish consolidation.

Start consolidation

Sequence consolidation is a process of organizing the tasks from multiple people, each containing multiple different steps with different breakdowns and different intents into one view of each task that shows the basic structure of the task, the order of the steps, the different strategies to get the same thing done, and the variation in intents and breakdowns.

From a process perspective, sequence consolidation is about lining up like parts of each like sequence, abstracting out and naming common activities and steps, and transferring over the intents and breakdowns also labeled in a general way. If you do this you will be able to see the real task that you need to support in your system.

Here we walk you through the process, to explain and show it in detail. Revealing the thought behind the decisions may make sequence consolidation look complicated; but once you get the hang of it, it goes reasonably fast. Remember, you are looking for the structure of the task as it is revealed by actual instances of work activity. So don't get lost in the detailed variation, and don't abstract so high you lose the meaning.

To help visualize what we are ultimately creating see the final eChalk example (Table 7-3) and the final Agilent example (Table 7-4). Now we will walk through the process to get to that outcome.

Pick the first three sequences for one task

Once you have chosen your starting task, choose three sequences from that task to start consolidating.

1. Hang the sequences next to each other.

2. Hang a long, vertical piece of butcher paper next to the sequences; you will build the consolidation on this paper. It is possible that you may need two or three pieces of butcher paper if your consolidated sequence is long or complex.

3. Write the name of the consolidated sequence at the top of the paper.

Example: eChalk

Like most teams, their sequences varied in length, and sometimes in thoroughness. Here are the three sequences that eChalk started with. We will use them to illustrate the sequence consolidation process (See Figure 7.1, page 145, to see the three sequences eChalk chose to start with).

Identify the triggers

Starting at the beginning of the sequences, identify the triggers. Remember: each individual sequence has only one trigger, at the start of the sequence.

1. Identify the trigger for each sequence. If the sequences have different triggers, decide if you can rewrite them into one abstract trigger. If not, list all the triggers.

2. Write the triggers on a 3x3 blue Post-it® note.

3. Stick the triggers' Post-it® note at the top of the consolidation page.

U8 5/22	U6 5/19	U2 5/23
Title: Communicate behavioral problems to parents (retrospective account)	Title: Communicate behavioral problems to parents	Title: Communicate with parents about behavior
Sequence #1 Page 1 of 1	Sequence #2 Page 1 of 1	Sequence #1 Page 1 of 1

U8 — Sequence #1

Intent: Inform parents of child's behavior problems in class
Trigger: Student disrupts class

Use form letter to create letter about disruptive behavior
↓
Give letter to student to be delivered to parent
↓
Parent signs note, promising to "rectify matter"
↓
Student returns with letter
↓
Parent calls main school number for more detail
↓
School secretary writes pink slip
↓
Student courier delivers pink slip to U8's desk
↓
U8 goes to office to make call
↓
Parent is home, answers phone
↓
Talk about how parent can assist with behavioral problem
↓
Two weeks later: student's behavior degrades again
↓
Regular parent/teacher meeting
↓
U8, problem student, and parent discuss
↓
Parent suggests further communication by email
↓
Parent does not have email (does have Internet access)
↓
U8 suggests free email service
↓
Parent sends 10 emails
↓
U8 responds to emails
↓
Student behavior improves

U6 — Sequence #2

Intent: Report behavioral problem to principal
Trigger: Student misbehaves in class

Create note describing time incident occurred, description of incident, and request to meet with mother of student
↓
Give note to principal's secretary
↓
Principal's secretary calls mother
↓
Waiting to set up meeting with mother

U2 — Sequence #1

Intent: Communicate about state of child's behavior problems
Trigger: Has a few spare minutes between classes

Signs on to email
↓
Intent: Check email since it's been a couple of days

Sees message waiting for two days
↓
BD: Because computer performance is slow, only signs on 2–3 times a week

Reads email from parent of child inquiring how child is doing
↓
Waits until after school to telephone parent instead of emailing a response
Intent: Interact more personally than email offers
Intent: Wait until it is more likely parent will be at home

Call parent
↓
Discuss how child is behaving
↓
Hand write on form provided by child's counselor
Intent: Counselor wants the report weekly and she just told the parent

Wait until tomorrow to send the note home via child
Intent: Use child as "student courier" to get the note home because that's a fast, cheap, reliable method
Intent: Follow procedure of not contacting counselor directly

145

Example: eChalk

The triggers in the individual sequences are:

- U8 Student disrupts class

- U6 Student misbehaves in class

- U2 Has a few minutes of time between classes

For their design, the specifics of the student's behavior problem don't matter, so U8 and U6 triggers can be rewritten as one abstract trigger e.g., "student misbehaves." However, "Has a few minutes of time between class" is a very different trigger. So, that trigger cannot be combined with the other two. The team could rewrite it a bit more abstractly as "Teacher has some extra time" unless they think it is important to make distinctions about when extra time is available. See Figure 7-2 for an example of a how you would write the two triggers on a Post-it® note.

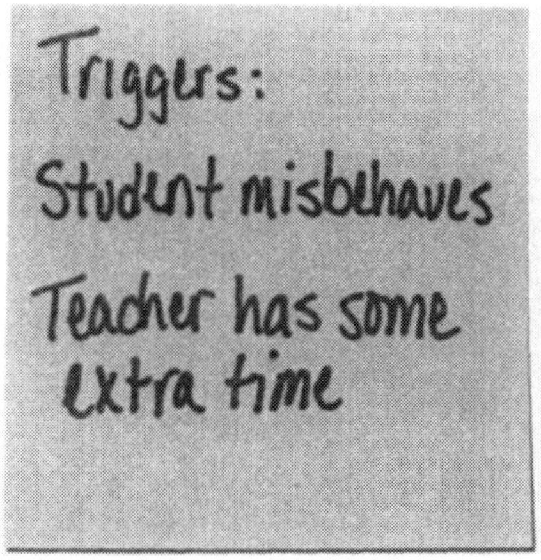

Figure 7-2:
Representation of eChalk's blue Post-it® note, placed at the very top of their sequence consolidatedsheet.

Triggers:
Student misbehaves
Teacher has some
extra time

Look for chunks that are one activity

Identify high-level activities on each sequence: An activity is a set of steps, which taken together, achieve a particular job or intent. Activities are used to help you get a handle on what is happening in each sequence; they chunk steps into coherent units for easier consolidation. This is especially important since individual sequences may start at a different point in the overall task. A task is a set of activities, initiated by a trigger. So if we consolidate the activities and then line them up, we get a consolidated sequence.

1. Walk through the steps of the first individual sequence to identify activities.

2. Write each of the activities on a green Post-it® note, and stick it on the individual sequence next to the first step of each activity.

3. Go to the second sequence and repeat the process.

4. Go to the third sequence and repeat the process.

5. Scan across all three sequences and match activities across sequences.

6. For each unique activity, move one of the green Post-its® for that activity to the far left column on the consolidation page. Be sure to include all activities, not just those that are common to all three sequences. Leave lots of space between each activity; you'll be adding the steps next.

Example: eChalk

Scanning the steps of the three sequences, it's apparent that communicating about a behavior issue is happening at different times. The U8 and U6 sequences are in immediate response to specific student behavior. In the case of U2, the student behavior—if it was observed at all—occurred at some earlier time.

To identify activities, the team walks each individual sequence, looking for chunks of steps that hang together. Looking at U8's sequence, the first set of steps are about Creating a Communication, so that is written on a green Post-it® and placed on the sequence next to the activity's first step: "Use form letter to create letter about disruptive behavior" (See Figure 7-3).

Activity Name	Steps
Creating a communication	Use form letter to create letter about disruptive behavior ↓ Give letter to student to be delivered to parent ↓ Parent signs note, promising to "rectify matter" ↓ Student returns with letter

Figure 7-3: Example of adding activities to initial sequence steps.

The second coherent chunk of steps starts with "Parent calls main school number for more detail." This step and the steps that follow it are about following up and ongoing communication.

If the sequence consolidators think the team needs to remember that following up is important, that can be called out in the activity name Following Up (see Figure 7-4).

Activity Name	Steps
Following up	Parent calls main school number for more detail ↓ School secretary writes pink slip ↓ Student courier delivers pink slip to U8's desk ↓ U8 goes to office to make call ↓ Parent is home, answers phone ↓ Talk about how parent can assist with behavioral problem

Figure 7-4: Adding additional activities to original sequences.

The same process is followed for U6's sequence, which has only one activity: Creating a Communication (see Figure 7-5).

Figure 7-5:
Reusing an activity
for U6's sequence.

Activity Name	Steps
Creating a communication	Create note describing time incident occurred, description of incident, and request to meet with mother of student ↓ Give note to principal's secretary ↓ Principal's secretary calls mother ↓ Waiting to set up meeting with mother

U2's sequence reveals a new activity that hasn't been seen before. This user isn't starting by creating a communication; he is reading one written by someone else. This activity is described as Receiving a Communication, and goes through the step "Reads e-mail from parent of child." The rest of the steps in the U2's sequence—phoning the parent, completing the form for counselor, and sending the form home with the child—are in Following Up (see Figure 7-6).

Figure 7-6:
Activities added to
U2's sequence.

Activity Name	Steps
Receiving a communication	Signs on to email ↓ Sees message waiting for two days ↓ Reads email from parent of child inquiring how child is doing ↓
Following up	Wait until after school to telephone parent instead of emailing a response ↓ Call parent ↓ Hand write on form provided by child's counselor ↓ Wait until tomorrow to send the note home via child

Notice that the end of U2's sequence has steps for writing a communication to a school counselor about how the child is doing. Is this part of the Following Up activity or a whole new activity? Since there are only two steps, they don't want to chunk into a new activity. Only if other sequences had similar, and more, steps would the team think again if a new activity needed to be created. The purpose of activities is to help the team understand the distinctions in the work and that's not needed here.

At this point each individual sequence has its set of activities, which need to be transferred to the consolidation. If any of the activities are essentially the same, only the wording is different, they are rewritten into one label. For eChalk, each of their unique activities is written on a green Post-it® and transferred to the left column of the consolidation sheet, with a lot of space between each activity for the steps and intents.

Create abstract steps

Within each activity, consolidate the steps in the actual sequences to create a series of abstract steps. An abstract step represents the activity of at least one user written in general terms.

The same step may appear in multiple sequences with different wording and referencing data very particular to that user. In this case, write an abstract step to represent the common user activity and generalize it. For example, in grocery shopping, "Select item from shelf" is the abstract representation of "Picked a can of beans off the shelf" and "Took applesauce."

Even if a step appears in just one sequence, it can also have an abstract step that captures the activity more generally. An abstract step in the consolidated sequence does not imply that every user or even many users performed this step. The consolidation is the superset of all activities that people might do—if you design to this superset of steps you will hit the proverbial 80 percent coverage of variation among users.

Each user may do a slightly different combination and order of steps in the task. Supporting the superset—without locking users into any required steps or order—will ensure that you can cover your whole user population quite well.

To fully consolidate an activity:

1. Choose the first activity.

2. Look across the sequences and identify each step in turn.

3. Fill in implied steps or steps that are missing, if necessary, to make matching steps easier (decision steps are often missing).

4. Write an abstract step on a blue Post-it® note for each set of corresponding steps, even when there's only one actual step. An actual step should not have more than one abstract step.

5. Stick the abstract steps (in a column) on the butcher paper, to the left of the activity. Leave enough space between the activity and the steps for one more column; you will be adding intents later.

6. Add breakdowns as you come to them in the actual sequences. Write the breakdown in red on a blue Post-it® note, labeling the breakdown either with BD: or the breakdown symbol.

Identify alternative steps or strategies in the sequence

Sometimes you will find that users follow the same strategy, but take different steps inside that strategy. Other times users will take entirely different strategies to complete the same task.

1. When the steps are different, but the strategy is the same, write the alternative steps on blue Post-its®, and put them in a horizontal row next to each other.

2. If the users follow different strategies, create a branch to show the different strategy. Use arrows between steps when needed to make the flow clear.

3. Repeat for each activity in the sequences.

Identify loops in the sequence

If a step loops back to an earlier activity or step:

1. Break the actual sequence at the point where it loops.

2. Move the remaining part of the sequence next to the steps already consolidated for that activity, so the first step after the break lines up with the consolidated step it corresponds to.

3. Continue consolidating the rest of the sequence from its new position.

4. To help you follow the flow on the consolidation, you can write an abstract step that indicates the loop.

Example: eChalk

After identifying the activities, the eChalk team went on to the next step, consolidating the steps within each activity. Tables 7-1 and Table 7-2 shows the process they used to account for steps in the U8, U6, and U2 sequences.

Identify intents

Identify intents after working on all the steps of a coherent activity. You will need to identify an overall intent for the entire consolidated sequence, and subintents for as many activities as you can. There may also be subintents for a group of steps inside an activity, or even a single step.

During the interpretation session the team should have indicated intents on the original sequences. Now we will look across them and consolidate them. But many times the intents don't become apparent until consolidation because of the fast pace of the interpretation session. Consolidation is the time to step back, look at the data, and clarify the intents of the users.

1. Look at the entire consolidated sequence. Identify the overall intent for why the users did the task.

2. Write the overall intent on a pink Post-it® note and stick it at the top of the sequence, next to the trigger.

3. For each activity, look across its set of steps and identify the reason for doing the activity.

4. Write the intent on a pink Post-it® note.

5. Place the intent next to the activity, in the empty space between the activity and the first step.

6. Look at the individual abstract steps inside the activity and identify whether there are additional intents for either a set of steps or an individual step.

7. Write the intents on pink Post-it® notes.

8. Stick the step intents next to their abstract steps. Remember, activities and steps can have more than one intent.

See Figure 7-7 for an example of an actual consolidated sequence.

U8 actual steps	U6 actual steps	Rewritten abstract step	Alternative step	Reasoning
Use form letter to create letter about disruptive behavior	Create note describing time incident occurred, description of incident, and request to meet with mother of student	Use a form letter to write the parent	Write a note to the parent	The steps could be rewritten into one abstract step. Or, the project focus may lead a team to writing two alternative steps, calling out that form letters that prescribe certain content are used, or that teachers have the latitude to write notes that imply less structure. Both strategies need to be supported in the eChalk design, so steps are captured as alternatives.
Give letter to student to be delivered to parent Parent signs note, promising to "rectify matter"	Give note to principal's secretary	Give communication to student	Give communication to administration	These steps cannot be abstracted into one since there are two different strategies here. In one case the student is the messenger. In the other case, a member of the administration is the messenger.
Student returns with letter		Student delivers communication to parent Parent acknowledges receiving communication Student returns communication to school		U18 and U16 take very different steps here, so the steps cannot be consolidated. These are two different branches in the sequence. There is also an implied step that has been added: The student delivered the communication to the parent.
	Principal's secretary calls mother Waiting to set up meeting with mother		Administration contacts parent Wait to hear from parent Set up meeting with parent	This step has an implied step: Wait to hear from parent. Since communication delays are important to the eChalk design, the team will want to break this into two steps.

Table 7-1:
Initial consolidated sequence with abstracted steps for creating a communication activity.

151

Table 7-2:
Partially consoli-
dated activity with
abstract steps for
the following up
activity.

U8 actual steps	U2 actual steps	Rewritten abstract step	Alternative step	Reasoning
Parent calls main school number for more detail		Parent calls school to speak to teacher		
School secretary writes pink slip Student courier delivers pink slip to U18's desk		Message delivered to teacher		Here we have consolidated two steps into one since the message delivery method is not important for the design.
	Wait until after school to telephone parent instead of emailing a response	Decide to wait to contact parent after school hours		The original step has both a decision step and an action step embedded in it. For the eChalk team's design, it matters that teachers have a strategy of when they try to reach parents, as well as how they contact parents. That strategy could be buried if it's not broken out.
U8 goes to office to make call	Call parent	Telephone parent		Here the two strategies are coming together. On the consolidation we'll draw a line to make this clearer.
Parent is home, answers the phone		Parent is available		This step is implied for U2. We've left it as a separate step since eChalk will want to capture any times calls are missed, if that occurs.
Talk about how parent can assist with behavioral problems	Discuss how child is doing	Discuss on phone with parent		

Example: eChalk

The final step for the initial eChalk consolidation is to add in the intents. After analyzing the steps to consolidate them, the sequence consolidators are immersed in these three sequences, and may understand them better than the original inter-viewers. Therefore, their job is to look at the intents as originally captured and decide if they need to be rewritten or if missing intents need to be added.

The overall intents in the individual sequences are:

- U8 Inform parents of child's behavioral problem in class

- U6 Report behavioral problem to principal

- U2 Communicate about the state of child's behavioral problem

The U6 intent as written isn't correct. The ultimate intent was to communicate with the parent; going through the principal's office was just an interim step. All three sequences are about establishing a dialog with the parent about the child, so the overall intent could be written as:

- Establish dialog about an issue

We've abstracted out the behavioral problem from the intent so the consolidation can support other kinds of communications. Table 7-3 shows the eChalk sequence with intents added (see Figure 7-7 for an example of an actual consolidated sequence).

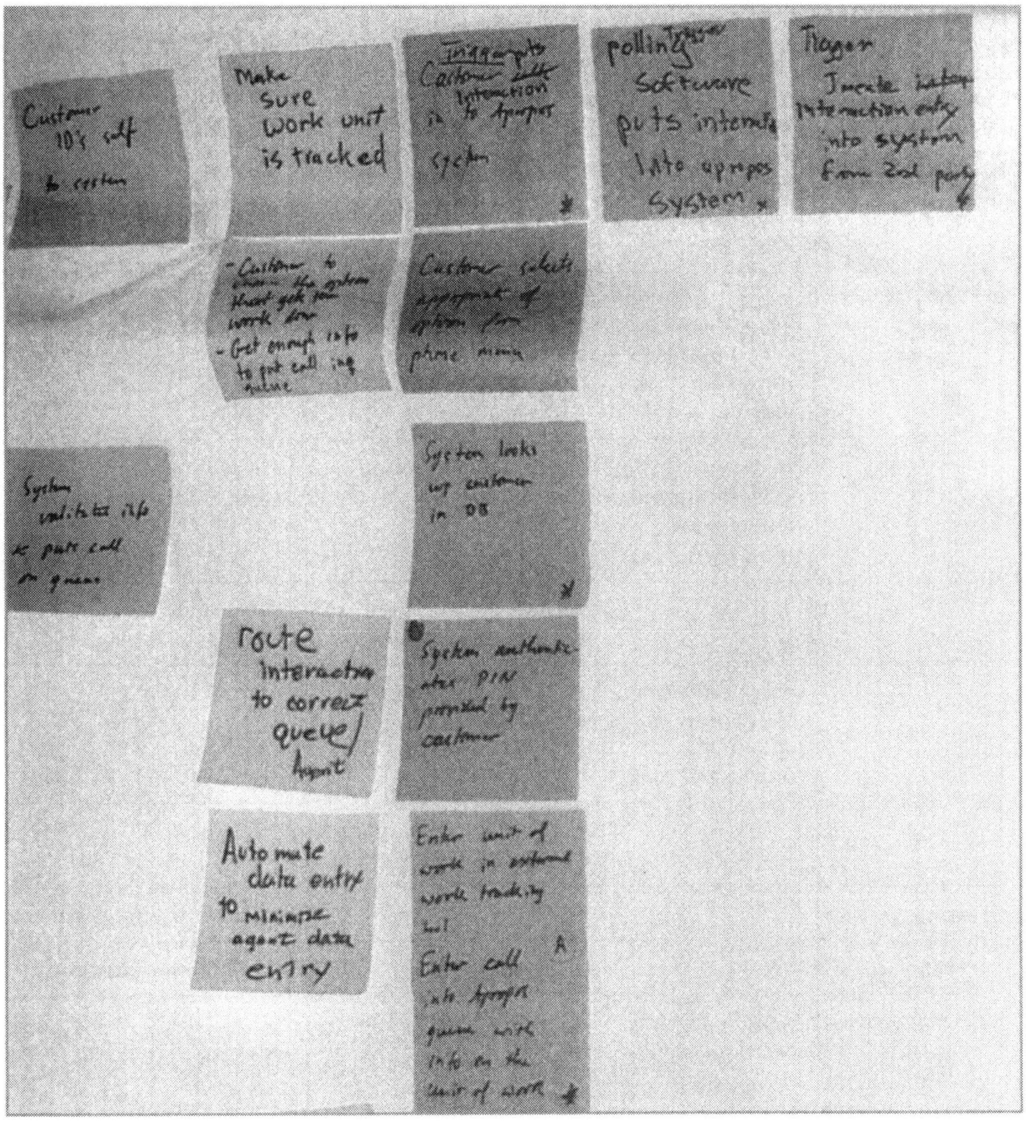

Figure 7-7: A partially consolidated sequence for Apropos's call center project built in paper. The team was able to visualize the sequence by seeing it in paper first. They moved the finished consolidation online.

Table 7-3:
The entire consolidated sequence, intents added.

Communicating with parents			
Triggers: Student misbehaves Teacher has some extra time	Overall intent: Establish dialog about an issue		
Activities	**Intents**	**Abstract steps: Strategy 1**	**Abstract steps: Strategy 2**
Receiving a communication	Be reachable by parents		
		Sign on to email	
		See message has been waiting for multiple days	
		Breakdown: Poor computer performance discourages email use	
		Breakdown: Delay in responding to parent	
Creating a communication	Keep parents informed		
		Reads message from parent asking about child's behavior	
	Follow the school policy for how to write communications	Use a form letter to write the parent	Write a note to the parent
	Follow the school policy for how to communicate with parent	Give communication to student	Give communication to school administration
		Student delivers communication to parent	Administration contacts parent
	Get confirmation that communication was received and read	Parent acknowledges the communication	
		Student returns communication to the school	
			Wait to hear from parent
			Set up meeting with parent
Following up	Keep up ongoing communication with parent		

Communicating with parents			
Activities	Intents	Abstract steps: Strategy 1	Abstract steps: Strategy 2
	Communicate quickly with teacher about problem	Parent calls school to speak with teacher	
		Message delivered to teacher	
	Increase chance of reaching parent at home	Decide to wait to contact parent after school hours	
	Interact more personally than email offers	Telephone parent	
		Parent is available	
		Discuss on phone with parent	
		Need to discuss again arises	
	Take advantage of already scheduled meeting	Discuss in regular, face-to-face meeting	
	Communicate in a faster method	Decide to communicate via email	
		One person doesn't have email	
		Person gets email account	
		Email sent	
		Email responded to	
	Have regular, immediate communication about a problem	Continue sending email	
		Discussion ends	
	Do the weekly report	Write report to a third party about the child	
	Use child as a courier, a fast, cheap, reliable method	Send the third party report home with the child	
	Follow procedure of not contacting certain third parties directly		

Table 7-3 continued: The entire consolidated sequence, intents added.

155

Finish the consolidation

After finishing the initial three sequences, roll in the remaining sequences in the set:

1. Line up steps in each remaining individual sequences with the consolidation.
2. Insert new triggers, steps, breakdowns, intents, and as needed.
3. Create new branches to deal with new work strategies.

Tips

Here are some tips for the sequence consolidation process. See the box, **Scheduling considerations and time estimates** for time management tips during consolidation.

Understand the purpose of the activities versus abstract steps. Activities are simply used to group the actual steps to better reveal the work.

Keep the activities at a high level. As a general rule of thumb, a consolidated sequence will have four to eight activities.

Include implicit steps. These may be thought steps or steps that are implied by the language of the step itself. Separate these into different unique steps.

Accurately reflect strategies. Make sure the team identifies real strategies and doesn't get hung up in the fact that one user did one step before another. Take note of this but realize it doesn't denote a new strategy or the need for variants.

Clearly separate the parts of the sequence. Visually separate intents and abstract steps so they easily can be identified during redesign.

Don't lose the detail. Don't consolidate steps together that don't really fit together. Make separate steps.

Roll in the rest of the sequences by visual inspection. The first three sequences should be consolidated in great detail. They will provide the structure for the rest of the sequences that exist for that task. For additional sequences scan each one to see what is new and add it directly to the consolidated model.

Scheduling considerations and time estimates

Following are some issues to keep in mind when planning your sequence consolidation schedule:

- Choose the sequences most important to your work to consolidate first.
- Start with the three sequences for each task that have the most complexity and consolidate them first.
- Get helpers if you are a two-person team so that you can consolidate your critical sequences quickly. A project will usually have four to six critical sequences, and a sequence takes three to eight hours to consolidate depending on its length and the number of sequences that have to be consolidated together.
- With helpers you can complete all of the primary work of consolidation in two days.
- Don't let the process drag out: You can spread the consolidation over several days or even a couple of weeks if you have only a couple of people or very demanding schedules. However, you may find it difficult to get reoriented to where you are in the consolidation if there are several days between the times you work on it.
- Roll in the rest of the sequences by visual inspection looking only for missing steps, intents, and breakdowns to add.

Wait to draw lines until you are sure you are done. Because the sequence consolidation will be done in several passes and things will change until you are finished, you don't want to draw the line or arrows for branches and loops directly on the paper. One trick is to draw them on removable tape.

Example: Agilent consolidated sequence

Table 7-4 is a partially consolidated sequence for the analytical lab, showing how a lab decides whether it can take on new work. Samples from the actual data are maintained as illustrations. This sequence model lays out the strategies in an outline.

Intent	Abstract steps with strategies	Sample user data
	1. Study or project is proposed or assigned to a department or group or lab	
	a. Project proposal notification.	U11: Client services carries worksheet to appropriate section manager. Section manager plans personnel, supplies, and other resources based on worksheet. U45: Project information and ID comes in (paperwork).
I: Notify manager that project has been assigned	b. Project arrives or is assigned to lab.	U4-1: New 1000 sample study arrives. U5: Project coordinator is selected. The project coordinator is responsible for project team coordination with synthesis lab, pilot plant, and analytical development.
	2. Estimate time to do study or project	
	a. Check resources to predict timeline	
	b. Strategy 1:	
	i. Look at manpower budget	
	c. Strategy 2:	
	i. Plan based on fixed date	U5: Production date is already defined by International project team and is not flexible.
I: Get an idea of when things need to be done for all functionality groups; need to coordinate.	ii. Check feasibility of lab	U5: Talk to synthesis group about technical feasibility (checklist).
	iii. Determine date that plant needs methods	U5: Talks to pilot plant to determine when they need methods for raw materials.

Table 7-4: Activity: *Planning for Work.*

Table 7-4
continued:
Activity: *Planning
for Work.*

Intent	Abstract steps with strategies	Sample user data
I: Get rough estimate based on lab's past experience and performance and on the predicted sample load.	d. Begin calculations based on assumed number of samples per day.	U4-1: U44 Assumes 60 samples/day Monday-Thursday, 120 samples over Friday-Sunday presuming the use of autosamplers.
	e. Calculate (study) time in weeks from number of samples per day.	U4-1: Calculates # of weeks by # samples/(4*60 + 120).
	f. Get staff input on number of samples per day.	
I: Refine estimate to include "overhead" and other "fudge" factors.	g. Add reserves for overhead to account for others staff work and replicate testing.	U4-1: He adds reporting and replicate determination time (for suspicious data). Replicate determination = 15% overhead If less robust method or inexperienced technician, or large scale project he adds additional replicate overhead. This factor varies with the project stage. He adds GLP overhead. 1-2 extra days for internal audits. This varies with the project stage. He pads all projects with overhead-like instrument.
	h. Factor in a client expectation of receiving results online.	U4-1: He looks at expectation from client on how quickly results are available on line. This varies with project stage. If results are needed instantaneously then he must reduce the batch size, because smaller batches can be turned around more quickly.
	i. Add extra time for sample delivery issues.	
	j. Discuss estimate with staff for accuracy.	U4-1: He discusses with his coworkers the accuracy of the estimate and commitment. U5: Supervisor meets with staff to plan projects (Resources).
	3. Determine what resources are required.	
	a. Create a plan based upon lab resources.	U11: Section manager plans personnel, supplies, and other resources based on worksheet. U5: Figures out who'll work on it from his group: who is available now, what stage are various projects. It is not practical for one individual to have more than one project in the same phase.

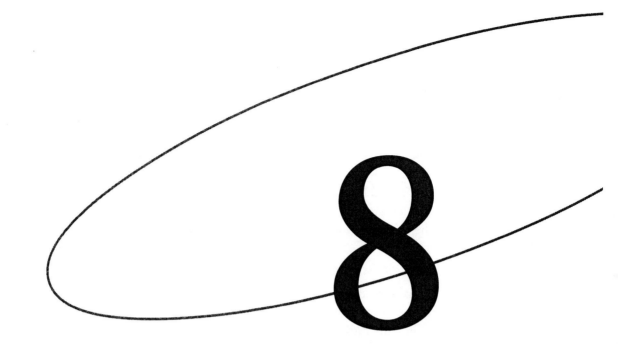

Building an Affinity Diagram

Rapid CD Process	Lightning Fast	Lightning Fast +	Focused Rapid CD
Affinity Diagrams	✓	✓	✓

The affinity diagram (see Figure 8-1) brings issues and insights across all customers together into a wall-sized, hierarchical diagram. In the interpretation sessions you captured individual notes representing the users' data. We call these interpretation session notes affinity notes because you are now going to use them to build the affinity diagram.

The affinity diagram is relevant for any form of Rapid CD. It is your fastest and best method to see all the issues across your user population. System design must address a whole market or user population. It must take into consideration the issues of the population as a whole, the structure of work, and the variations natural to that work. Consolidating the affinity notes and individual work models enables you to see the issues for your whole user population, not just one individual. This chapter guides you to build an affinity.

The affinity diagram is built from the bottom up, grouping individual notes that reveal key themes in your data. We let the data suggest the labels for these groups rather than starting with predefined categories. Groups are then labeled using the voice of the customer—saying what they do and how they think. This process exposes and makes concrete common issues, distinctions, work patterns, and needs without losing individual variation.

The affinity diagram for Rapid CD can be built in one day with a few helpers or in two to three days by a two-person team depending on how many notes you have.

Once built, you can "walk" the affinity and let the data stimulate design ideas appropriate for your project. Walking the affinity, and for Focused Rapid CD, your consolidated sequences to prepare for creating your recommendations and high-level project vision are covered in Chapter 10.

Definition

The affinity diagram organizes the individual interpretation session, or affinity, notes into a wall-sized, hierarchical diagram grouping the data into key issues under labels that reveal the customer's needs. The affinity shows in one place the common issues, themes, and scope of the customer problems and needs. The affinity acts as the voice of the customer and the issues it reveals become the basis for user requirements.

Key concepts

Affinity diagram. This diagram is a hierarchical representation of the issues for your user population built from interpretation session affinity notes. Since it is initially built on the walls of a room, it's also referred to as the affinity wall or "the wall."

Affinity note. The interpretation session note and the affinity note are the same thing. The affinity notes will be printed so that a team can group them on a wall into the affinity diagram. The affinity notes are sometimes referred to as yellow notes or Post-its® because they can be printed on yellow Post-it® notes.

Blue labels. These labels collect together a coherent set of notes representing a theme or work distinction. The labels are written in the first person, as though the customer was directly talking to you.

Pink labels. The next level of label, these collect together a set of Blue labels with a common theme. Pink labels abstract the data another level and characterize the Blue labels under them. The language of Pink labels is also in the voice of the customer.

Green labels. The highest level of affinity label, these summarize the Pink labels under them. Green labels also can be written in the voice of the customer but may be more general in nature. Each Green label denotes a big piece of the user story. Most affinities have five to eight Green labels.

Affinity building process

☐ Prepare for affinity building

    ☐ Decide when to build the affinity diagram

    ☐ Identify affinity building team

    ☐ Prepare to build the affinity

☐ Build the affinity

    ☐ Introduce the affinity building process

    ☐ Place all affinity notes

☐ Add Blue labels

☐ Reorganize the wall—add Pink and Green labels

☐ Creating the final affinity—rolling in new data

Figure 8-1 shows a section of an affinity. This section has a Green label at the top, the Pink labels below them, and the Blue labels in columns below each Pink category. The angled sticky notes are design ideas the team has attached to the data after the "wall walk" described in Chapter 10.

Figure 8-1: Section of the affinity showing label hierarchy.

Decide when to build the affinity diagram

For a typical Rapid CD project you will have a total of eight to 10 users at two or three work sites for the entire project. Generally, each user interpretation session yields 50 to 100 notes, so affinity diagrams contain about 500 to 1000 notes. You can choose to build your affinity all at once after you finish interviews or you can build it in two rounds.

Two rounds of affinity building make each session easier to deal with and allows for refocusing the project mid-way. You can start building your affinity diagram after you have completed roughly half of your interviews and have 300 to 400 notes. After you have completed your initial build, walk the wall to find holes in the data and areas where you need more information. This will drive whom you interview next and what you focus on during the interview. After completing your remaining interviews roll the additional data into your initial affinity.

Whether you build the affinity all at once or in two rounds it will take approximately the same length of time. Lapsed time in affinity building is determined mainly by how many notes you have, how many people are building at once, and how finicky you become about groupings and labels.

Do not try to build an affinity all at once if you have more than 1000 affinity notes to put on the wall. For two people large numbers of notes quickly become overwhelming. Even if you get a large number of people to help, you then need strong moderation. So with that many affinity notes build your affinity in two steps.

Monitor your interpretation sessions to see how many notes you produce during an average interpretation session to predict when to build your affinity. You can get a quick overview of your progress in the CDTools project window.

See the box, **Distributed teams and affinity building**, for tips on how to manage the affinity building process with team members and interested parties in multiple locations.

Distributed teams and affinity building

Affinity building is one of the best times to get your distributed team together. It allows the team to form a shared understanding, and since it is preparation for visioning and design anyway it can precede other design work.

But if you can't get your team into the same place, consider splitting the building process into two locations, each with several team members and stakeholders in each place. Simply divide the affinity notes randomly or by user type, equalizing the type of user in both places. Let the team build separate affinities.

Then if you are using CDTools each team can enter their own Green, Pink, and Blue labels. Affinity owners from each group can review the affinity, consolidating labels and creating new groupings in the tool. Just display the affinity builder in a meeting support tool so you can both see the affinity and normalize the final affinity together. Moving affinity notes and labels around is easy to do electronically.

Then print out your final affinity in both places and hang it up on the team room walls in your multiple locations. Now everyone has the same user data to work from for the design step.

Identify the affinity building team

Decide if you have the resources to get helpers to build the affinity. Remember this is not just a resource issue—affinity building is also a great opportunity to involve your stakeholders. A half- to one-day commitment is usually something that stakeholders will be able to commit.

To build an affinity in a single day, get one person for every 50 to 80 affinity notes. So if you have 400 notes you will need six to eight people to build your affinity in one day. If you have less people then the affinity building will take longer. Go back and look at the suggested schedules in Chapter 2 to set expectations for time and resources for affinity building.

Never let your affinity building drag out over more than two to three days; the team will become tired and start to think it takes too long. Remember even if the manpower is the same, time is experienced as short if the task is completed in a day. This lets the team move on to the next step of design, speeding up the overall project schedule.

Your affinity building team can include your team members, stakeholders, and anyone who understands the project focus and is interested in the data. The people who sat in on your interpretation sessions would make excellent helpers. You could also invite:

- Marketing
- Management
- Business analysts
- Developers, information architects, usability professionals, UI designers, interaction designers, and others who have to build products but are not on the team
- People on related projects
- Documentation writers
- Technical support staff

Your helpers do not have to stay the entire day. As long as they can commit two- to three-hour chunks of time their help will speed up the process and create buy-in. Be sure to explain how to build the affinity before any helpers start. Try to start many helpers at the same time so they can hear the rules and process.

Note: Prior to building the affinity, send non-team members copies of the project focus and any other documents that will provide them with context.

Prepare to build the affinity

Your preparation includes getting your online notes formatted, and then printed out. You will also need to set up the room beforehand and gather supplies.

You need a conference-size room with enough wall space for the affinity to spread out. Line the walls with butcher paper, hanging the paper vertically in 6-foot vertical lengths, overlapping. Cover all walls of your team room, including the windows if there are many of them.

Do the following tasks before you start building the affinity:

- Print the interpretation notes on sheets of laser Post-it® notes or in label format on paper that has been cut into notes. If you don't use Post-its®, use removable tape to place notes on the wall. If you use CDTools, it will automatically format the notes for printing as 3x5 notes.

- Mix up the notes. Shuffle the notes so each person building the affinity has a mix of users in the notes they are working with.

- Break the notes into stacks of 20 or so. Smaller piles are less intimidating.

- Print a copy of the interpretation notes printed in numerical order (not as Post-it® notes) in a running list format. This can be used for reference if a particular note doesn't make sense; sometimes reading the note written before or after it will clarify it.

- Print a copy of the user and organization profiles. These can also help you better understand an unclear note.

Note: If you are using CDTools, its Print features automatically format the notes for printing as 3x5 notes, prints them in random order, prints the profiles, and also prints a list of notes in numeric order.

See the box, **Set up the room**, for a detailed supply list to have in the room.

Set up the room

Ideally, the session will take place in your design room; if not, then in a large room (approximately 15x15). In your room you will need:

- White, waxless butcher paper or craft paper to cover all the walls of the room. Hang the paper vertically in 6-foot vertical lengths, overlapping. Cover all walls of your team room, including the windows if there are many of them.

- One or two flipcharts to create additional places for organizing notes if needed. These are back-ups.

- Masking tape to secure the butcher paper to the wall, and removable tape for the notes when you have finished the wall and want to tape it down to move it. You never want to use regular tape—affinity building is all about moving notes around.

- Yellow 3x5 Post-it® notes. You will need these while building the affinity in case you need to break any existing notes apart into multiple notes and add them to the wall.

- 3x3 square Post-it® notes for the affinity labels, in approximately this number: Blue (8 packs), Pink (6 packs), Green (2 packs). Use high-end sticky notes like the Post-it® brand because other, less expensive brands will fall off the wall more easily over time.

- Fine-tip felt colored pens. You will need enough blue, red, green, and black pens for each person with a wide enough point so that the writing can be seen from a distance—extra-fine is too small (use fine point, not extra-fine). If anyone is color blind, use black instead of green.

Introduce the affinity building process

If you are a two-person team building the affinity, review how to build an affinity and start building your wall. If you have helpers you will need to do an introduction to help them understand what is going to happen. As soon as you have helpers one person needs to run and moderate the session—he or she will also build the affinity but one eye must be kept on the process and progress (see the box, **Managing people during**

affinity building). After people have built lots of affinities this watchfulness won't be needed because people will know what to do.

Managing people during affinity building

Building an affinity is not an easy process for some and people will react to the process in different ways. Here are some guidelines.

Response	Advice
The number of affinity notes and the lack of structure overwhelm some. These people can organize a limited part of the affinity, but find it hard to put up the original groups.	Talk about this before starting so people who get overwhelmed will know it is normal to feel this way. Reassure them that they will find it easier later in the process, and that at the end when the wall is organized they will have the structure they need. Explain that building the affinity this way is the most practical way to get the affinity notes up and organized, while taking advantage of multiple perspectives.
Some get concerned about creating the "right" affinity.	Help them see that there are many ways to put an affinity together and you will produce only one. This is okay—the purpose is to push your understanding of the customer by revealing key distinctions for the users. As long as your affinity makes you think new and appropriate design thoughts it is good for your purposes.
Some people need to clear out distractions and focus on just a part of the problem.	They may not be able to deal with working with someone else to do it. If you have two people who work like this, suggest that they pair up because they will work in parallel but engage in some discussion.
Some will get frustrated trying to track "their" section of the wall or Post-it® notes when others add to these groups or move their Post-it® notes somewhere else.	Coach people to be comfortable with multiple people creating the diagram, without anyone keeping the whole thing coherent. Tell them to trust that something good will come out. This is how to move quickly.

Explaining everything about affinity building in advance will not clarify what to do. You need to give a brief overview to set expectations and then guide people each step of the way. Here is an introduction script you can start with, which will also help you see the big picture of what happens in the affinity building process.

Example script: eChalk

Affinity building is a group process that relies on inductive reasoning—you look at instances of data and ask yourself what this point is really about and whether it can be grouped with other data points already on the wall. The groups emerge from paying attention to the data—not by predetermining categories to sort things into.

So this note says (Read one of your affinity notes and discuss it like we do in this example with this affinity note from eChalk).

"The principal includes a personal note on each printed e-mail that he sends to the teacher"

This note has the word "e-mail" in it, but it isn't really about e-mail or even about the fact that the school principal prints e-mail. This note is really about the need for a sense of personal or person-to-person communication.

We want to look beyond the key words in the affinity note and see the work issues relevant to this project that they reveal. Create your groups based on that kind of reasoning.

So let's get started. Everyone will get about 20 Post-its® to start. First we are going to stand at the wall and get these notes up into these natural groupings. I'll lead you through this process—we'll move from doing it together to acting individually until all the notes are up on the wall with no labels.

Then we will stop and label the notes. We'll start with Blue labels for each of our groupings. All labels are in the voice of the customer as though you were writing a story to read later. We use "I" language in the label (substitute a possible label language for your project) "I want every parent to feel they are special." Our goal is to have all the relevant issues expressed in the Blue labels so we don't have to read the individual interpretation notes again. We don't want category labels like "Strategies I use with parents." This label would make me have to read all the affinity notes under this section to find out what the strategies are.

After we create Blue labels we will then group the Blues under the Pink labels and the Pink's under Green labels. Then we will have our whole affinity and we can read it back, hearing the voice of the customer as we read it from the top down—Green, to Pink, to Blue. (If you have another affinity group read them the labels so they get the idea of creating a story.) Think of the affinity building as happening in multiple passes or stages where we iterate and clean up in each pass.

Let's get started (pass out piles of affinity notes to each person).

This is a conceptual description of the affinity building process—but to build an affinity requires working in stages. Here we will describe each stage so you can build your own affinity and help others build with you.

At the start of any affinity building session remind everyone on the team of the project's focus. Tell them about the following rules of thumb and watch for compliance during the process.

Building columns (groups of affinity notes)

- A column of affinity notes (groups) is started with any kind of observation note, but not a design idea note or question note.

- Once a column is started, design ideas and questions are treated like any other affinity note.

- If a group doesn't hang together, separate out the notes that don't fit and make new columns.

- Anyone can move any note without justification—it's a group process.

- The eventual goal is to have three to six notes in each column. If you have more than six notes, you are probably burying a distinction that needs to be pulled out into a new column.

Making sense of individual affinity notes

- If a note doesn't make sense, go back to the affinity note list and read the note before or after this affinity note. If it still doesn't make sense, talk to the person who did the interview or someone who was in the interpretation session. Once you have figured out what the note means, place it or hand-edit it if necessary.

- Every affinity note is supposed to contain just one idea. If an affinity note needs to be broken up because it contains more than one idea, handwrite a new affinity note on a yellow Post-it® for the second idea and cross out the duplicate information on the first note. Give the new note the same user code and number and write the note number like this: #A (e.g., U01-22A). See the box, **Can one note go into multiple columns?**, for more help on knowing when to split up a single note into two.

Note: If you are using CD Tools, just write the user code and number; CD Tools will automatically assign the next available note number when you eventually enter the note into the software.

Can one note go into multiple columns?

The rule is that a note can go into only one column. Decide where is seems to fit best; often putting it in a column that has only one or two notes is the best and fastest choice.

It's not a good use of time to agonize or spend a lot of time discussing it. But, if the note has multiple points in it, do separate it into multiple notes. Just take a blank yellow Post-it® and rewrite it. For example:

U9-25 He keeps his own attendance book, because this is more accurate than the bubble sheet because he can't make changes (95% accurate); doesn't have access to the Scantron system so he can't modify the Scantron

The eChalk team realized that the note has two points in it so they made new notes:

U9-25 He keeps his own attendance book, because this is more accurate than the bubble sheet because he can't make changes (95% accurate)

U9-25a He doesn't have access to the Scantron system so he can't modify the Scantron

Weeding out the "bad" notes

- If you can't find an immediate home for an affinity note, set it aside and come back to it later. Go back to any notes that were set aside during the building process and try to find them a home in the affinity. Or give it to someone else and see if they can find where to place it.

- Look for work implications hidden in Question notes and add them to groups. If there are none, put them in a Questions category that's separate from the affinity.

- Some affinity notes hold demographics or say nothing about the work. Put them in a Junk category to be reviewed later to see if the notes can be integrated into the affinity. If they ultimately are deemed to be junk, CDTools users can mark them as Junk notes to be ignored.

Place all affinity notes on the wall

The first step is to get all the affinity notes up on the wall in loose groupings with no labels. Run the process as follows:

1. Start with one person reading aloud so everyone can hear any affinity note that is not a design idea or question. This person then puts the affinity note on the wall to start the first column.

2. Everyone reads through the affinity notes in their hands to find any affinity notes that go with the one that's already up.

3. If related affinity notes are found, read them aloud and put each under the first affinity note.

4. If you can't find an affinity note telling the same story, read another affinity note with a different focus aloud and start a new column.

5. Repeat this until you have about 10 columns with two to four notes in each. Don't let people just start putting up individual notes with nothing grouped under them.

6. If someone disagrees with placement and wants to move an affinity note from one column to another or group it with one being held, let them do it and remind them that this is done without argument or discussion. This is not a time for discussion or group agreement about where each note goes. Anyone can add or move a note—no one owns an affinity note so it can be moved without justification or consultation.

Starting together this way makes everyone aware of the notes and the groupings as they go up. It focuses everyone on building the wall together. And it is a time when people can remind each other not to keyword the notes. The second step starts to reduce the overall group coordination. See Table 8-1 for tips on placing the first affinity notes.

Run the next part of the affinity building process as follows until all the notes are up on the wall or until people really can't track where the groupings are—that is usually with 60 to 80 columns or so.

1. Keep adding new affinity notes but don't read every one aloud; read aloud only notes that start new columns to make people aware of a new grouping to consider.

2. Watch out for groups of only one or two notes—push yourselves to fill in the groupings before putting up a new column.

3. People can talk and yell out if anyone has seen a certain type of work practice, but avoid talking in categories: "Has anyone seen other things about e-mail?" Focus on work practice distinctions.

Dos and don'ts for placing first affinity notes	
Don't	Do
Start from a set of categories and try to fit the affinity notes into them.	Move affinity notes around. Avoid pre-conceived categories.
Worry about putting an affinity note in the right place.	Create new distinctions by moving affinity notes. If moving it won't create a new distinction, leave it where it is. The labels are what we care about, not the individual data points.
Find a "keyword" in the affinity note and assume it belongs in that category.	Read the affinity note to find the underlying implication. For example, all the affinity notes with the word "printing" do not automatically go into a column about printing.
Take a lot of time in the initial step of getting all the notes up.	Get the notes on the wall into rough groupings to allow the next layer of sorting and structuring by the group. It doesn't have to be perfect in this first round. Use a time metric to get all the affinity notes up. Plan for two to four hours depending on the number of notes and the number of team members.

Table 8-1:
Tips for placing the notes during the first step of affinity building.

4. When everyone seems to know what they are doing and are putting up notes, getting new ones, and filling in columns, stop reading anything aloud and then just get all the notes up.

5. When people run out of notes give them notes from others who still have some—the goal is to get all the notes up or reach the point where you need to put up labels to track the groupings on the wall. For anything under 600 notes you should be able to get them all up before labeling.

6. When almost all notes are on the wall give yourselves 10 to 15 minutes to get all the notes up in a big push in the end. If you started first thing in the morning this will be around noon, so promise lunch as a reward. If you have a smaller affinity, promise a break.

We don't write summary labels or label the groupings formally until all the affinity notes are up on the wall to encourage the team to read the groupings when they add a new Post-it®. This keeps them focused on the content instead of the category and helps keep the grouping more coherent. But don't be surprised if in this first round you get long columns focused on key words—that is part of this initial bottoms-up sorting process. It will be corrected in the labeling process.

Add Blue labels

We add labels to the wall from the bottom up so the first set of labels are the Blue labels describing what is going on in the Post-it® groupings themselves. The wall will reach a critical point when Blue labels are needed—when the team can no longer keep track of the groups.

Assuming you have more than two people working on the affinity, break up into pairs to put up the initial Blue labels. You want to work in pairs so that you can bounce ideas and label possibilities off someone else. Working in pairs also helps to avoid key wording and results in a better affinity.

Start labeling with the longest columns. Your goal is to have an affinity with two to six notes in a coherent grouping. If you have only 300 to 400 notes, make groupings of one to three Post-its® to ensure you don't lose key distinctions. If you have 500 to 1000 notes, aim for groups that are deeper—up to four or five notes. Long columns bury requirements—the first mark of a good affinity is how long the groupings are.

After all the affinity notes are up on the wall without labels, most teams have some columns that end up being anywhere from 10 to 30 Post-its® long. These are usually Post-its® surrounding one semi-coherent theme or story. So when you break it up you will start to see some groupings that show the key work distinctions and issues for that theme.

To break up a group each pair will:

1. Walk through each column of notes looking for notes that hang together in one coherent distinction and regrouping them into these smaller groups.

2. Discuss between themselves any issues or ideas for new groupings.

3. Separate out any notes that don't fit, and when appropriate give them to other pairs in the room working on that topic.

4. Start new columns, if necessary.

5. Write Blue labels for the resulting groupings.

6. If the Blues seem to hang together in a higher order grouping, write Pink labels for those groups.

Once the team identifies the distinctions hidden in the long columns and writes labels for them they can look for other notes that further support these same issues. Usually, there are. So writing a Blue label for one Post-it® when it belongs with a group of other Blue labels will help you start to construct a larger story of the work. And an initial affinity may have some Blue labels with only one note—later data gathering may be able to flesh out this issue.

The general rule of thumb is two to three notes per Blue label in a preliminary affinity and four to six notes per Blue label in the final affinity. If there are more than six notes under a Blue label, examine the column and check if there is a distinction you could pull out.

Good Blue labels have design relevance

A good Blue-level label tells you what matters about the notes underneath it. When your affinity is built and you walk it, you'll be reading it top-down. The goal is to create an affinity where you never have to read the individual affinity notes to understand the labels. If you have to read them to find out what the strategies are, why something is liked, or the details of how people work, the label is too categorical and needs to be rewritten. A good Blue label raises the detailed work issue up into the label language (see Table 8-2 for tips on writing good labels).

Example: eChalk

Both of the following are good labels because they remind the eChalk team that they can't be seduced by technology; they can't assume that the mere act of putting communication online will be useful. The team needs to think about how their product can support person-to-person and informal communication.

Blue: Person-to-person communication is important to me

U04-27 Principal includes a personal note on each printed e-mail that he sends to the teacher

U01-16 Schools are small; teachers talk often

U20-18 There's lots of informal verbal communication between the teachers (e.g., "You must create your students' files so that I can add in my comments")

U16-8 He walks around while students are doing the "do now" and talks one-on-one about the last day's homework

U04-28 DI: Personalized notes on e-mails when forwarding

Blue: When teachers are nearby we communicate informally and verbally

U03-4 She communicates easily with the other first grade teacher; their rooms are across the hall

U12-34 Mostly face-to-face informal communication goes on in the hallways

U02-26 The school teachers communicate in a morning prayer circle

U05-12 Communications take place mostly in verbal form and are informal

U10-2 Informal communication is used to schedule meetings with the vice principal (VP is expected to be in his office)

U11-2 Communication is very informal at the school and is all verbal

A good Blue label will both characterize the work of the users and push home an issue to the team that they need to consider to build the right system for this population. Labels that hide distinctions also hide user needs and aspects of the work that the team must consider in their design. For this reason, the Blue label is the most important driver of design thinking. If your groupings are too long, if your labels are too general, you will not get the full advantage of a well-built affinity.

Because the Blue labels drive design thinking the exact location of one particular Post-it® is not relevant. If one Post-it® can go under one of two Blues and both Blues have some other Post-its® there already it makes no difference where that Post-it® goes because you already have these two labels. But if moving a Post-it® can create a new Blue label—can raise up a hidden distinction—then move it. Or if moving a Post-it® from a group of five to a group of one can bring greater clarity and weight to the label, move it.

But don't get crazy—massaging an affinity for days on end to make it perfect is not a goal. It just needs to be good enough to stimulate good design thinking.

Note: Often a Blue label will be too high level because it is trying to characterize too many Post-its®, but after you break up the affinity notes underneath it and create new Blue labels, the old Blue label will become the Pink label, collecting the Blue labels into a coherent story about the users' experience.

Table 8-2:
Tips for writing
good labels.

Dos and don'ts for creating affinity labels	
Don't	Do
Write labels in the third person.	Write labels as though the user is speaking to you. Use I and We.
Write labels that are too abstract.	A good label captures what its group is saying in detail.
Use your own jargon.	Write clear labels that everyone can understand.
Use pre-defined categories.	Let the data tell the story, don't assume that your preconceived notions are the best way to organize the findings.
Force a label on a group.	Reorganize a group if it's too incoherent for a good label; make sure the label talks about the work.
Bury distinctions that are potentially important to the design.	Surface important design points in the labels so they'll be very visible to the team.

Bad Blue labels hide or misrepresent distinctions

The following label does not reveal a distinction that clearly drives the design—what content drives which mode of communication. You have to read the individual notes to find out what is really going on.

Example 1: eChalk

Original Blue label: My mode of communication with parents is determined by content of conversation

> **U11-8** She is pleased with success of communicating via e-mail with parents, especially because emotion is removed from the situation

> **U2-12** Responds back to parents' e-mail by phone because there's more opportunity for interaction with the parent

> **U12-60** He makes a distinction between schoolwork e-mail (Yahoo) and personal mail (AOL)

> **U6-7** She has to records of all parent communication that deals with behavioral issues

Indeed this label is hiding four more valuable distinctions. With these distinctions revealed the team can look for other affinity notes to flesh out the groups. Here's how the blue label could be rewritten.

Rewritten Blue label: I use e-mail to diffuse potentially emotional communications

> **U11-8** She is pleased with success of communicating via e-mail with parents especially because emotion is removed from the situation

Rewritten Blue label: I want face-to-face interaction with parents

U2-12 Responds back to parents' e-mail by phone because there's more opportunity for interaction with the parent

Rewritten Blue label: I need to keep my work and personal e-mails distinct from each other

U12-60 He makes a distinction between schoolwork e-mail (Yahoo) and personal e-mail (AOL)

Example 2: eChalk
Original Blue label: I need to document certain types of communication with parents

U6-7 She has to keep records of all parent communication that deals with behavioral issues

Similarly this label could be improved—it is already known that the school uses information. A better label might be:

Rewritten Blue label: We are using manual processes that are comfortable to us.

U6-7 She has to keep records of all parent communication that deals with behavioral issues

Example 3: eChalk
Blue: The school district or parish uses information from our school

U5-4 When the parish needs information they send a spreadsheet to U25, who manually fills it out

U11-43 She is already comfortable with the school's existing data management program and uses it on her own

U2-3 Manually records all daily attendance into a spreadsheet. The parish uses this to figure out school buses.

This label focuses the team on the real competitors to their tool—existing processes. If this Blue label sits on a wall with other Blue labels that talk about discomfort with change, the team can see their challenge as developing a design that is equally comfortable to the user population.

Reorganize the wall—add Pink and Green labels

When all of the relevant affinity notes are placed on the wall and you have your initial Blue labels you can reorganize the wall to put things together by like themes. By now the team will naturally have started to move Blue labels together that seem to group into related themes. These large chunks of the user story foreshadow your Green labels.

To make building the wall easier, after the Blue labels are up, walk the wall and create temporary Green labels with labels that reflect, for example, big steps in the process, communication strategies, how tools are used, how the organization is structured. In all likelihood these categories defined themselves while you were building the wall (aim for four to six Green labels depending on how large your affinity is). These temporary Green labels help you designate certain space on the wall to work out the details of that theme. Now you can move all the Blue labels that go together under the Green, and start working on identifying the appropriate Pink labels, and then the ultimate Green labels.

When you are done reorganizing the room, assign a Green label to each pair of people you have to work on the wall. If you have experienced people, let one person work on each Green area. At this point you may be thinking that it would be easier to build the affinity online. See the box, **Build your affinity on the wall, not in a tool**, for an explanation of why you shouldn't build online.

Build your affinity on the wall, not in a tool

CDTools helps you to put the paper affinity online efficiently and quickly. And it also has an interface that lets you move the affinity notes and groupings around, edit the labels, and create new ones. So why not just build the affinity online?

Well we can, when we have wall-sized displays! Walls give the team a large space to spread out all the affinity notes, to quickly scan and regroup the labels, and to pair up to complete the affinity building quickly. A tool interface is optimized for one person and although one person could build an affinity one affinity note at a time it would take an awfully long time. More importantly the affinity would represent the perspective of only that one person. The value of having multiple people build the affinity at once is that simply by mixing up the people, the affinity notes, the pairs, and the general group discussion, the affinity comes to represent the thinking process of the whole team. Affinity building is a way of creating a shared understanding of the user data among the team and stakeholders without trying to do it. The simple process of building makes it happen.

It is true that we could imagine a team of 10 sitting around the room, each working on their separate computers putting in their set of affinity notes, seeing each other's groupings, and talking across the table. But come on! Let's just wait for the wall-sized display so we can move things naturally, communicate simply, and not get stuck in manipulating a tool while we are trying to think.

Each pair will do the following within their Green area:

1. Restructure the Blue labels to eliminate redundancies, make appropriate length Blue groupings, and write your final Blue labels. Move out groupings and Post-its® that don't belong to the themes in one area and place them within other Green areas to be worked on later.

2. Create coherent Pink groupings by grouping like Blue labels together. At the Pink level, as a rule of thumb, there should be two to six Blue labels per Pink label.

3. Group the Pink labels to create your final coherent Green labels and write the real Green labels. A Green label should have four to eight Pink labels. Too many Pink labels under a Green label make it hard to see the structure of the findings; but too many Green labels make the themes too granular. Five to six Green labels is a good number for a good affinity.

Remember the affinity is a communication device; the team will walk the wall and use it to stimulate design thinking. Too many labels in one section make scanning difficult and represent too many concepts to think about at once. And since the labels all are written on Post-it® notes you can keep changing them until they truly reflect the data and the voice of the customer.

Finally, watch out for ownership issues; no one owns wall sections. If you have helpers, move people around and mix up people into pairs to gain a shared perspective on the data. If you are building with a two-person team, start out working together and then split up. But trade areas of the wall so both of you eventually touch all areas of the wall.

Good Pink labels reveal key issues in the data

A good Pink-level label tells you what matters about the Blue columns underneath it. You should not have to read the Blue labels under the Pink label to figure out the key theme of that section; it should be clear in the Pink label.

Example: eChalk

The following label tells a strong story at a glance, letting the eChalk team know which one of the values they'll want their product to support. The team also did a good job of calling out all the ways that teachers use technology to encourage student creativity.

Pink: Technology gets my students excited and allows them to be creative

  Blue: I use technology to allow my students to be more creative

  Blue: My students are excited about technology

  Blue: I tell students to incorporate their own interests into technology projects

  Blue: I encourage students to use technology by playing games

  Blue: My students use technology to display their work

eChalk also needs to think about their business case, and how they can leverage and extend what the schools do to encourage teachers to use technology. The following Pink label draws attention to this issue, capturing all the current things schools are doing.

Pink: The school supports teachers learning about technology

  Blue: Teachers get monetary incentives

  Blue: The schools support my learning technology by giving me time

  Blue: The school supports my learning technology by sending me to outside classes

  Blue: I can use computers during free time

  Blue: The schools don't support my learning technology

Bad Pink labels don't provide enough information to understand the issue

Bad Pink labels hide the theme suggested by the Blue labels and do not represent the customer data well. The Pink labels help designers orient to the data—curing the wall walk (see Chapter 10) they draw you in or encourage you to skim a section. So, bad labels inadvertently encourage the team to skip the issues in that section.

Example 1: eChalk
Original Pink label: I need to do it, to know it

  Blue: The more I use technology, the more comfortable I am

Blue: I will use technology if you give me features that are useful

Blue: There's no point in training me if I can't apply it right away

Blue: I know as much "tech" as I need to be successful

The wording of this label isn't very clear. Once you read its Blue labels, this Pink label doesn't represent the customer story well.

Rewritten Pink label: I only learn the technology I need to get my job done

Blue: The more I use technology, the more comfortable I am

Blue: I will use technology if you give me features that are useful

Blue: There's no point in training me if I can't apply it right away

Blue: I know as much "tech" as I need to be successful

Example 2: eChalk

Original Pink label: I support technology use

Blue: My students have computers and access to the Internet—I take advantage of this

Blue: My students do not have computers and access to the Internet

Blue: I give students access to computers all day every day

Blue: Students' use of the Web will motivate the school and teachers to adopt technology

Blue: I want to know if technology is being used at home

Blue: I support technology in the school by providing students with e-mail

Blue: I am concerned about content on the Internet

The more general wording, "I support technology use" in the previous Pink label is perfectly acceptable. However, some of the Blue labels are really about when and how students have access, and might be broken into separate groups characterizing those distinctions. More importantly the Blue label, "I am concerned about content on the Internet" belongs in a very separate category and is buried under this label.

Good Green labels group Pink labels that tell a core story of the work

Green labels group together Pink labels and their notes to form a coherent piece of story that is important to the project focus. Unlike Blue and Pink labels, Green labels can be more categorical and abstract. The goal of the Green label is to chunk the wall—to give designers an overview of the key issues so that they can move from section to section easily without getting disoriented. Also, later the Green labels help chunk the information so you can find the information you are interested in quickly. CDTools can help you get your affinity online and into an HTML data browser. Then you can use the Green labels to easily revisit data you are interested in.

Example: eChalk

The "Resources & Funding" Green label below is perfectly appropriate because it indicates what that area of the wall is about even though it is not written in the first person like the second grouping. You'll also notice that there are only three Pink labels under this Green label.

This is the only Green label in eChalk's affinity that has so few labels under it, but the team wanted to call it out. That's appropriate for central issues that would otherwise be buried, but if several Green label sections are this small, you may want to think about whether you are breaking up the story too much.

Green: Resources & Funding

  Pink: There are too many restrictions to spending our money

  Pink: We must come up with creative ways to supplement the budget

  Pink: Getting supplies is slow and difficult

Green: My world is impacted by standards and controls

  Pink: Bureaucracy and red tape impede my success

  Pink: Approval is required so that control can be maintained

  Pink: There are standards for the classroom and school

  Pink: Our electronic ordering system is impacting how I work (the principal's work)

  Pink: Privacy and security issues are important and need to be understood

  Pink: I know what I need so let me do it

Bad Green labels don't represent the Pink labels beneath them

Bad Green labels act like a catchall for the Pink labels, sometimes when the team doesn't know where else to put them. But if the label doesn't match the content it suggests that content is missing when it is not or simply makes a confusing story to read.

  Example: eChalk

  Original Green label: Communication inside the school

    Pink: I need to reach school administration

    Pink: I need to reach students

    Pink: I communicate with other teachers and students

    Pink: The Administration/principal communicates with the whole school

    Pink: I need to reach parents

    Pink: I need to reach other teachers

    Pink: This is what I communicate about with other teachers

    Pink: We need to promote and show off the school

The wording of this label is fine if all the Pink labels below it are all about communication that occurs inside the school. Some of the Pink labels below this Green label are about communication outside the school (reaching parents), and one (promoting the school) is about community relationships. eChalk's affinity does have other Pink labels about communicating outside the school elsewhere in the affinity. Bringing them together under a Green label such as "Communication between the school and the outside" would highlight an important part of the work. Since eChalk wants to support this kind of communication, the issues around it should be surfaced.

Creating the final affinity—rolling in new data

Once you have put on all your labels and ensured that your columns are not too long your affinity is complete. If you built your affinity after you collected all your data you are ready to walk the wall (see Chapter 10).

But if you built a preliminary affinity you will now go out and collect more data. Look at your initial affinity and identify any holes in your data—where you'd like to flesh it out. Make sure you cover those topics in subsequent interviews. Or change some of your interviewees to ensure you get the data you need.

Once you finish all your interviews you will have new notes to add to the existing affinity structure. To roll in new data use the following procedure:

1. Print the new notes.

2. Quickly sort the notes by the existing Green labels they fit under. This should be a "gut level" exercise, something on which you spend only a few minutes. Notes that don't seem to fit under an existing Green label should go in an "Other" category.

3. Clean up the Green labels. Within each Green grouping, read each new note and stick it on the wall next to the Pink or Blue label it seems to fit with.

4. Start new columns for notes that don't fit with the existing labels because they address completely new issues.

5. Repeat until all notes are placed.

6. Go back to each label with new notes and rework the group.

7. Create new Blue and Pink labels to pull out new distinctions.

8. Organize any completely new sections of the affinity into Blue labels and Pink labels.

9. Create new Green labels, if necessary

Remember, you are pushing to create new distinctions—work to discover new implications and new meaning—work *against* just placing notes wherever they will fit (even if they do fit). And don't let your groups get too long—that is another indication that you are burying data.

Once you have finished your affinity you will need to protect it against damage. One way to do this is to put it online. See the box, **Putting your affinity online**, for suggestions on how best to store your affinity.

Putting your affinity online

To make sure you don't lose any affinity data (from Post-it® notes falling off the wall, getting moved, etc.), you should put the finished affinity online. Use CDTools to get your affinity online and publish it to an HTML browser (see Figure 8-2). Having the affinity online is especially critical for distributed teams. See Chapter 10 for an example of an affinity published to HTML.

Also, you can keep your affinity up in paper to share with other stakeholders and to use during design, but secure the physical affinity. Tape down the affinity notes and labels with removable tape strips. This also lets you easily transport the walls if you need to move them to a new location. If you have CDTools and Microsoft® Visio®, you can also use the Export to Microsoft Visio® feature to print out wall-sized diagrams that look like your original paper wall.

Assign a team member to own the affinity to keep track of it and make sure it is kept clean and intact. This is especially important if you have to move your affinity from room to room.

Figure 8-2:
CDTools screen for putting the affinity online to share with the team and others by publishing to HTML.

Using CDTools to Put the Affinity Online

Putting the affinity online in CDTools affinity Diagram Builder both stores it and places the data in an environment where it can be re-used and shared. Once online in CDTools, the Affinity can be published to an html data browser (see Chapter 9) that acts like an online data library, providing an interactive data repository for communication and reuse. The Affinity can also be printed in wall-sized diagrams by exporting it to Microsoft® Visio® (not included with CDTools).

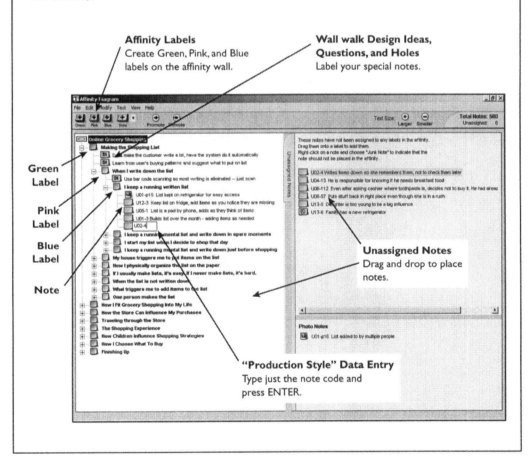

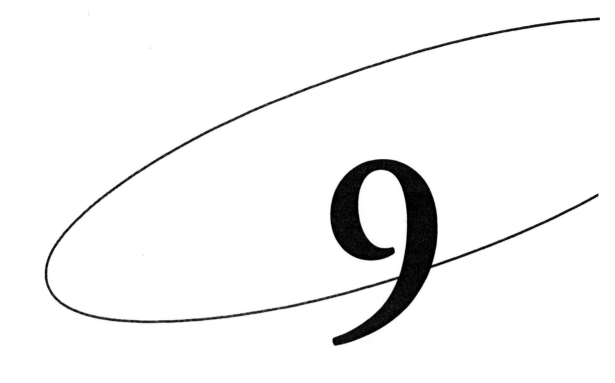

Using Contextual Data to Write Personas

Rapid CD Process	Lightning Fast	Lightning Fast +	Focused Rapid CD
Personas and Scenarios			✓

When your cross-functional team has worked together to gather, interpret, and consolidate customer data, you've developed a shared understanding of the users and their issues. You haven't just *built* the data—you've *experienced* it in a way that others haven't. So you may find the consolidated models and affinity to be evocative representations of the customer data you experienced, but others don't share that experience and can't assimilate these models as easily.

Most teams need to communicate their understanding of user needs and their design plans to stakeholders—management, customer organizations, product groups, and so forth. These stakeholders, with no background in CD and no experience with the data, don't embody the memories of the real users from the field interviews. When they walk the data they can see the issues, needs, and breakdowns, but the power of "knowing" the users and their issues personally is not as poignant or personal.

Personas can help bring users alive and focus the stakeholders on the relevant issues when they are built from rich contextual data. Popularized by Alan Cooper,[1] a persona describes typical users of the proposed system as though they were real people. Their use is becoming more widespread with mixed success. According to Harley Manning, "a persona that's not backed by rich contextual data isn't valid, which accounts for much of the mixed success." But when backed by rich contextual data they can help developers and designers not involved in the data collection focus on the needs and characteristics of their users.[2] Anyone—trained in CD or not—can read this vignette and if done well will gain a sense of the typical user they are trying to support.

Teams like LANDesk that use personas as part of their development process find that the stories and characters help the developers focus on the needs of the users. They talk about the characters like Dan Means (see the box, **Dan Means—IT administrator software distribution specialist**) and how they are supporting them and their problems. The persona helps to create the same kind of personal relationship and commitment to solve their problems as the design team gets by going to the field.

In this chapter we'll discuss how to write personas and user scenarios from consolidated data and give you pointers on how to make your personas as rich and expressive as possible.

Definition

A persona is a one-page textual description of a typical user. This typical user is an amalgam of elements drawn from several users who share common job roles, demographics, and user need characteristics. The persona is given a realistic username, a "head-shot" photo expressive of the nature of these users, and a textual description. The description covers who they are, a little of their background, and key goals. It summarizes their tasks and the primary roles they play (see the box, **Agilent: John Merriwether, analyst** for an example).

Key concepts

Persona. A description of a typical customer, a composite drawn from the actual data you collected.

User scenario. A description of a particular task performed by a persona, told in a story as though it were actual observed behavior.

Goal. High-level achievement a persona is working toward or strives to maintain.

Task. An identifiable piece of work for which the persona is responsible.

Role. The primary jobs that the persona plays, the hats they wear to get the job done, a collection of a set of responsibilities which taken together achieve an intent.

Personas

☐ Choose the personas to write

☐ Identify representative users for each persona

☐ Identify goals, roles, and tasks for each persona

☐ Write the persona

☐ Write a user scenario—an extended task description

☐ Check your personas

Dan Means—IT administrator software distribution specialist

Having the users download software themselves doesn't always work well," Dan Means explains as he selects the custom query he will use as the target for his software package. "No matter how simple the instructions are, we'll get calls if they have to click more than once."

Dan Means speaks from experience. As a network administrator at Indeco, Inc. for the past 7 years, he has handled his share of calls from confused end users. Dan is the go-to guy for software deployment for his 7,000-node company. He uses LDMS to update software OSs to the latest security levels and refresh the custom applications his customers use for mission-critical duties.

"You can't work in a vacuum. You have to let the users know what's going on." Typically, Dan sends an e-mail announcement to let customers know what changes to expect. Dan often pushes vital security patches out immediately, but he lets customers pull some less-critical application updates at a convenient time. "You don't want to make a sales guy download a 20MB file while he's trying to get a presentation ready in his hotel room," Dan points out.

"Sometimes you have to force it (upgrades or patches) with the department heads from a political standpoint. People don't like to change."

Even with vigorous lab testing and careful scripting, Dan concedes they get some phone calls with nearly every update, so Dan always lets the help desk know his plans so they are ready.

Dan has been using Windows since the 3.0 days and has current MSCE certifications tacked on the wall. He's used LANDesk for several years now, but he still doesn't know all the features available to him. "I don't have much time to explore much. Sometimes we're just fighting fires around here."

Dan checks the manufacturer requirements for all software updates, but he knows undocumented idiosyncrasies or requirements are a way of life. "No one tells you everything. The docs are usually written to the best-case scenario." Because of this, Dan phases his deployments to smaller groups of clients at a time, even at the main site where bandwidth isn't too much of a concern. "If you try to blast it out all at once, bad things *will* happen," says Dan authoritatively. "My last deployment? It was only to 50 nodes."

Dan checks each job to ensure it was successful. If it fails once, he assumes the computer was turned off or disconnected, but he never really knows for sure. Finding out why a machine didn't get updated or why the package doesn't work on a specific machine is a manual, time-consuming process.

Dan only builds packages once every couple of weeks, and bases them on an existing script that he then cuts and pastes. He says he'll often get the package about "80% finished" before he runs into some issue with a specific platform or configuration in the test lab. Then it's a matter of troubleshooting the dependencies to finish it.

Most of Dan's queries are already set up. He admits he isn't a database expert, so when he needs something special, he asks the team's SQL expert for help.

"These people are busy with other things so I don't want to break things," says Dan of his customer's computers. And, if things break, Dan's team will take the hit. "If something breaks my team will have to spend the time fixing it. And if we can't do it remotely we'll have to go out to their desk."

Dan's goals:

- Distribute software successfully the 1st time.
- Send updates without maxing out network pipe.
- Keep help call traffic from updates to a minimum.

LANDesk built this persona from their user data, affinity notes, and consolidated sequences. There is no real Dan, he is a composite character, representing the key issues that the team wanted to highlight to development. The key to a good persona is to base it on field data collected from multiple users; it's much richer and more complete than a description of any actual real user could be. It's the best of both worlds—the breadth and depth of field research with the immediacy of anecdotes about real users.

Choose the personas to write

The first step in building personas is to determine which of your real users the persona will represent. A Rapid CD project will have anywhere from six to 12 field interviews to draw upon, covering one to four job roles. Remember, a job role describes the work people do; multiple job titles may do the same job role. A persona represents the job role, not the job title.

To aid communication to management, business, and development you can create one persona for each job role. One of these personas may be primary—the most important user to consider for this version of this project. The rest will be secondary, supporting characters. Remember that personas are a focusing device—they help keep your attention on the most important issues for this release, and help you cut through the fog of distractions and competing priorities.

More personas are not better. Too many personas create their own distractions. In fact, if you can't come to agreement on a small set of personas, it may well be that your project lacks a clear focus. After you finish the following analysis look over your set of personas and make sure you have not sliced them too thin.

Create a persona for core roles. If you collected data from multiple job roles you know whether all the job roles you interviewed turned out to be core to the problem. If so, do personas based on each job role. If not, choose only the job roles core to the issues and problems you want to address.

Determine if there are more job roles than you identified originally. Your initial identification of job roles might not be the right way to cluster users to create personas. They may have been identified as a target group by marketing or by job title, but do they really characterize the way the work is distributed? Review the users for each of your job roles and see if they are similar enough that one persona can cover them. For example, in one project we gathered data from IT professionals and developers. But when we interviewed them we realized that there was a third character, the hybrid developer who engaged in both of these activities. So we created a third persona for that role as well.

Challenge market segmentation categories. Sometimes you will gather data based on demographics like age, location, or income range, particularly with consumer products. But do the users, often grouped by marketing into demographic segments, really care about the same issues? Are they approaching how they live their lives and make their choices in the same way? In a study of youth (about 18 to 25 years old) we found that 20-somethings are very different, depending on whether they are still in school or have entered the work force. So we needed to create more than one persona for this age class; effectively 20-somethings played more than one life role.

Pay attention to skill level and power differences. When you focus on a job role or task as the defining characteristic in your user selection you may find that people that do the same job have different skill levels, tolerance for technology, and power in their organizations. Even though the way they do the task may be the same, you will have to focus on different design considerations to deal with issues of acceptance. So for example, in the analytical lab, senior scientists run experiments following predefined procedures, just like lab techs. Doctors take blood from patients, just like nurses and lab techs. But they have different intents and different tolerance for and requirements for technology support. Define your personas for this combination of task, skill, and cultural differences.

Identify representative users for each persona

Once you know what personas you are going to write you need to map your users and their data to each persona. You know through the interpretation sessions which of these users had a rich story or was more representative of the overall consolidated data. At this point you can weed out the less interesting users so you have fewer to deal with. Keep the users where you saw a lot of ongoing work or got a lot of insights, or those that had interesting strategies or perspectives or were unique in some important way. Eliminate users whose interviews were short, sketchy, high-level, or that repeated data you got better elsewhere.

Now you know whose data you will focus on. Quickly review the profiles that you captured and their issues by scanning their affinity notes captured in CDTools or your word processing documents. Look at the consolidated sequences, if you have them, that characterize their key tasks to augment this data.

Now pick the base user to build up for the persona. This will be the person whose real story is closest to everyone's story and whose data is the richest. Often one user is particularly evocative and important to the team—the user they keep referring to during design conversations. If not, some users simply will have better data than others. Choose one user who is evocative and for whom you have good data. You'll use this interview to provide the primary structure for your persona, integrating data from other users as needed.

Persona writing is just like writing a short fiction story inspired by real life. Stick close enough to the base user's life story to provide the realistic setting and personal flavor but expand the activities to incorporate the strategies and issues of the other users. In this way your persona will be a "super" user, characterizing the issues of their part of the market. This guides the team to focus on market issue—not just the story of one user.

Identify goals, roles, and tasks for each persona

Now that you have identified your base user and have the background information you need it's time to harvest data to fill out the core descriptors of the persona's activities.

For each persona identify the following for each user behind this persona (see the Agilent example):

Goals. For each user related to the persona, ask: What is this user trying to accomplish? What do they care about? What makes them feel good at the end of the day? This includes goals related to your project focus, but also a wider set of goals that will characterize them and their life experience in general. For this exercise, focus on high-level goals related to each user's overall job, not the low-level intents you might find on sequence models. List three to five goals for each user.

Roles. When someone says, "I wear three hats in this position," they are talking about the roles they play. They are chunking their work into coherent groupings of responsibilities that can be thought about independently. What hats are your users wearing? How would they divide up their responsibilities? Give your role an evocative name that makes you think about the intent of the role—avoid job titles. If you have chosen to build a flow model you will easily find all the roles related to your persona. (See pages 89 and 163 in *Contextual Design: Defining Customer-Centered Systems*, to learn about flow models.) Identify and list the primary roles each user plays. Again, no more than five per user.

Key tasks. What are the most important tasks for this user? What sequences did you capture for these users? Often each role will be associated with one or more primary tasks. List the tasks for the user based on what you saw and heard in the interviews. If you collected sequences you should have a consolidated sequence model for each task in your focus.

Once you have finished finding the data for the base user and the other users that will be combined with the story of the base user, check that the data across the users is consistent enough to create a coherent persona. Look for substantial overlap in goals, roles, and tasks. If so your persona will hang together. If the lists are different, ask if the differences simply complement each other and can fit together in the story of this super user. Perhaps some users stand out as being different in interesting ways. If so, you might lift their stories for color.

Also look at the data for the other personas. Do the goals, roles, and tasks truly suggest a different persona? Each persona should represent significant differences relevant to your project focus. If you have data in one persona that doesn't seem to fit it might be better represented within another persona. Looking across the data within and between personas will ensure that your personas represent a set of discrete job roles, each of which create a coherent story of user needs and activities relevant to your project focus.

Example: Agilent, John Meriwether, analyst
You already know the story of the users whose data will form the persona. Looking through your interpretation session notes you can pull out relevant observations to remind you of their data and help you think about goals, roles, and tasks. See the box, **Agilent: John Merriwether, Analyst**, for the finished persona.

U2 profile
This is an R&D facility, at a large pharmaceutical company. They make the active ingredient for bulk quantity. U2 has been an analyst here for two years. Started as

part time student then went full time in the Q/C lab (1 year, 3 months). Has a degree in biology with a major in toxicology. Works in three shifts of eight hours each. Rotates the shift every seven days. Two to three analysts per shift. During the time we were there, there were three analysts. Referred to as analyst rather than chemist or technician.

U2 goals

- Keep samples running through analysis at speed. He has procedures and habits for running multiple tests at once, and depends on them. Minor shortcuts, such as keeping measurements in memory rather than writing them down immediately, are okay.

- Operate as a competent member of the lab. He is in control of his lab, his procedures, and his equipment.

- Manage multiple analyses in parallel. He's able to track them all at once.

U2 roles

- Analysis Runner—He runs predefined analysis processes on samples.

- Dishwasher—He spends a lot of time cleaning up after experiments, cleaning instruments, and disposing of samples.

- Scheduler—He has to track all the samples as they come in and juggle their priorities against work already in the queue and the characteristics of the tests themselves—for example, whether it requires a lot of his intervention.

- Recorder—Much of his time is filling out forms and adding to his lab notebook, recording the work he's already done.

U2 tasks from sequence models

- Run predefined analyses on sample material as it comes in.

- Identify problems with equipment and fix when within his competence.

- Keep lab notebook up to date.

- Report results of analysis.

U9 profile

U9 is one of 12 Lab Technicians, and usually is paired with one other tech on his shift. He had a biology degree when he started, then got a chemistry degree while working at Org. 5. Has been at Org. 5 for 10 years.

U9 goals

- Get sample analyses done as rapidly as possible.

- Never slows down—enough of the work is routine and repetitive that he can just zoom through it.

U9 roles

- Analysis Runner—Runs analyses on samples.

- Recorder—Reports on work done.

U9 tasks

- Run predefined analyses on sample material as it comes in.

- Keep lab notebook up to date.

Write the persona

Now that you have organized your data and know which user you will use as your base character you are ready to write each persona as a coherent story, pulling bits from all the different users in this group. Do the following:

Name the persona. Choose a realistic name—but not the actual name of any of your interviewees, of course. The sex of the user will be the sex of the base user driving the persona. Give the user a job/position title that may also be the same one as the base user. (A consumer product might choose a title like "Jane Green, single mother.")

Review the data. Reread the lists of goals, roles, and tasks; reread the user profiles you collected in the interpretation session. Skim the consolidated sequences for any key tasks in this grouping. Scan the affinity for issues relevant to this grouping and read those sections. Read the insights from these interviews and remind yourselves of any user quotes from these users. You're priming your brain to synthesize all this into a single story.

Start writing about the user. You should start with an introduction—either with a characteristic user quote in which the user introduces him/herself or as though you were introducing a third party. Summarize the user's job, including demographic information in your description. Describe a day in the life of the user, or how the user accomplishes key tasks in their day. Pull in elements and quotes from your other users as you go, building up a composite that integrates all these elements. Write a few paragraphs—remember, a persona is a focusing document, don't make it longer than a page.

List the persona's goals. Choose three to five goals from all the goals you identified for this grouping. Describe each goal briefly.

List and describe the persona's roles and tasks. Choose three to five roles and their primary tasks from all of the roles you identified for this grouping. Describe each role and show the persona performing its primary task.

Choose a photo to represent the persona. You want a picture that communicates what these people are like: a senior scientist should be middle-aged and serious; a starting system manager should be young and either geeky or punk. If the point of the scenario is that the person is worried and harassed by the job, don't choose a photo that looks serene and happy. (You may want to buy access to a photo art service. The free collections tend to show only happy faces.)

Remember that writing a persona is telling a story. You are describing this interesting person to people who don't know him or her. Make the person sound as interesting as possible. Use quotes and actual events from the interviews to make the description as concrete and illustrative as possible.

Use simple, direct, and informal language—if it doesn't sound right when you read it out loud, it's probably too formal. On the other hand, don't make up detail just to make the story better—you should have enough real detail from real interviews that you don't need to add anything you didn't see.

Aim for no more than a page, including the lists of goals and tasks and the photo. The persona is a focusing device—if you write too much, trying to include every aspect of every user, you'll make it too hard to understand the persona as a coherent person. Every decision you make about what to include or exclude from your persona will affect how the team thinks about the problem—so choose mindfully! Your persona should support the design direction for the project by highlighting the aspects of work practice that matter most for these users.

A good persona should take about an hour to write if you are familiar with the data.

Agilent: John Meriwether, Analyst

If John seems perfectly at home in his lab environment that's because he is. He's been working in the analytical lab at Acme Pharmaceuticals for five years and seems to be a part of the place. From start of shift to the end—and since he works a rotating schedule that may cover any part of the day or night—he's on the move, ensuring that samples are processed and tests are run with all deliberate speed.

Samples arrive and are dropped off at a designated location, but there's no official notification when they arrive so he checks by the coolers and shelves of the drop-off location regularly throughout the day. As the sample comes in, he notes their priority and special requirements and plans in his head how to schedule them into his day.

He rarely has fewer than four tests running at a time, using procedures that have been worked out ahead of time. Many of the procedures are standard and run several times a day, so he's got them memorized. Others are written down, and are kept by the apparatus as the analysis runs. For speed, he'll cut minor corners on the "Generally-accepted Lab Practice"—only pulling out the written procedures when he doesn't have them memorized, pouring amounts rather than measuring them when he knows having the exact amount isn't critical.

The lab has attempted to streamline the work with introduction of an in-lab computer. As he takes the test he writes down the results on his paper pad. When all is done he goes to the computer corner and enters the data from all the instruments used in the test. The company has a LIMS (Laboratory Information Management System) but with indifferent success. Most of the machines he uses aren't hooked in, so data transfer is manual. Since he also records results in his lab notebook to track his own activities and on the analysis report sheet, there's a lot of redundant data entry. Furthermore the methods definitions are all in paper or on the computer across the room so he's continually moving from instrument, to online system, to paper.

John's goals

Keep samples running quickly through analysis. John has procedures and habits for running multiple tests at once, and depends on them. Minor shortcuts, such as keeping measurements in memory rather than writing them down immediately, are okay.

Operate as a competent member of the lab. John knows his instruments, his procedures, and the tests that need to be accomplished to keep the business running smoothly.

Manage multiple analyses in parallel. John works on multiple tests in a day and on multiple tests at a time and knows how to track them all at once.

Never slow down. John's work is routine and repetitive so he can just zoom through it.

→

John's roles

Analysis Runner. John runs predefined analysis processes on samples following the agreed upon methodologies defined by the business.

Dishwasher. John spends a lot of time cleaning up after experiments, cleaning instruments, and disposing of samples.

Scheduler. John has to track all the samples as they come in and juggle their priorities against work already in the queue and the characteristics of the tests themselves—for example, whether it requires a lot of his intervention.

Recorder. Much of John's time is filling out forms and adding to his lab notebook, recording the work he's already done, and entering it into the computer system.

John's tasks

- Run predefined analyses on sample material as it comes in.

- Identify problems with equipment and fix when within his competence.

- Keep lab notebook up to date.

- Report results of analysis.

Write a user scenario—an extended task description

Personas can be extended with *user scenarios*—detailed descriptions of how this persona accomplishes a particular task. Some IT organizations want to characterize the current work practice (the as-is process) in high-level use cases, user scenarios can help. The scenario presents the information in a consolidated sequence as though it were the story of one user doing the task on a particular day. It's much easier to understand than the consolidated sequence itself.

Write the scenario in the same manner you wrote the persona itself. Collect the consolidated sequence models for each task to be characterized. You may want to revisit the actual sequences to get more detail and color to put into your story. Then write a user scenario walking your persona through the consolidated sequence. You want to tell the story of this person doing this task on a typical work day, using actual examples from your observed data. Where there are multiple triggers, choose the most common or most important. Where the consolidated sequence branches to show different strategies, choose one path; choose the most typical strategy or the one that will reveal the most opportunity for streamlining the process. If you need to show other strategies, you can tell the story of a second event where the user follows a different strategy.

As with the persona itself, you are using the actual data to inform and extend your description. Don't be afraid to include illustrative detail from several users when fleshing out the story.

Check your personas

The last step is to do a final cross check. Look from your persona back to the original users behind it. Are there user characteristics that you haven't been able to represent? Were there stories from the data or insights from the interpretation sessions that you haven't revealed?

Identify any of these missing elements and add them to the persona. Now you are ready to use your persona to communicate to your stakeholders and developers. This is a great addition to the visioning process covered in Chapter 11.

Endnotes

[1] A. Cooper. *The Inmates are Running the Asylum: Why High Tech Products Drive Us Crazy and How to Restore the Sanity*. Sams Publishing, 1997.

[2] H. Manning. *"The Power of Design Personas,"* IT View and Business View Report, Forrester Research, December 18, 2003.

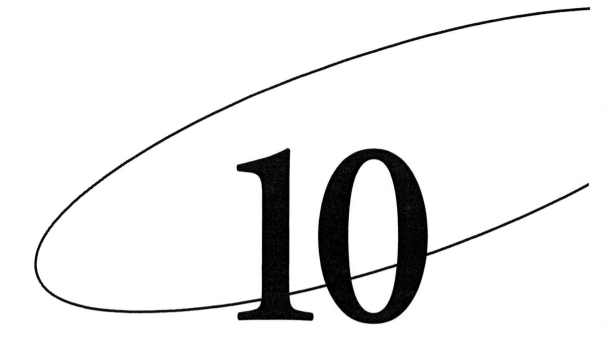

Walking the Affinity and Consolidated Sequences

Rapid CD Process	Lightning Fast	Lightning Fast +	Focused Rapid CD
Wall Walk and Visions	✓	✓	✓

After consolidating the data, you are ready to use it to drive design conversations. The team will create a vision and recommendations for their project based on their understanding of the data. Visioning will be covered in Chapter 11. To prepare for visioning, the team and any relevant stakeholders "walk" the data to start to articulate, share, and record the design directions they started to form during the affinity and consolidation processes. The "wall walk" occurs in your design room by walking the physical data that hangs on the wall.

This chapter leads you through the process of interacting with, or "walking," the affinity diagram and consolidated sequences to come to a shared understanding of the issues the data reveals relevant to your project. All Rapid CD projects will walk the data, but only Focused Rapid CD will have consolidated sequences.

Walking the affinity enables all the team members to immerse themselves in all the information that was collected about the users and to generate design ideas based on the data. The affinity shows you the scope of the users' problems and issues organized into a coherent story. If you create them, personas introduce stakeholders to the users (see Chapter 9). Generating design ideas in response to this coherent organization of information helps the team develop a coherent, systemic response to the data rather than individual feature fixes.

During a wall walk, individual team members, stakeholders, and interested people "walk the wall" thinking about the data and generating individual design ideas in response to the data. These design ideas are written down on Post-it® notes and attached to the affinity near the data that drive the design thinking. Similarly if people see "holes" in the data, places where more data is needed, these are also posted.

Walking the consolidated sequences is a similar process. Team members walk each consolidated model capturing design ideas and issues.

Note: "Walking the wall" may be your last step in Rapid CD. After you have collected and organized your data, walk it to drive your design thinking. Then proceed with your design process in the usual fashion for your organization knowing that you have put an understanding of the user in the center of your process. Or continue on to the visioning step in Chapter 11.

Definition

Walking the data is a process that enables each team member and stakeholder to interact with the data, become familiar with it, generate design ideas, or find holes in the data to drive additional data collection.

Key concepts

Data walk or wall walk. The process of the team walking the data or sequences displayed on the wall and becoming familiar with the issues, adding design ideas, and posting holes in the data. This may be done as a group or individually.

Design ideas (DI). Design concepts that are grounded in the data and developed as a result of surrounding yourself in the consolidated models. Design ideas may include product or system concepts, features, training, market messages, implementation possibilities, business rules, process reengineering suggestions, help and learning concepts, or any other relevant aspect to the system solution being developed.

Holes. Areas of the affinity or sequences that seem to have missing data or whole areas of user behavior that seem to be missing. Holes can be areas of data that people expected to show up in the data. Sometimes holes are the result of real missing data and sometimes they are the result of inaccurate expectations.

Questions (Q). Areas of the affinity that raise questions. Questions are similar to holes, but offer a way to raise concerns or issues that are not about missing data.

Process for walking the data

☐ Prepare for the wall walk

    ☐ Prepare the data and the room for the data walk

    ☐ Gather people to walk the data

☐ Walk the affinity

    ☐ Introduce visitors to your project

    ☐ Introduce the wall walk process

- ☐ Walk the affinity and monitor the process

- ☐ List key issues and hot ideas from the affinity

☐ Walk the consolidated sequences

- ☐ Introduce the sequence walk process

- ☐ Walk the sequences

- ☐ List key issues and hot ideas from the sequences

Prepare the data and the room for the data walk

Hang your data and personas up in your team room or a large conference room. If your team room isn't large enough to hang the affinity and sequences simultaneously, try to use a second room nearby for the consolidated work models, or even use the hallway. You'll need this extra space only during the data walk. You will need to prepare and organize your data for display.

- Organize your paper affinity to ensure that the columns are spaced out reasonably and your labels are legible. Or put your affinity diagram online in CD-Tools, export it to Microsoft Visio®, and then print wall-sized diagrams that look like your original wall. A printed affinity is particularly good for sharing with stakeholders.

- Format the consolidated sequences and print them. Be sure they are printed in a large enough font to be read while standing. Hang the consolidated models up around the room.

- Display relevant example artifacts either hanging on the affinity, on the sequences, or organized in folders on a table for people to examine.

- Hang examples of physical models if they are showing relevant information.

- If you have created personas (see Chapter 9), print them flipchart-size and hang them around the room also.

You will also need to have a couple of flipcharts and a computer with a projector or large screen so that you can capture issues after the data walk. Alternatively, you can just capture your issues on flipcharts and put them online later.

If you are visioning, plan your wall walk in the morning and start visioning in the same room in the afternoon. Or get the room for two half-days and do the wall walk the day before.

Gather people to walk the data

The project team should walk the data even if they collected and built it. Walking the wall is a process of stepping back and systematically thinking about the data for the purpose of design. The subsequent conversations help bring the team into a shared understanding.

Invite your stakeholders and other interested parties to become familiar with your data. If you have an extended team that will be producing the system or has a stake in the specifics of the requirements or the design, you want to invite them to walk the wall.

Also, anyone who will be involved in the visioning session needs to walk the data before they can participate. The goal of user-centered design is to ensure that design thinking is driven by user data; so anyone participating in the formal process of determining the product or system direction needs to be immersed in the data before offering design concepts. Our rule of thumb is that no one designs a system who has not been immersed in the data.

Walking the wall is a good way to communicate your findings to others and to gather their comments, design ideas, and worries about holes, or missing issues, in the data. Walking the wall is a formal way of "listening" to those on your extended team. When they share their design ideas by writing them down, knowing that you will read and consider them, you are by this very act valuing their input. So walking the wall is a good way to generate buy-in to your processes.

If you are walking the wall before a visioning session, hold a group session to walk the wall. Allow two to three hours for this process, depending on how much you want to talk afterward and how much you are introducing beforehand (see the box, **How long does wall walking take?**).

How long does wall walking take?

Walking the affinity should take one to 1.5 hours. If the team is walking the data with no visitors, plan on two hours to capture issues. But if you are inviting stakeholders add 15 to 30 minutes to introduce the project and your users. If you are going to capture issues and hot ideas, add another 20 to 30 minutes.

If you have consolidated sequences add another hour for walking and talking. So if you are planning a pre-visioning wall walk with stakeholders you can do it all in three to four hours.

But if you are just doing a bag lunch, do it all in an hour for the purpose of sharing the data—just introduce your project and then point everyone to a good part of the wall for them to start walking. They can come back later if they are interested.

And if the team is just walking the preliminary affinity to look for holes to be filled in the next interviews you can do this in 45 minutes or so.

If you are inviting people to walk the wall as part of an overall communication process, visitors can come in alone if you hang up instructions on how to walk the wall. Or you can organize a formal time, a bag lunch, or an internal marketing event for them to visit your data. You may have multiple groups of people walk the wall at different times if you are trying to generate buy-in from different parts of your organization. Or you may have data relevant to more than one project, so you may choose to invite them on separate occasions.

Since each wall walk will generate design ideas and holes, you may need to collect and remove some of them before each new wall walk. But leave some up as examples. Catalog removed ideas by the labels to which they were attached for later reference.

Prepare visitors to walk the wall

If you are walking the wall with visitors you need to orient them to your project before they start the wall walk. They are not aware of what you have done, who you talked to, or your customer-centered design process. So prior to the wall walk, give them a brief overview:

- Cover your project scope, its goals, and a description of the number and type of users interviewed.

- Explain where the data came from, describing the field interview.

- Prepare a little story of two or three users including who they are, what you observed, and what their world is like. This helps make the users real. Or, optionally, introduce your personas if you developed them.

- Explain how the affinity was built, introducing them to the structure of the wall by reading one section of labels (Green, to Pink, to Blue).

- Introduce the wall walking process (described later).

- Point visitors to sections of the wall in which they will be most interested if they are a related team and you are sharing your data with them.

Once you have everyone in the room, give them the supplies they will need to walk the data. Make sure everyone has a:

- Pad of yellow, 3x5 Post-it® notes

- Blue Sharpie® Fine Tip pen, for issues, questions, and design ideas

- Green Sharpie® Fine Tip pen for holes in the affinity data

Introduce the wall walk process

Introduce everyone to the process, even if someone comes late explain what to do before they start walking the wall (see the box, **Encourage systemic design**).

> ### Encourage systemic design
> The affinity diagram helps encourage systemic design. Most people look at user data and see some small problem and can design a small fix or define a needed function. But lots of small ideas don't add up to a system that coherently supports the whole of the work. Instead we want to encourage teams to generate design ideas that support more of the overall work intent, more of the overall process, and solve the larger problems or issues.
>
> Systemic thinking sees a person's interaction with the system, with others, and with their organization as part of a larger work practice system. Innovation and new product function that has high value comes from this systemic viewpoint.
>
> With the affinity, this systemic design is easy to encourage because within the context of the affinity it is easy for people to understand. If one yellow Post-it® note, one observation from one user, is the source of a design idea it is considered a "one off": a small quick fix to some existing problem or issue. But if a design idea addresses a Blue label, and so a collection of issues, it is a more systemic idea. A design idea that addresses a Pink label is more systemic still, and a design idea that addresses a Green label is even more likely to solve the large issues revealed in the data.
>
> Introduce walking the wall with this challenge—generate design ideas at the level of the Blue, Pink, and Green labels. This creates a game for the walkers—they are prone to try to generate ideas that will address larger issues. The wall walking process makes systemic design thinking concrete and physical; it is therefore instrumental in generating new concepts and solutions.

Explain the following as part of your introduction:

- Wall walking is a preparation step for the visioning process or for more informal discussions about product ideas and features. Wall walking takes one to two hours.

- Walking the wall is like going to the art museum. It is a silent, personal process, where you move from one section of the wall to the next, reading the wall, thinking about it, and generating design ideas. Later, you will have time to discuss what you are thinking.

- Read the wall from top to bottom, using the labels to stimulate design thinking. Read the individual notes only when necessary to help understand the meaning of the label when needed.

- While you are reading ask yourself, "If this is what's going on what could we do?" Design ideas are the answer to these questions. If you get a design idea, write it on a yellow Post-it®.

  The purpose of a wall walk is to let the data drive your design thinking; filter out design ideas you may have had already that do not make sense given the data and generate new ideas because you are encountering the real user issues (see the box, **What qualifies as a design idea?**).

- You may see holes in the data, places where more data appears to be needed; areas you expected to find data and did not. If you see a hole, write it on a yellow Post-it® note and place it wherever there is something missing in the data. Later the team will look at the holes and decide if they need to collect additional data to fill them.

What qualifies as a design idea?

A design idea is any possible response to the customer data. It can be about technology, a feature or piece of functionality, a marketing idea, a documentation or help system need, a business process or strategy, pricing—any idea that comes to mind that is driven by the customer data in the affinity can be a design idea. Design ideas can be highly specific (add the existing search function to every screen) or very general (make it easier to search). Here are some of the design ideas the eChalk team posted on their affinity.

Green label: How I communicate

DI: Marketing message: eChalk is not technology for the sake of technology—it is technology for the sake of learning, enhancing communication, and fostering collaboration

DI: Student profile/progress report that teachers, students, and parents can access

DI: Have users select at initial login which listservs, discussions they want to subscribe to and then automatically sign them up

Pink label: I'm throwing information out there for general knowledge

DI: Create distinctions between messages that appear in mailbox: general announcement, individual students

Blue label: I use the public address (PA) system to communicate daily/important announcements

DI: Get principal to use PA to drive users to eChalk, i.e., "for more details about today's pep rally, check out your school homepage"

Make sure everyone is aware of the ground rules for walking the wall:

1. Read from the top down: the Green label, then a Pink label, and the Blue labels under it, and then go on to the next Pink label until you are finished with the whole Green area.

2. Respond with design ideas. Try to come up with ideas for your design that address whole areas of the wall: entire groups of Blues, Pinks, or Greens.

3. Write your idea in blue marker on a Post-it® note. Put your initials on the note in case your handwriting is difficult to read.

4. Stick the design idea to the part of the wall it responds to. Don't cover the label.

5. Look for holes in the data. Write holes in green marker on a note and stick it to the wall near the data you think is incomplete.

6. Go around the room at least once reading silently until you get back to where you started. If you make noise the moderator will ask you to be quiet or step outside to talk.

7. If you have time, walk the affinity again, reading everyone else's design ideas and holes during a second pass through the affinity to see if it stimulates any new design thinking. Don't worry if others have the same ideas as you.

8. Remember, we aren't committing to any design implementation. You are walking the data to understand it and to see what it means for the design. In our design discussions we will decide what we will actually do. So don't worry about silly ideas or things you don't agree with.

Walk the affinity and monitor the process

For the team, read the wall in parallel, but silently. Start at different places. If you built part of the wall, don't start there. Figure 10-1 shows an affinity section after a wall walk.

Review the labels from top to bottom, asking these questions:

- What does this part of the wall tell me about what to design?

- What more do I need to know? Are there holes in the data?

Write your design ideas and holes, ignoring those of others. You may find that your ideas start building on each other as you go around. Or you may find that your ideas are quite divergent, responding to each section of the wall with something new (see the box, **What do we do with all the design ideas**). On your second pass, read others' ideas and see if they help you generate new ideas.

What do we do with all the design ideas?
The ultimate purpose of the wall walk and posting design ideas is to have each person actively engage the data. At this point you are still uncommitted to the design ideas. As in the interpretation sessions, just because you think of it doesn't mean you need to build it. The design ideas are not a to-do list. The ideas that the team believes in—those that work for the user and for your company or client— naturally surface when you vision. For that reason, cataloging the design ideas is not necessary. But, some teams like to do that for a feeling of completion or tracking. That's fine too.

See the box, **What do we do with the holes and questions?**, for more about what you will do with the holes and questions you generate during the wall and sequence walks.

What do we do with the holes and questions?

Identifying potential holes in the data or questions to ask users is very valuable if you are building an interim affinity. Before your next interviews, go through the holes and questions so you can be looking for data on them in your interviews.

If this is your final affinity, focus on the design ideas now, not the holes. But if you do find a really important hole, flag it. You may need to do a few interviews to fill it. If you do another round of interviews later, go back and look at the holes.

Finally, identifying holes is an opportunity for your stakeholders to tell you where their worries are. If they walk the wall before visioning, you want to review the holes to see both what you are missing, and what you need to handle to maintain buy-in.

Team members may note groups that are duplicated or misplaced in the affinity, don't fix them during the wall walk. Just mark them for cleanup later.

During the wall walk, one team member acts as a monitor . While walking the wall, the monitor is tasked with keeping the group on task and quiet (see the box, **Handling people: web thinkers and bouncers produce good designs together**).

Handling people: web thinkers and bouncers produce good designs together

Different people handle wall walking in different ways—not because of their personality but because of the way they think. If you know about these different cognitive styles you can manage their reactions and the walking the wall process better.

Web thinkers

Web thinkers read the affinity labels and start creating design ideas. As they move through the affinity their design thinking gets bigger and more systemic. Why? Web thinkers weave everything together. As they read each label they start to create a picture of the user's problems and they start weaving a solution. Each part of the wall stimulates them to connect more and more into their story and their design solutions. Web thinkers are good at developing whole system solutions, but their solutions will follow the thread of thought that they are developing. Web thinkers are synthetic, but they are not naturally divergent thinkers. Web thinkers are weaving their web, so they don't like to be interrupted because it will cause them to lose their train of thought.

Bouncers

Bouncers respond with design ideas to whatever they happen to be reading at the moment. They are good at generating lots of design ideas in response to user data. But bouncers don't hook up the ideas; it's like their minds bounce off the wall. So bouncers introduce diversity. Bouncers also like to talk about their ideas because they get excited. So, bouncers like to share what they are thinking when they are thinking it. They will naturally disrupt web thinkers who want it quiet. So encourage bouncers to write their ideas down or talk with another bouncer outside the room.

Good system design needs web thinkers and bouncers

We don't get to pick what kind of mind we have, so there is no value judgment in being a web thinker or a bouncer. Besides, good design needs both. Web thinkers weave things together into a coherent system, but weave only along one track. Bouncers have divergent ideas but they don't hang together. But if bouncers put their design ideas up on the affinity they introduce divergent thinking. If web thinkers walk the wall a second time reading the bouncer's ideas they will naturally open up their own thinking to incorporate these new ideas. So, good design needs both synthetic and divergent thought. The affinity wall walk encourages the team to engage in both.

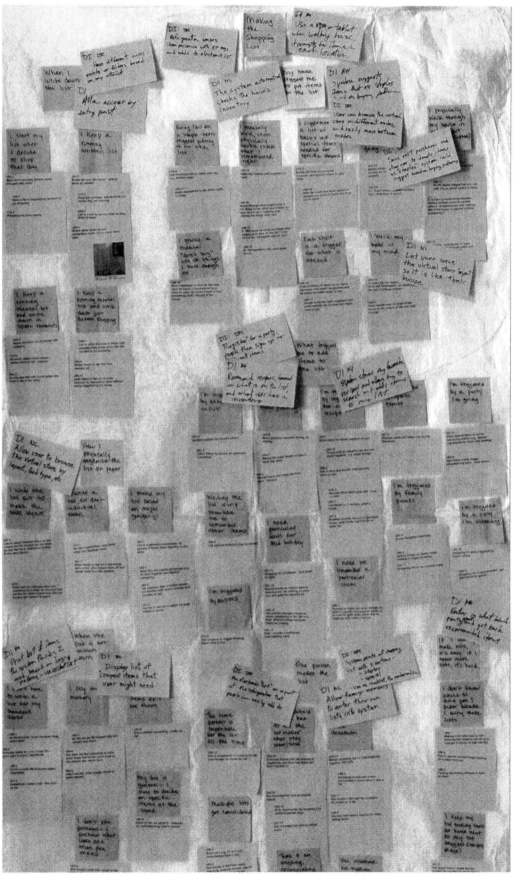

Figure 10-1:
An affinity diagram decorated with design ideas (large, handwritten notes).

List key issues and hot ideas from the affinity

Right after walking the affinity, gather the group together to create two lists. Creating lists is a formal way for the group to start sharing their experience of the data and their initial design thinking. It is also a preparation step for visioning.

List key issues

First, list the key issues: the most central aspects of the work practice and the key user issues that the system must address. These are not design ideas; these are the top user needs as the group has experienced them by walking the wall. Write the issues on a flipchart for all to see, or capture them online, projected on the wall.

The issues list is an implicit prioritization. It helps the team focus on the key user issues present in the affinity. These key issues will direct and focus the team's design thinking. Writing an issues list is not meant to be a formal prioritization process. We find that people will "freeze" if we tell them they are prioritizing. They often worry that they have committed to something irrevocable. But the simple act of walking the wall will create a natural emphasis of one set of user needs over others—whole sections of the wall will jump forward for attention given the project focus. This natural prioritization is what we are trying to capture to help focus the team's subsequent work.

Example: eChalk

Here is a sampling of eChalk's affinity issues:

- Attendance taking and reporting is a major deal.

- Get real (and eChalk has dependencies):

  - Some bureaucracy may be out of our control.

  - Availability of Internet is not guaranteed.

- The technology proficiency level of users is not high, so we need to keep it simple. But, also need to support more experienced users.

- Different schools have different needs; we need to have modules.

- Students are the center of the teacher's world.

- The technology teachers are early adopters of new technology and will try their best to get other teachers to accept new technology.

Example affinity issues: Apropos

- We need consistent terminology and semantics for problem/interaction handoff no matter what the medium.

- The interface we show when an agent takes a problem must be consistent.

- Managing screen real estate is a problem—especially when some belong to the CRM software.

- We can't make assumptions about what media the user will reply with—it won't necessarily match how the problem came in.

- We need to integrate the address list with the speed dial tool.

→

- The user cannot currently get to the AutoSuggest list while on a call.

- The QA tool currently works only on e-mail—what about all the other ways Agents give answers?

- We can't transfer problems outside the company.

Example affinity issues: Purchasing
- Purchasing depends on existing, known relationships. It's easier to work with people you've worked with before.

- People maintain a pool of connections—people they have had dealings with and trust. New deals will tend to be made with these people.

- Purchasing happens within the context of a known community. Purchasers know who is a player in the overall community.

- Evaluating a product is best done by touching the product itself. When that isn't possible, people do all kinds of other things, like visits to the manufacturer, to get close to the product.

- Purchasers have a different motivation than the users of the purchased item. Purchasers evaluate themselves by how much they got the supplier to reduce their prices.

- Making the deal is its own activity with its own lifecycle, with shared documents, discussions, and outcome.

List hot ideas

Second, list your hot ideas. After walking the affinity, the team should be bursting with ideas about what they could do in the design. Now is the time to start a hot ideas list. You'll need the hot ideas for your visioning session (see Chapter 11), so you can create a list and add to it after walking each model.

A hot idea is a big design idea, one that you can imagine driving a story of the customer's new work practice. Hot ideas are not small design ideas that might address a small user problem. They are starting points for generating a coherent, systemic response to the data given the project focus. For example, an idea like "Online glossary of technical terms" is not a big design idea that would drive a big story. "Online classroom" is a larger idea that you could imagine telling a story about.

Hot ideas are design ideas that can capture the imagination of team members, a slogan that the team wants to commit to, or a metaphor for what the work could be like.

Example: eChalk

Here are a just a few of eChalk's hot ideas after walking their affinity:

- Virtual support person that supports people as they move through the application

- Multiple interfaces that are driven by the user's level of expertise

- Customizable desktop that the user can create

- Online classroom—everything to do with the class is online

Here are some hot ideas from other projects. These are good starting points relevant to each project focus and the corporate goals of the companies producing the products. A hot idea will stimulate wide-scoped solutions to real customer problems but still reflect the corporate mission of the team.

Example hot ideas: Agilent
- The lab should be like Federal Express tracking packages—you always know the state of every experiment.
- Integrate all data from every instrument and automatically produce a report.

Example hot ideas: Apropos
- Show all data for a call customer in one overview interface with the ability to manipulate the data and get detail.
- Create a comprehensive time-tracking system to record minutes spent on each call and type of problems.
- Provide all caller information automatically with an easy way to capture notes online during the call.

Example hot ideas: Purchasing (generated when using the Web in business was fairly new)
- Online support community for communicating credibility, similar to eBay's trust markers.
- Create a "negotiation environment" where the dealmakers from supplier and purchaser can share information and track the state of the deal.
- Give suppliers a way to have a "virtual presence"—virtual visits to the factory, process audits, history of past products, etc.

Each of these ideas is a seed, a starting point for the team to elaborate into a whole approach to a design problem. Some hot ideas are bigger and some are smaller. As the team lists hot ideas they tend to start to generate smaller related design ideas. Remind the team that they can build up the ideas later.

Now you just want to capture good starting points. Write the hot ideas on a flipchart for all to see or capture them online, projected on the wall.

At the end of the wall walk you may want to consider communicating out to your stakeholders and other interested parties who were not a part of this process. Putting your affinity online now and using it as a communication device will make it easier to bring other people into your data (see the box, **Communicating with slide shows—the language of managers and corporations**).

Communicating with slide shows—the language of managers and corporations
You can easily turn the affinity into a slide show presentation. Managers like slide shows and many organizations communicate to each other and even document their product ideas mainly with slide shows. Let your affinity help you create good slide shows to share your data.

If your team has walked the affinity, use the issues list to define the key issues you want to present. Organize the slide show to tell the story of your users.

Start with who you interviewed and their demographics, share any personas you created, then section your slide show by Green labels telling the story of the data within each section. Pink labels are your slide titles and Blue labels your bullets. Use quotes and examples from the data to illustrate your points.

End your slide show with your design challenges and some of your hot ideas. Or if you have done visioning, create slides sharing your vision.

Introduce the sequence walk process

If you have consolidated sequences you walk the sequences after you walk the affinity diagram. The purpose of walking the sequence models is to develop a shared understanding of the work process users currently are performing, as well as to look for ways to improve their processes. It is similar to the affinity walk but it is done in small groups to allow for more discussion of how to redesign the tasks the users perform.

Prior to starting the model walk you should:

1. Introduce the consolidated sequences pointing out where they are on the wall. Give guests a brief overview of where the data came from and how the sequences were built, and introduce them to the model walking process.

2. Hand out copies of the design questions discussed below.

3. Pair people up, if you have multiple sequences, so they can start examining them in parallel. Try to pair guests with people who know the data. If not, team members will have to rotate to explain things.

4. Point to the related artifacts for the small groups to examine in support of the tasks.

5. Make sure everyone has Post-it® notes to write design ideas and holes on.

Prior to the sequence walk you should design questions to remind the group about your project focus and design issues while they are walking each sequence. In addition to using design questions during the sequence walk, have them team do the following:

- Read each sequence one activity at a time to understand the flow of the work of that task.

- Pay attention to triggers; thinking about how the system might support or replace this trigger. Ignoring triggers when automating the work may break the process.

- Look for problems or breakdowns in the work you can ameliorate in your design.

- Think about how to support all the strategies so that the design allows flexibility.

- Look for underlying intents that you can support more directly or by eliminating steps; generate new steps or ways to achieve the intent that would increase productivity or user value.

- Look for process changes that are not technical. If your system is for internal use you can change roles, process, policies, and other organizational elements that can improve the work independent of or in conjunction with technology.

- Identify ways to eliminate redundant work or automate steps; think about business rules that might help improve the process.

- Identify what parts of the sequence the current product or product set already supports so the team can get real about what they need to do.

Walk the sequence models

When everyone is ready, each pair should walk each of the consolidated sequence models. The sequence walk will take about an hour depending on how many sequences you have. If you have only two sequences the sequence walk should take about 30 minutes total.

Read the sequences discussing the issues as you go:

1. Read the trigger and overall intent.

2. Read each activity.

3. Read the steps within each activity and their intents.

4. Generate design ideas to address the issues and to redesign the task, activities, and steps.

5. Write any design ideas in blue marker on a Post-it® note and attach it to near the steps they address.

6. Identify any holes in the data and write it on a note in green marker. Attach it to the sequence.

7. Scan and examine the relevant artifacts and use them to generate design ideas to improve how they are used within the tasks.

The sequence walk is not a silent experience like the affinity walk. Groups of two and three people can discuss with one another what they are seeing. If you have a lot of sequences, just be sure that someone covers each one. Then they can share their observations during the discussion of issues and hot ideas. Expect that people will want to look at the sequences in more detail on their own after the meeting. Come back together to share issues immediately after the sequence walk.

List key issues and hot ideas from the sequences

After walking the sequence models, gather the group together again to generate additional issues and hot ideas. List these on flipchart paper or online as we did for the affinity process.

Don't worry if the hot ideas seem lower level—sequences tend to focus people on lower level detailed streamlining of the work practice. The affinity diagram generates wider solutions.

Example: eChalk

Here are some of the issues the eChalk team identified from their sequences:

• There are multiple strategies for creating homework assignments and reminding students about homework assignments.

• Teachers have routines they fall into—support all of them.

• Teachers lack a basic understanding of technology and this is a problem.

• Different levels of support are needed for different levels of expertise.

eChalk generated some additional hot ideas after they walked their sequences:

- Link to state standards
- Web templates for lesson plans, news, surveys, lesson plans
- Attendance monitor

Sharing and re-using your data

You have now finished walking your data, gathering issues, and hot ideas. This is a good point in the process to put your data online and share it with stakeholders and other groups conducting similar research in your organization (see the box, **Making customer data a corporate asset—share it across the company**).

Figure 10-2 shows the the CDTools Publish Window where you name and build the browser. Figure 10-3 shows what the affinity looks like after you have exported it to a data browser from CDTools.

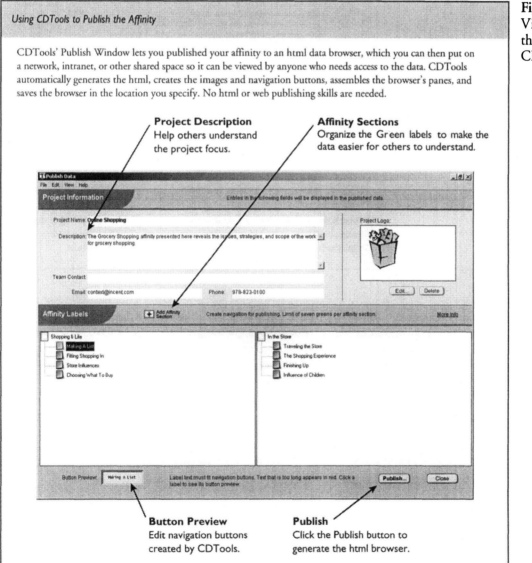

Figure 10-2:
View of building the data browser in CDTools.

Figure 10-3:
The shopping affinity online, published to HTML using CDTools.

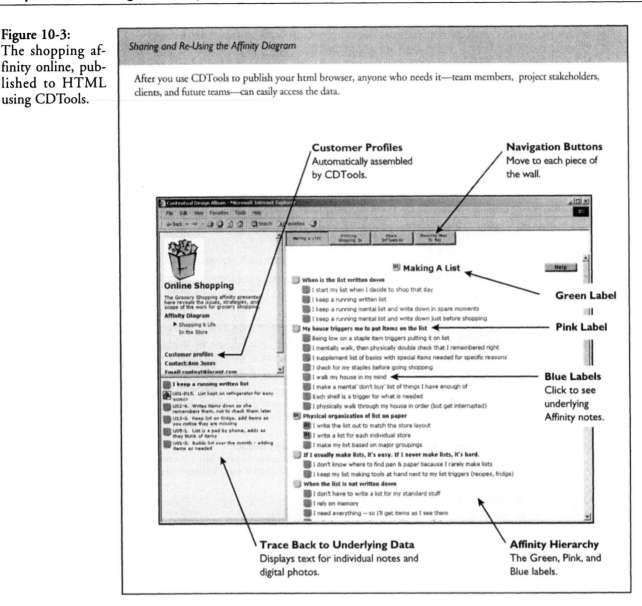

Sharing and Re-Using the Affinity Diagram

After you use CDTools to publish your html browser, anyone who needs it—team members, project stakeholders, clients, and future teams—can easily access the data.

Making customer data a corporate asset—share it across the company

Once your affinity is finished, we recommend putting it online. If you have CDTools, you can easily put the affinity online, and publish it to a data browser outside CDTools so anyone can access the information. If you don't have CDTools, then at a minimum you can enter it into a word processing program, using either styles or outlining to reflect the affinity's hierarchy.

The value to the team, the project's stakeholders, and your organization of having the data online is difficult to overstate. Distributed teams can do *virtual wall walks* if they can't travel to the team room. Stakeholders, including developers and others who may have the requirements or design handed off to them, can access the source of the design thinking directly. More importantly, you now have *reusable data*; teams can reuse each other's data. What you discovered in this project can inform other projects in the organization—if not now, then in the future.

Data does not get stale—at least not for approximately five years. In our experience, that's how long customer data can be used with confidence. The technology may change, but the structure of the underlying work practice and intents do not. Once your data is online, share it, extend it with more interviews to keep it fresh, and let new projects start from an existing base of knowledge.

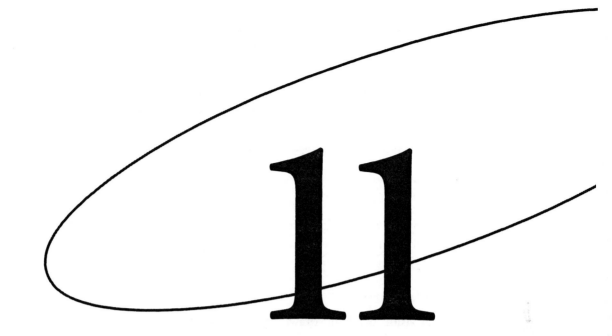

Visioning a New Way to Work

Rapid CD Process	Lightning Fast	Lightning Fast +	Focused Rapid CD
Wall Walk and Visions	✓	✓	✓

After you create an affinity, consolidate the work models, and analyze them for the issues and design implications, you are ready to create the vision of how your new or redesigned system will better support your users' work or lives. Remember, tools or systems are meant to support real life activities. The elements of these activities are represented within your affinity, your sequences, and your personas. A good system fits well within, extends, and supports the activities of life. So don't start your redesign by brainstorming function—start your redesign by telling the story of what the new life will be like if you introduce new technology. This is the essence of visioning.

We recommend visioning for any Rapid CD process. Visioning can be done in one to two days and will help you conceptualize a bigger picture of what your product can do far more than simply brainstorming function or starting to sketch UI ideas. Visioning encourages you to think more systemically about your redesign—it focuses you on fitting technology into the overall intents and flow of the work process your system is situated within. This ensures that your products and systems will consider all the relevant elements of work and not break the existing work practice.

Visioning is both a "grounded brainstorm" and a storytelling session. It is grounded because the team walks the wall and collects data before they start imagining future function. It is a brainstorm because within the needs of the customer data the team members are free to present any idea without evaluation. It is storytelling because it is a process wherein the team weaves a story of how their users (which they may have characterized by personas) address the issues uncovered in the affinity to accomplish the tasks described in the consolidated sequences.

Visioning is a method to lead groups in future scenario building, grounded in user data. Like the artist who first sketches the whole drawing structure on a canvas before filling in the detail, the team sketches the new work practice on the flipchart without getting bogged down in the details of the user interface or implementation. Storyboarding (see Chapter 12) is where you work out those details.

The philosophy behind visioning is described in Chapter 13, "Design from Data," pg. 273, in *Contextual Design: Defining Customer-Centered Systems*.

Anyone who participates in the vision must walk the affinity and consolidated sequences before they can vision. In this chapter, we outline the process for leading a team through a visioning session.

Definition

A vision is a hand-drawn, graphical representation. It is a high-level story of the customers' new practice. The vision describes what is in the new environment and how it works as told from the user's point of view. It includes possible changes in technology, user interface function, underlying business rules, role definition, and process. It can also include help, training, and overall support and services.

Key concepts

Pluses and minuses. After each vision the team evaluates both the positive and negative aspects of each of the visions generated.

Consolidated vision. The team generates multiple visions that are all evaluated. After considering what to keep and what to change the team creates one consolidated vision, which operates as the overall guide to detailed design.

The Pen. The person who draws while the rest of the visioning team tells the vision story.

The Poker. The person who reminds the team of issues they have not yet covered in the vision during the visioning process and helps ensure that the story is complete.

Process for visioning

☐ Preparation

    ☐ Prepare for visioning

    ☐ Invite people to vision

☐ Run the visioning session

    ☐ Review how to vision

    ☐ Review issues and hot ideas

    ☐ Define parameters for the vision

    ☐ Select a hot idea for first version

☐ Run the visioning session

☐ Evaluate the visions

☐ Create one consolidated vision

Prepare for visioning

Plan to do your first vision right after you walk the data. You can walk the data the afternoon before and vision the next morning or do both activities in one day. Remember that anyone who did not walk the data needs to do so before the visioning starts.

Try to hold your visioning session in the room where the affinity and sequences are displayed so that you can refer back to the data if you need to. Hang up or display the issues you generated and have the hot ideas available. The entire team should rewalk the data, rereading the design ideas if a considerable length of time has passed since the data walk.

In addition to the data you hang up on the walls you will also need to have at least one flipchart stand and pad of paper in the room. You will also need:

- Yellow 3x5 Post-it® notes, a half-pack for each person, used after visioning to put up design ideas during the evaluation

- Blue Sharpie® Fine Tip pens for everyone

- Tape to hang flipchart paper on the walls and to tape pluses and minuses to the visions

- 8½x11 or larger paper for capturing pluses and minuses

Note: Good visioning sessions need energy, especially mental energy, from all the participants. Try to avoid scheduling the session at the end of the day or other times when people aren't fresh.

Invite people to vision

The people at the visioning sessions will be the ones who generate the high-level design for your products. As such they should represent the core team, any stakeholders who wish to contribute, and anyone else who has knowledge that you need. Remember, we do not recommend that anyone participate in the visioning session without walking the data.

Visioning sessions work best when you have enough people to stimulate ideas and get multiple perspectives. Your goal is to get the people in the room who have the design skill and the technical, market, process, and business knowledge that taken together will inform the new design (see the box, **A vision is only as good as the team's combined skill**).

But, too many people in the session can make it difficult to manage: everyone will be talking at once, quiet people will have a hard time contributing, and the story may become less coherent. Plan to have no more than 10 people at the visioning session; an optimal size is between four and eight people. If you have more than eight people, run parallel sessions with each group visioning a different hot idea.

211

A vision is only as good as the team's combined skill

Customer data is the context that stimulates the direction of invention. But there is no invention without understanding the materials of invention: technology, design, and work practice. The visioning team needs to include people who understand the possibilities and constraints of the technology. If the team is supposed to design web pages and none of them has ever designed a web page, they will not be able to use web technology to design. When the people who always designed mainframes were told to design WYSIWYG interfaces, they replicated the mainframe interface in the WYSIWYG interface. Similarly, if the team has no interaction designers or work practice designers on it, the resulting vision will not be as powerful as if they did. This is why we recommend that design teams include people with diverse backgrounds representing all the materials of design and the different functions of the organization. Only then will an innovative design, right for the business to ship, emerge.

Review how to vision

The visioning process has three major steps. First, create three to four individual visions on flipchart pages. Each will take about 30 minutes. Second, evaluate each vision and identify what works and doesn't work about each one. These steps are continued until the team feels they have covered the key issues identified. Finally, take the good parts of each vision, overcome the bad parts, and create the final consolidated vision that will guide the team's work. Depending on the scope of the work visioning can be completed in one to two days.

Like all Contextual Design meetings, the visioning session has a process, roles, and ground rules that you'll need to review with the team before starting.

Introduce the visioning process

Explain how to vision. Tell the team that a vision is a group storytelling process in which every one participates, much like the chain ghost stories they told as kids. One person starts the story and others chime in adding to the story as it unfolds. This is the story of the users we interviewed performing the tasks we saw with the new technology and processes we are going to invent.

Everyone's ideas are welcome as long as they are developing the story from the point of the hot idea being developed or the task being explored. A vision includes manual processes and technical aspects. It has UI concepts and human interactions. It has automatic function and simple walking, reading, and talking. It is the story of the entire work practice or life activity that will be affected by the introduction of the technology.

Explain the perspective of the story. The vision is told as a story from the perspective of the user, not from the system or the product. Encourage this by starting the vision by asking "Who am I?" and "What am I doing?"

Describe the level of detail. The vision is high-level in that it doesn't work out the details. However, high-level does not mean "vague." The vision works out a specific set of user stories based on the tasks in the sequence models but it does not work out detailed UIs or underlying technology implementation. The vision focuses on what the user sees and does and what the system monitors and automates at the level of function, not at the level of detailed design.

Explain that visioning is iterative. You will do several visions, each taking about 20 to 30 minutes to complete. After doing three to four you will evaluate them, identifying the good parts and those parts that don't work. Evaluation comes after visioning, not during it.

Tip: The story of the vision feels like making a movie. Just like a movie there are characters that have thoughts and actions. Show them in the vision. Remember, it does not have to be a linear story; there can be flashbacks and flash forwards.

Figure 11-1 shows the whole process. Notice that the simple UIs are showing the function that will be available under different conditions and not explicit low-level UI design. Different function is associated with different characters within the process. Automatic function and what has to be managed under the hood is denoted in the cans.

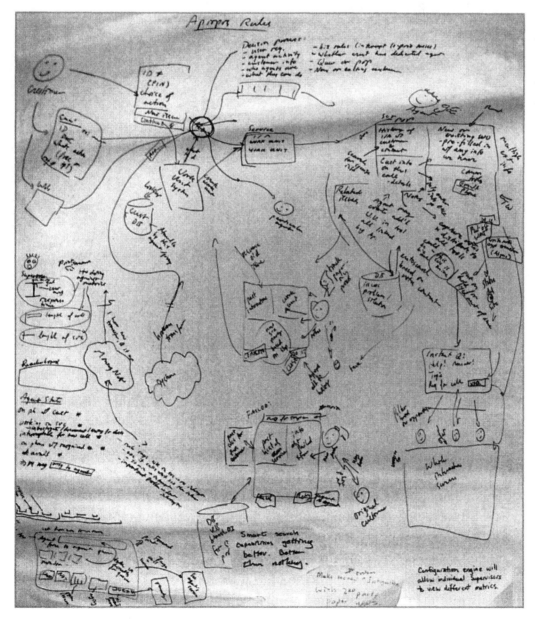

Figure 11-1: Apropos' call center rules vision shows the way the process works and the UI functions.

Figure 11-2 illustrates that there are user–interface–like areas but they do not imply layout—only coherent collection of function. Also that they show the process of use within the workgroup and what happens under happy and upset conditions.

Figure 11-2: Apropos' web vision is an example of how to represent functions needed without worrying about the UI.

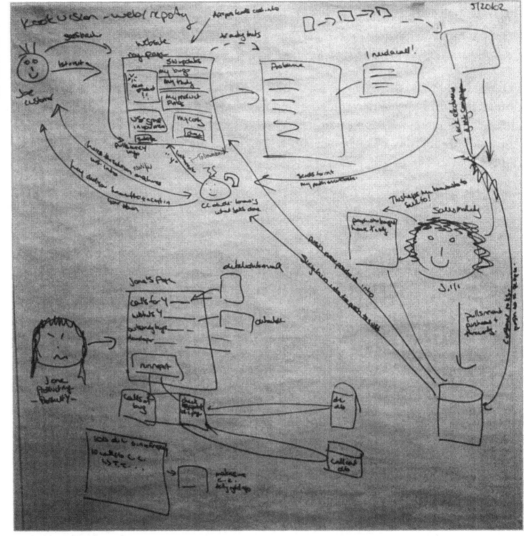

Introduce the roles

The Pen. The Pen is the person drawing the vision as the rest of the team tells the story (see Figure 11-4 for examples of vision drawings). The Pen is in service of the team, which means that they cannot contribute to the story. The Pen can ask questions for clarification, and may throw in a design concept or two. But the Pen cannot start telling the story as a major contributor. If someone feels strongly about a hot idea and wants to participate in the telling, they should not be the Pen. If they know the visioning process, an outside facilitator can act as the Pen.

The Pen has two roles: encourage people to talk, and fit their ideas into the vision as it is developing. The Pen listens for ideas that are on the story thread, postponing ideas that are too far off the main line for another vision. When an idea conflicts with the thread the team is working on, the Pen adds it to the list of hot ideas—this keeps the thread coherent, while assuring the team member that his idea has been heard and will be dealt with later.

The Pen also moderates the rate of talk, asking people to wait if he or she needs to catch up, calling upon someone who had been trying to contribute, and generally making sure everyone's ideas are heard. The Pen is not a gatekeeper for ideas and will frustrate the team and the flow of the story if they do not draw quickly enough and include the ideas of all team members.

Figure 11-3 shows a complete workflow. To reveal what the system needs to do to support the entire process, process steps like the telephone conversation are included, communication across multiple people playing multiple roles are explored, and multiple devices (PCs and handhelds) are included.

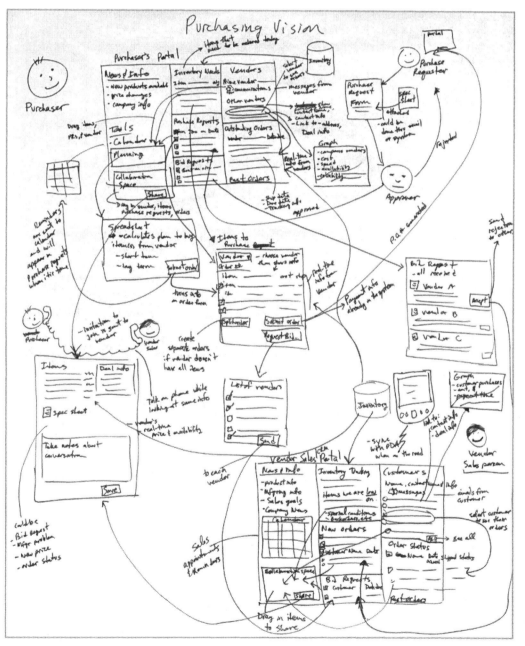

Figure 11-3:
Vision of B2B purchasing across the web. The UI is visioned in the context of the users' total workflow.

The Poker. The Poker can be anyone on the team. The Poker participates in the vision but also has an eye on the issues the team said they wanted to address. When the team reaches a lull in the storytelling the Poker will remind the team about an issue that has not yet been addressed. This will stimulate additional storytelling and lead to a more complete solution.

When moderating, this person's job is to be sure the rules are being followed, that everyone has a chance to be heard, and that no one person is dominating the story.

Participants. Except for the Pen, the entire team participates in the telling of the vision.

Figure 11-4: Examples of how to draw components of the vision.

Explain the rules

- There is no evaluation of ideas as good or bad during the initial visioning. There is a separate evaluation period later.

- No idea belongs to a person; everyone participates in elaborating a group vision.

- Talk to the Pen (drawing the vision), not to each other. You are creating what is on the flipchart—if it isn't on the flipchart it won't be in the design.

- Offer design solutions and user actions—don't ask the team questions about what we want to do about this or that issue. Visioning is not a discussion, it is a time for all to cocreate the story of how things will work in the future.

Review issues and hot ideas

The intent of reviewing issues and hot ideas is to prime your brain in preparation of the vision. Prior to starting make sure you:

- Make or review the list of issues generated by walking the affinity and consolidated sequence models. You want to do this so you know where you need to take the design. You also need to know what the problem areas are so that you can correct them.

- Make or review the list of hot ideas. This list comes from the hot ideas the team generated while walking the data. It is the starting point for the vision.

- Optionally, make a list of technologies available to you. This step can be very useful because it reminds the team of the technologies available to them for invention. If anyone does not understand one of the technologies it can be explained or even demonstrated. People can design only from what they know, so be sure everyone on the team understands the technological assumptions for your project.

Define parameters for the vision

Prior to visioning the team needs to understand the parameters within which to vision. The most important of these are technological, business, and time constraints.

If *technology platforms* have been picked the team needs to know what it can and can't do. Manage this by asking a technologist to present the technology platforms to the team before visioning. Let the team ask questions so that they can understand what they can and cannot envision.

Business constraints can take many forms. The team needs to understand the business goals whether they are designing products or internal systems. They need to understand the value that the business is expecting from the system. If it is an ERP (Enterprise Resource Planning) system or an internal business system the team needs to understand any process reengineering expectation or upcoming business changes that they must consider. Ask someone from the business or from marketing to present the business goals and expectations to the team before they start visioning. Clarify how "set in stone" these decisions are to understand how widely you can vision.

Time, meaning expected timeframe until shipment, is the aspect the team most often worries about. The danger of over-focusing on time is that the team will vision so narrowly that they will not see how different parts fit into a whole solution. Remember that a broad vision can be broken into parts and developed individually. But if it was all visioned together each release is more likely to hang together for the user, particularly if you ship within a reasonable timeframe.

Our general recommendations are as follows:

- For a standard development team, use only current shipping technology and invent a vision that can be shipped in three to five years.

- For an advanced research team, use technology that will mature within five years and vision in a five- to 10-year timeframe.

- For a team that is trying to ship a release within one year but wants to develop within a bigger picture, use only current shipping technology and invent a vision that can be shipped in three to five years. But then back off the vision and do a one-year vision based on the longer term vision. Don't start with the short vision.

- For a team that only wants to identify the top things to fix in the next release, don't vision at all. List the top key fixes in order of value to the user; then work with development to determine which of these are easy and hard to implement. Create a final list balancing user need with engineering effort.

- For a team using XP, use only currently shipping technology and invent a vision that can be shipped in two years. Then break up the vision into chunks of related function and start with the chunk most central to the work. Use the vision to direct work after that, changing priorities based on the continuous user feedback you are getting.

In general, remember, a team will not feel empowered to vision more widely if they do not feel that there is a reasonable plan to identify the first release. Explain how the vision and the visioning process can be used to direct both short and longer term decisions. Discourage a tightly constrained vision; it usually doesn't work for the user because their work is not being imagined as a whole. Rather let the team vision more broadly, and then create a last vision of the next release. In that way you can get the best of both worlds.

Since visioning itself is quick, it pushes a Rapid CD process forward while it creating a shared understanding across functional groups and other people that have a stake in the ultimate solution.

Select a hot idea for the first vision

If you built a hot ideas list after walking your affinity and the consolidated models, you already have a list. If you haven't, your first step is to get your list (see Chapter 10).

Because hot ideas are listed in a brainstorming-like fashion, you may have overlapping hot ideas, or several smaller ideas that could be combined into one big idea. Take a few moments to consolidate the list and identify the top groupings of hot ideas. This also helps the team see that smaller ideas can combine to create more systemic ideas.

Example: eChalk

eChalk's hot ideas list started off as having over 30 hot ideas—big and little. This is very exciting, but also a little overwhelming. In several cases they had related ideas that were combined into one big idea.

For example, in this list the first idea—Virtual Classroom—is the hot idea. The other ideas are extensions of that one big idea:

Idea: Virtual classroom—everything to do with a class is online

Idea: Bug tracker for the students—keep track a student's progress throughout the year and use this data to generate a progress report

Idea: Student files—an area where students can store their information as they move through a school district

Idea: Centrally store all communication that relates to a student (e.g., field trip forms, student work, etc.)

Idea: eChalk pen pals

After about 10 minutes eChalk consolidated their hot idea list down to five bigger ideas that represented all the smaller ideas.

Idea: Virtual support person

Idea: My eChalk

Idea: School showcase

Idea: Online classroom

Idea: Forms life cycle

Whether you have five, 10, 20, or more hot ideas, the team needs a fast way to decide where to start. Rather than taking time to debate this, we suggest that you simply vote.

Where you start actually doesn't matter because you will do more than one vision anyway. More importantly, any vision naturally pulls in aspects of multiple hot ideas as the story unfolds. So try some fun ways to identify the first idea.

Here's the one we tend to use most often. It takes only about five minutes, and gets the team energized and excited.

1. Explain to the visioning team that they get to vote on which hot ideas they are going to vision.

2. Explain that a Post-it® flag is equivalent to one vote.

3. Pass out an equal number of Post-it® flags to each team member; six is a good number.

4. Let each person cast their votes anyway they want. They can vote for six ideas, or put all six votes on one idea, or spread them out in any other way.

5. Have everyone stand in front of the hot ideas flipchart, and remind them that they can't stand back and wait to see how the team is going to cast their votes.

6. Give the team enough time to cast all their votes. But don't let this go on too long; after three or four minutes, give them only two more minutes to cast all of their votes.

7. The hot idea with the most votes is the one you will start with.

8. Also, you can vote simply by a general applause or "noise" metric; the hot idea with the most noise wins. The goal is to eliminate debate and just get started!

Run the visioning session

The Pen steps to the flipchart and labels it with the title of the hot idea. Then the Pen asks "Who am I and what am I doing?" Once a team member starts providing ideas you are into the first vision. Watch that everyone is participating, make sure that the ideas get onto the paper, and listen to the Poker, who will remind you of areas to cover (see the box, **Managing the team**).

Listen for when someone suggests an option that would be better addressed by treating it as a separate idea. Each idea has a core theme, which you should state explicitly—if the option just extends the same theme, incorporate it. If it suggests a new theme or significantly modifies the current one, treat it as a new idea. Tell them you will elaborate the idea later. Don't try to stretch an idea too far.

When the first vision is finished go on to a second vision. Listen for when the team stops elaborating on an idea. Move on to the next idea quickly. Spend no more than 20 to 30 minutes on each vision.

Choose the next idea to cover a new area of customer work, draw on a very different type of technology, or allow for a different level of risk. Draw each idea on a separate sheet of paper.

Managing the team

Here are some problems with participants in the visioning process you may encounter.

Worrying about the vision. Seeing an idea drawn out will disturb some people. They will see all the flaws or get stuck on how to implement it. Remind them that you have committed to nothing—it is a flipchart page. Later we will evaluate for what works and what doesn't and change things.

Not speaking up. Make sure everyone is participating and feeling heard. Part of people not speaking up may be the number of people involved; visioning is difficult to do with more than 10 people. If necessary, break into smaller groups.

Too tight to vision. Some people or even entire teams will have a difficult time letting go and thinking creatively. To help them loosen up, have a silly break beforehand, vision while standing up, and generally help them let go physically. Remind them that thinking widely will lead to a more innovative product and that you will evaluate later. Alternatively, suggest some wild design idea to start the visioning session and push them wide. When they pull back, they'll most likely settle in a broader place than they were in before.

Meticulous group. Some people are very methodical and need to put every piece in place before they can go to the next. When the whole group is like that, don't try to push them faster than they want to go for the sake of time. Teams like this don't mind putting in the time if it means they can work their ideas out.

Mixed style group. When only certain team members are detail oriented and others want to be very open and visionary without detail, talk to them about appreciating what each brings to the vision. Let the visionary set the direction and let the detail person fill in the first layer of detail, without going too deep.

If your group is big, you can run parallel visioning sessions or start together and then split up.

Do at least two visions before evaluating—three to four is better. But this also depends on the scope of the project. The goal is to cover the work practice you are designing for and to touch upon your most interesting large hot ideas. See Table 11-1 for tips on running the vision.

Note: It is critical to a successful visioning session that you have a good Pen. This person needs to be able to listen and synthesize ideas quickly, without a lot of filtering or explanation. If the Pen is slow, the meeting gets boring. If people don't feel that their ideas are being written down, they will get frustrated. Change Pens and speed up the session.

Dos and don'ts for the visioning process	
Don't	**Do**
Use multiple pages for one vision.	Keep the vision to a single flipchart page. Running over multiple pages usually indicates you are trying to address more than one coherent task or perspective in a vision. Start fresh on a new page with a focused topic.
Talk in generalities.	Say specifically who the users are and what they are doing, saying, thinking, and seeing.
Over focus on the system or the UI.	Acknowledge databases, processors, web servers, and so on that are working in the background, but don't work out the implementation. Roughly sketch out UI screens or devices to represent what the user might do there. Don't worry about buttons and navigation.
Feel constrained that this will be your final design.	Create multiple visions and evaluate them. Imagine possibilities that may be too difficult to implement. Remember that the evaluation step comes next and the vision can be scaled back once you have it.
Be prematurely constrained or narrow in visioning.	Vision as broadly as you can within the constraints of your project focus. You can then pull back once you see the possibilities and evaluate them against resources, schedules, and technical constraints.
Try to work out all the details.	Wait for storyboarding to work out the details.
Talk to each other and not to the Pen or have side conversations.	Share your ideas with everyone. Side conversations are disruptive to concentration and then your ideas aren't captured. You aren't discussing the vision with each other and asking questions about how it works, you are telling the story to the Pen.
Worry about being neat or perfect when drawing.	Don't worry too much about neatness. Visions are rough brainstorms that are done quickly because that tells a more integrated story. Trying to make it neat will slow down the storytelling and destructure the story.

Table 11-1: Tips for running a productive visioning session.

221

Example: eChalk

eChalk's Online Classroom vision (see Figure 11-5) is based on the idea that core classroom tasks like scheduling class activities, making assignments, getting permission slips from parents, communicating with parents about student behavior, and taking attendance all need to be available in one web application. These are activities are from the sequences that eChalk collected and consolidated.

At first glance the vision might look linear, but in reality it reflects activities that are happening throughout the year, and can happen in any order. The story of the work involves multiple people, so each individual playing a role is shown with a little head, labeled with his or her identity.

Process steps like thoughts or conversations are represented in bubbles next to the person's head. Screens or web pages are shown as nothing more than rectangles, populated with content. At this point there is no attention to what the actual UI might be—checkboxes versus list boxes, shape of buttons, and so on are not relevant to expressing what functionality is needed to support the work in the story. When the user takes an action like checking something off or clicking a button, that shows on the screen drawing.

The underlying system that is storing information and populating screens is represented by databases or cans. What the system is doing is represented at a very high-level, sometimes with just a name for the database and other times a few words or bullet points. The vision isn't implying that multiple systems or databases will be needed; this is just a way to indicate what has to happen under the hood to respond to the users' actions on the various screens.

Evaluate the vision

The purpose of evaluation is to identify what works and overcome what does not work in the visions. Evaluation is not conducted to pick among competing visions. Each vision page has processes, function, and design elements that the team will want to keep. Treating the picture as a monolithic whole makes people think they have to implement the whole thing as is.

But good design is the invention, recombination, and iteration of parts within a sociotechnical system until it meets the needs of the user, the technology, and the business. Evaluating a vision by looking at its parts encourages creative redesign and keeps the team from rejecting the visions because of aspects that don't work.

Pluses and minuses, as we call it, is an informal way to help the team step back and review their ideas critically. It is through the critique that they will see what to keep, what to let go of, and how to change things that don't work so they do.

Pluses and minuses is a fast group process to raise issues and come to consensus—a process that is much better than long prioritization meetings. Do pluses and minuses with the same team that produced the visions in the first place, right after the visioning session.

An evaluation session covers about two to four visions. Do not evaluate each vision after you create it—evaluate a group of visions together.

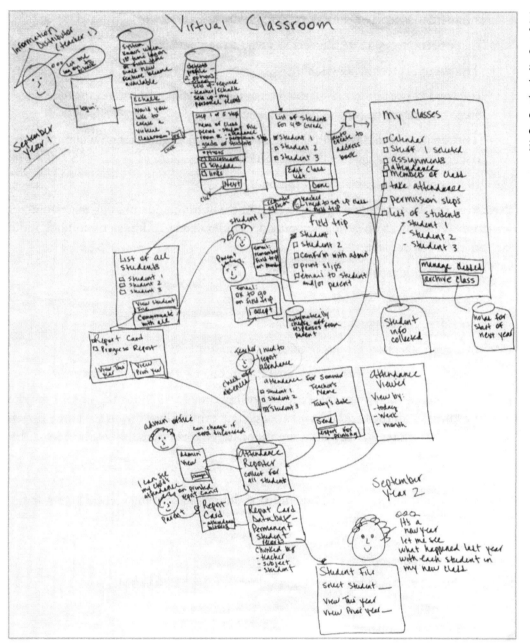

Figure 11-5:
The eChalk virtual classroom vision shows a high-level view of the new work practice. The details are worked out in storyboarding.

The team reviews each vision and then together lists all of the vision's positive attributes (pluses) and then all of the vision's negative attributes (minuses). Listing the positive before the negative forces the team to really look at the vision and not just react to the pieces each individual doesn't like. It ensures that the value in the vision is not lost.

As the team lists the minuses, they should be thinking of design ideas to overcome these problems. Team members then write their design ideas on a Post-it® note, and post them on the vision at the end of the evaluation.

If you have split up into more than one group to create your visions you will need to get back together and share all the new visions. This sharing can be done right before the visions are evaluated.

223

Pluses represent aspects of the design that work. Pluses are:

- It supports the work of the user as given in the data collected.

- The design is technically doable.

- It has good sales potential—it will create a good value proposition for the sales force to pitch to the buying decision-makers.

- This design is doable within our organization—the organization will be able to collaborate or manage its processes to deliver it.

- It supports the organizational mission.

Negatives are the opposite of the positives, but do not include missing issues, roles, or situations. A vision can be evaluated only on what it tried to address, not on holes it did not address. Minuses are:

- This design doesn't support the work.

- It isn't technically doable.

- This design has low sales potential.

- It isn't consistent with our organization mission.

- It requires too much organizational politics or new processes to succeed.

Sometimes people will be at the extremes of how they feel about the vision: they can love it or hate it. Tell the team that if anyone loves the vision, they must come up with at least three minuses. If they hate the vision, they must come up with at least three pluses.

Example: eChalk

Here are some of the pluses and minuses the eChalk team identified for their Online Classroom vision:

Pluses

- Shares student progress

- Organizes information by class and student

- Has different views of data

- Links to teacher home page

- Lets teacher distribute different information

- Gets teachers to do all of this—work practice is being supported

- Gets information to parent

- Gives teachers control over their information management

- Empowers the teachers, gives them more control—levels the playing field

Minuses

- Will this really save time, or is it more work?

- Need to get buy-in from the school administrators

- Are there concerns that student information is too readily accessible?

- Still have to have manual ways to communicate with parents and students who don't have access to technology.

Create one consolidated vision

After the team has finished creating and sharing the multiple visions they should create one high-level, consolidated vision. The consolidated vision combines visions to eliminate the negatives and reinforce the positives. It presents all the core elements into one vision on one page so that the team has a clear focus for their design work.

To create a consolidated vision, consider the following:

- If the visions do not conflict, draw a new vision, combining parts from each as needed.

- If the visions are actually working out multiple cases in a process, abstract out the overall work flow and core concepts and represent them on one page. Keep the other pages for backup.

- If the visions conflict because they operate from differing business assumptions or technology platforms, agree to the technology or business assumption from which you will operate. Then circle the parts of each vision that will work within those assumptions. You will be surprised how many elements of a conflicting vision can be quickly reconceptualized to fit within the chosen assumptions. Then draw one picture representing the new direction.

- If there are parts of the vision that need technical investigation before they can be considered viable, note them and start a technical team investigating. Design assuming that the technology is stable until otherwise notified. Identify a simplified way to achieve the same intent and storyboard that also.

A consolidated vision can be constructed by two people in a half a day. You may ask why it takes so long. Although it is a "redrawing" of what you already have, it is also an opportunity to clarify what you have drawn and create a coherent representation of what you will be designing. A good consolidated vision guides the team throughout the subsequent design process and keeps them from expanding the scope of the project.

When you are done, produce a clean drawing of the final vision on a flipchart or put it online. Consider writing a short narrative of the vision to ensure that you remember all the elements. This is your very high-level use case or user story.

Initial visions are working documents to help the team make their design conversations concrete. These visions do not really need to be put online. Once you have a consolidated vision that you want to use for designing the system, you want to put it online to help communicate to the rest of your organization. Use a drawing/graphics program such as Visio®, PowerPoint®, or CorelDRAW®.

Hang the consolidated vision on the wall in your team room. If appropriate, communicate your vision to stakeholders or management by walking them through the drawing or create a series of slides introducing the product or system concepts (see the box, **Communication out: Visions create a shared understanding across the organization**).

Example: Shopping

This is the vision for Online Shopping. It is an at-home system using a flat panel or tablet and a hand-held input device for making selections, entering text, and reading bar code labels. The household member can go to the refrigerator or other location where the panel is stored, and then move around the house with it.

Figure 11-6 is an online form of a vision that can be stored and annotated to remember what the team was thinking. The picture of the vision is supported by a narrative that describes it. Consider videotaping a narrative (see example) to save the vision as one of our clients did when they had to stop a project before it was complete. Having a written description or videotape record is very useful to help you remember the specific content of the vision if time is going to pass before you actually work out the details.

Figure 11-6:
Shopping vision picture that goes with the supporting narrative.

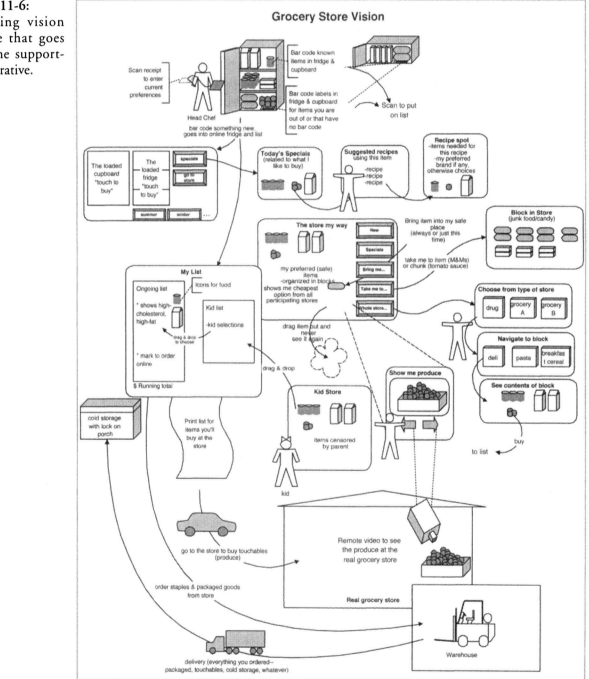

Example vision narrative: Shopping

This is the vision for Online Shopping. It is an at-home system using a flat panel or tablet and handheld device to make selections, enter text, and read bar code labels. The household member can go to the refrigerator or other location where the panel is stored, and then move around the house with it.

The underlying system stores information from prior purchases to create this household's buying patterns and preferences, and uses this data to populate what is displayed on the panel's screen. One way to add items to a shopping list that appears on the flat panel is to swipe printed bar code labels that are in the refrigerator, cupboards, and other locations of the house.

Another way to add items to the list is by viewing "virtual" household places and "virtual" stores and making selections from them. A virtual household place, for example a virtual cupboard, allows the customer to select individual items, shelves, or entire cupboards or refrigerators and add them to the list. The virtual store's contents—aisles, blocks, or departments; individual items and brands; seasonal items; and store specials—are displayed and organized the way this specific shopper approaches shopping, and displays only the preferred items, brands, and so on. Other household members can have their own special virtual stores, such as a Kid Store that contains only items that have been preapproved by the parents.

Recipes are linked to items. Multiple stores participate, so virtual household and store contents can come from any store and the shopper may opt to see which store has the best price for a given item or only to see items based on price. The bricks-and-mortar store has a video camera that displays real-time images on the shopper's in-home panel so the customer can see what produce or meat actually looks like before adding them to the list. Items are added to the list by touching the image. Items are permanently removed from the household place or store by dragging them out.

There are two ways to place an order and take delivery. The customer can create the list, order online, and then items are delivered to the home. A cold storage box with a lock at the residence is used when the customer is not at home for the delivery. Customers also can assemble their list at home, print it, and then go to the store to do the actual purchasing.

Communication out: Visions create shared understanding across the organization

Products usually do not slip because of technology. Products slip because organizations cannot settle on the real requirements and design early enough to operate smoothly. Design from customer data helps this because organizations can look to the data for guidance instead of arguing with each other over who knows the customer best. The vision, produced by a cross-functional team immersed in customer data, creates a shared direction for the product or system. Visioning creates the context for hearing and synthesizing individual design ideas into a coherent business direction.

The more complex the product, the more complex the organizational buy-in process. Everyone wants information and everyone wants their opinion considered. If you are in a large corporation, you will need to get buy-in for your design from other parts of the organization. The vision session provides an excellent opportunity to bring in divergent views, create organizational buy-in and at the same time communicate your work.

For example, one of our clients held five different visioning sessions across their multinational company, bringing in key stakeholders to walk the walls and brainstorm. The team found that everybody was inventing the same thing. Just as work practice is circumscribed by its context, when people from the same company, designing the same kind of technology, looking at the same customer data, considering the same business case, go through the visioning process, the visions overlap from group to group. But the team now had fabulous buy-in from across the corporation!

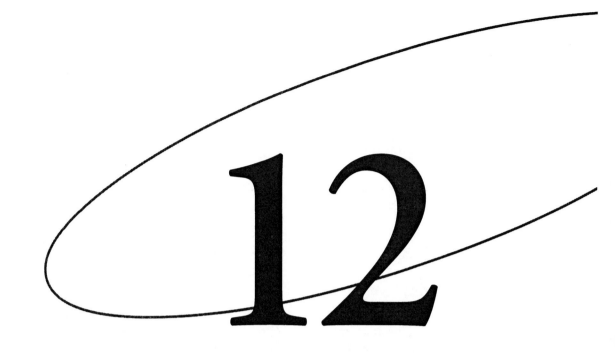

Storyboarding

Rapid CD Process	Lightning Fast	Lightning Fast +	Focused Rapid CD
Storyboards			✓

Storyboards take the broad view of the vision, and work out in detail how a person will accomplish specific tasks in the new design. You need to figure out the details of how work will be done in the new system to ensure that you don't break the users' existing work practice. Therefore, storyboards are guided by and checked against the consolidated sequences for tasks and intents that need to be supported.

Too often when people design, they break work practice because they jump from their big idea to low-level user interface and implementation design. As soon as designers start focusing on technology, technology and its problems become their central design concern. Storyboarding, guided by the sequence models and affinity data, ensure that the team does not overlook any intents and steps that are critical to the work. Storyboarding lets you work out the details of how to support the sequence within the new system, whether you support it by making sure users can still accomplish an activity in the old way, or by introducing new technology to better achieve the intent.

The vision is a natural prioritizer. You need not storyboard every sequence. Instead, identify which sequences are relevant to the vision, and storyboard those. The sequence models should represent the core tasks to achieve the work within project scope. Supporting those sequences will be enough for a next product release.

Storyboards are equivalent to future scenarios, to-be use cases in RUP, and the basis for user stories in the XP process (see the box, **Why storyboard: using drawings instead of** text-based use cases). See Chapter 15 for a more in-depth discussion of how storyboards are related to other methodologies. This chapter illustrates how storyboards are created.

Definition

Storyboards are like freeze-frame movies of the new work practice. Like storyboarding in film, the team draws step-by-step pictures of how people will work in their new world. Storyboards include manual steps, rough user interface components, system activity and automation, and even documentation use. Storyboards act like high-level use cases.

The role of storyboarding in system design is discussed further in Chapter 13, "Design from Data," pg. 287, in *Contextual Design: Defining Customer-Centered Systems*.

Key concepts

Low-level or mini vision. The storyboarding process starts with a low-level vision. This is a similar process to the visioning process described in Chapter 11. The low-level vision works out the details of a portion of the high-level consolidated vision. The low-level vision is tied to a task defined by a consolidated sequence—working out changes to every step and designed to support sequence intents while overcoming user issues. The low-level vision lets the team explore alternatives and have discussions grounded in their drawings in preparation for storyboarding.

Process for storyboarding

- ☐ Preparation
  - ☐ Prepare the room, data, and supplies
  - ☐ Gather people to storyboard
  - ☐ Choose where to start
- ☐ Review how to storyboard
- ☐ Create a low-level vision
  - ☐ Walk the consolidated vision
  - ☐ Collect issues from the affinity and consolidated sequence model that are related specifically to what is going to be storyboarded
  - ☐ Create a low-level vision for one task to be storyboarded
  - ☐ Identify pluses and minuses for the low-level vision
- ☐ Create the storyboards
  - ☐ Draw the storyboard frames
  - ☐ Check the storyboard against the consolidated sequence
- ☐ Share the storyboard with stakeholders or members of a larger team
- ☐ Refine the storyboard
- ☐ Go on to the next storyboard

Why storyboard? Using drawings instead of text-based use cases

Storyboards are equivalent to future scenarios or high-level use case instances and may be represented in standard use case document structure and Unified Modeling Language notation. We choose to represent the redesigned work in frame-by-frame drawings. They include manual steps, rough user interface components showing function, system activity, automation, and even documentation use.

By working with multiple teams we have learned that the best system design comes from this type of visual representation of the to-be models of work. Text versions of a scenario or simple user interface drawings alone fail to consider all the dimensions of the new work practice. Use case and object modelers are trained to use the text-intensive use case characterization of the redesigned work. We find that this ultimately focuses the team too much on system activities and business rules and not enough on necessary human processes and user interface function. But user interface designers who are concerned primarily with the interaction design tend to overlook the system steps and over-focus on UI detail. They get stuck prematurely in detailed discussions of layout that will become irrelevant when the implications of multiple scenarios of use are worked through.

One key principle of Contextual Design is to use the right representational form for the design conversation the team is trying to have. Even though it might be possible to represent the storyboard concepts with UML models, use cases, stories, a series of UI drawings or even a high-level business process drawing—none of these individual representations encourages the team to think about all these factors simultaneously. Storyboards by their very nature ensure synthetic sequential thinking and thereby a more complete design for the user, especially when guided both by the vision and the consolidated sequences.

Storyboards also provide a conceptual common denominator for design discussions with users; it is much more likely that a user will grasp the metaphor of a storyboard (e.g., as used in the creation of animations, comic books, and movies) over more abstract modeling techniques. When developing in-house systems we photograph our storyboard frames and display them for user groups and stakeholders. Then we run a "share" session, collecting their issues. In this way the team creates buy-in with future users and gets additional feedback that can be rolled into the next version of the storyboard.

See Chapter 15 for a description of how CD is used with other development methodologies.

Prepare the room, data, and supplies

In order to create the storyboards you will need to hang up the consolidated visions and sequences in your team room. You will also need flipcharts for drawing low-level visions and 5½x8½ sheets of paper for your storyboard frames. Bring removable tape to hang the storyboard frames onto flipcharts for review.

Gather people to storyboard

It is best to create storyboards in pairs. As with other parts of Contextual Design, you do not want to storyboard by yourself—with two people you can bounce ideas off each other. If you have more people on your team or want to include others in the process you can create several storyboards in parallel. Be sure that one core team member works on every storyboard to ensure continuity.

If you have core team members who work all the time and adjunct team members who work part time be sure that the same people are always responsible for the same storyboard. Moving people on and off a storyboard slows everyone down because the work has to be reviewed and agreed to over and over. Assign two people to each storyboard and then run a formal share session later.

Choose where to start

Before jumping into storyboarding you need to pick a place to start. Your sequences represent the key tasks for your project. Select the sequences you will storyboard starting with the work that is core to the system.

If you are storyboarding in parallel with stakeholders or a larger team, assign two people to each sequence to storyboard. Ensure that the sequences do not have overlapping activities—if so, indicate what team will address the overlapping piece. If you have very long sequences consider breaking them up to give to teams working in parallel. If you are a two-person team, simply start with the core storyboards.

Review your consolidated vision to see if it implies tasks that do not correspond to your sequences. You may want to get additional data to guide the storyboarding—field interviews focused on collecting data for one task are very quick. Even having one real instance to guide the storyboarding will be quicker and more productive than making up the storyboard with no data.

We have seen teams spin their wheels and argue when they have no clear idea of how an activity is accomplished. The vision alone is not enough of a guide, particularly for a complicated or unfamiliar task.

Review the vision for different cases or conditions. Your consolidated sequence will also have different branches and strategies—storyboard each of these as well. Sometimes new process design plans within a business will imply that the same activity will be storyboarded under different assumptions. Make a list of all cases implied by the vision, the consolidated sequence, and any process plans, and storyboard these cases.

Review how to storyboard

Be sure that everyone participating understands the following:

- The storyboard works out in more detail the new work practice described in the vision. It is made up of both pictures and words representing the complete story of the work, not just interactions with the product.

- A storyboard is a set of hand-drawn pictures that let people think concretely about how the new work practice will work. It includes manual steps, interaction with the new system's user interface, system automation, business rules, and interaction with other systems and products. See Figure 12-1 for examples of different types of storyboard frames.

- Storyboards are guided by user data. Each storyboard will be associated with an existing consolidated sequence and will take into consideration other user data gathered from the affinity and artifacts. When the storyboard is done you want to check it against the sequence to be sure that users can still accomplish the task and achieve their intents.

- Each storyboard frame is one step in the story. Each step in the storyboard represents one interaction with the system, one interaction with another person, one manual step, or one behind-the-scenes step where the system responds.

- Just like a movie a storyboard can have flashbacks and flash forwards to deal with strategies and cases—it doesn't have to be one straight path.

- A storyboard should have enough detail and text for someone who did not create it to read and understand the proposed process. You also want others not on the team to be able to understand them. So in a business, your employees or business customers can review the storyboard to see what the new process will be like.

Figure 12-1: Examples of different types of storyboard frames.

233

Describe the order of the process:

1. Collect the data relevant to your sequence.

2. Create a low-level vision of your sequence accounting for each activity, intent, and step while staying within the constraints of the vision and the agreed to technology platform.

3. Do pluses and minuses on the low-level vision and fix the minuses.

4. Create the storyboard frames. Be sure to put only one interaction or step within each frame.

See Figure 12-2 for an example of a completed storyboard.

Figure 12-2:
An example of an actual storyboard. Note the different types of views on the work—process, UI, and human interaction. The Post-it® notes are issues that were gathered after a storyboard share.

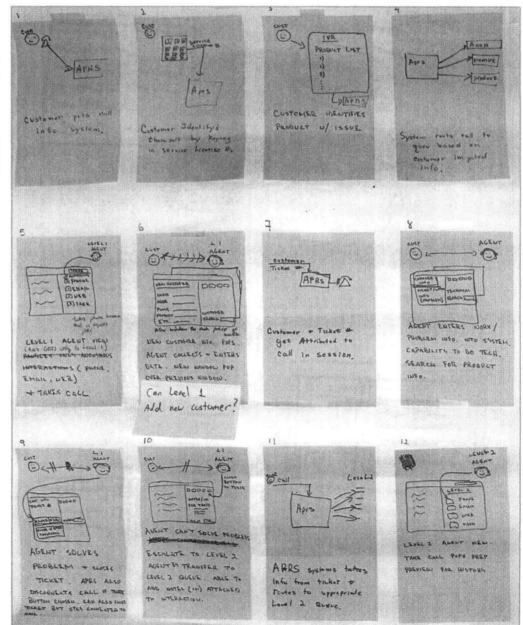

Walk the vision

If there is a break in time between visioning and storyboarding, have the team walk the vision to re-orient themselves to how the task and system will change in the new system or product. If people in the group are not familiar with the vision have someone walk the group through the story. If everyone is familiar with the vision just review it silently.

Collect issues from the affinity and consolidated sequence

Prior to low-level visioning collect issues from the affinity and any consolidated work models. Your vision issues tend to be broad or high level. You need to go back to the affinity and sequence model and quickly walk them for lower level issues related to what is being storyboarded, looking for parts of the affinity related to the task you are going to storyboard. Walk the sequence, paying special attention to strategies, intents, and breakdowns. The entire subteam does not need to walk both the affinity and the sequences. They can assign themselves different parts to look at, take notes, and come back together to share.

Spend 15 to 20 minutes on collecting issues, and another 15 minutes to share them with your subteam.

Work out your approach to the task in a low-level vision

Once you are grounded in the data you are ready to start the first step of the story-boarding process. However, before you start drawing the individual storyboard frames you need to work out alternatives for how to support the task within the framework of the vision. A low-level vision is not the same as the whole system vision you created after the data walk. The low-level vision is smaller in scope and is focused on working out the details of the sequence and cases that you are storyboarding.

Follow the same process as you did in the larger visioning session, only go into more detail. Unlike in the visioning session, in a low-level vision your Pen does actively participate in the conversation; both of you may also draw. The two of you talk together about how to address each activity, each intent, and each case. Like with the vision, you are focused on what the user will be doing manually, with others, and when interacting with the system.

Let the activities in the sequence chunk your thought process. If you have more than one idea of how to approach the task or section of the task, do multiple low-level visions. Your goal is to work out your ideas on the flipchart paper—quickly drawing the possibilities, evaluating them, and fixing the minuses. Think of the flipchart as a conversation board capturing your conversation physically.

The low-level vision is still about user experience and process including interaction with proposed technology; it avoids exact interaction design or underlying object or data modeling. This is your opportunity to work out the details and determine what will work from the vision for this particular task. It is also the time to determine, now that you have had a chance to examine it in detail, what is simply not viable. You are figuring out the next level of detail about the functions and UI, but you are still not yet having a conversation about the specific UI.

In a storyboard you want to show the process, the exact underlying business rules or automation desired, the content of the interface and an initial layout, the collaboration expectations, the reliance on other technology, back-end systems that need to be accessed, and any other elements relevant to getting the work of the task complete. You are working out the functions needed to support the work but within the context of the whole work task and preliminary concepts of how to chunk access to function in the user interface.

Creating a low-level vision should take 1 to 1.5 hours per task or central case. More complicated tasks with many conditions may take longer.

Caution: When feeling pressed for time, don't be tempted to skip the low-level vision and go directly to creating the storyboard frames. It actually takes longer to go straight to the storyboard because you haven't taken the time to think it through. The low-level vision does that for you, and then creating the storyboard frames is essentially a transfer process from the low-level vision to the frames.

Identify pluses and minuses for the low-level vision

Once you have your possible approaches, identify pluses and minuses just like you did after visioning. Do this even if you had only one approach because it causes you to step back and think critically about your solution.

Generate design ideas for the minuses and fix them in the low-level vision. If you came up with alternate methods of doing the same task, run pluses and minuses on the alternates in order to choose which you are going to use.

If you have competing possibilities you must choose one to storyboard. If you can't agree on the storyboard direction after pluses and minuses, pick the more radical solution (see the box, **How to choose between two ideas**).

Keep track of your alternatives—you can always fall back on them if the user doesn't like the design you choose to present. We call these alternatives test cases. They help define your focus for paper prototype testing (see Chapter 13), so keep track of them.

How to choose between two ideas

When low-level visioning you may have two alternatives that are equally good. Within the Rapid CD process storyboards will drive development of the paper prototypes, which will then be tested with the user (see Chapter 13)—so you don't need to worry about having picked the "best" solution of the two. But how do you choose between them? A good rule of thumb is to pick the more radical of the choices, the one the user is least likely to expect. Your storyboard is on the way to becoming what you test with users in a paper prototype. If you give the users what they are accustomed to seeing, you won't elicit much of a reaction. However, when it is unexpected, the user will react—either positively or negatively—and you can use that reaction to drive a conversation.

So we recommend picking the solution that challenges the users' habits but better supports their intents. You can always fall back to a more traditional approach after testing.

Then create a list of test cases so you know what you want to test when you are out in the field. Remember, the final arbitrator of the goodness of the design is the user, not you.

Draw the storyboard

Now you are ready to capture the storyboard according to the new work practice. Remember, each frame represents one step in the story. If there are branches to a step, let the storyboard branch and number each frame; for example, 1A, 1B, 1C.

Once you are finished, tape the frames to a flipchart page so the storyboard can easily be seen and used. Write a title for the storyboard, and number each of the frames.

When drawing the storyboard frames remember the following:

- Draw rough user interfaces annotated with usage.

- Describe manual actions—draw pictures where needed for clarity.

- Sketch documentation used.

- Draw cartoons of people interacting for interpersonal steps.

- If the system will take over a step draw what the system does and describe any data it relies on.

- When the user does a series of actions with the system, draw a separate step for each action with rough layout of the user interface.

- Annotate with role names to indicate the players performing the tasks.

- Annotate with any business rules, implementation notes, constraints, hardware or software expectations, etc.

- Include words to explain what is happening, state assumptions, and anything else where a picture is not sufficient.

- Assume that you are creating "documentation" of the process in the storyboards so that someone that wasn't in the design meeting could read the storyboard and understand what is happening.

Drawing the storyboard frames should take about one hour if you think things through the steps in the low-level vision.

Example: eChalk

Figure 12-3 shows a flipchart page with 15 frames of eChalk's total storyboard for their Online Classroom vision. Two two-person subteams worked on the storyboards, and then the storyboards were brought together and shared to be sure the overall story hung together.

They did a total of 34 frames to represent the following tasks:

- Creating a class calendar

- Making and receiving assignments

- Creating class events

- Taking attendance

- Entering grades

- Communicating with parents

237

Figure 12-3:
eChalk storyboard section with issues from review session posted.

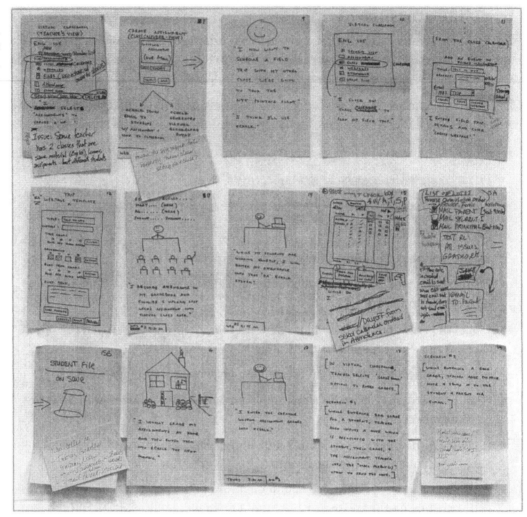

Different cases or scenarios were run for some tasks like grading, which had two cases: one for a good grade and another for a poor grade. Classroom assignments also had two cases—the teacher's perspective and the student's perspective.

The eChalk team wanted to be sure they thought through the interactions between teacher and eChalk throughout the day. So they indicated the transition of time during the day as the teacher goes from task to task (i.e., Wed. 8:30 a.m., Wed 9:30 a.m.). Manual steps flesh out the story and ensure that the team is thinking about how the technology fits into the work practice smoothly. System behavior is storyboarded to show when it drives what the user sees onscreen, and when data is stored for future use.

The team is not worried about making neat or beautiful storyboards; they are focused on driving out the details of the work. They have tried to make each storyboard frame have enough detail that someone familiar with the project understands the work practice being represented.

Figures 12-4 through 12-8 show a closer look at some of eChalk's storyboard frames.

Figure 12-4 shows a screen with all the functions in eChalk. The team is using this frame to start the story with the equivalent of an opening scene. This sets the stage for the various functions the teacher will use in the upcoming frames. In this sketch the user selects the New Assignment function to create a new classroom assignment.

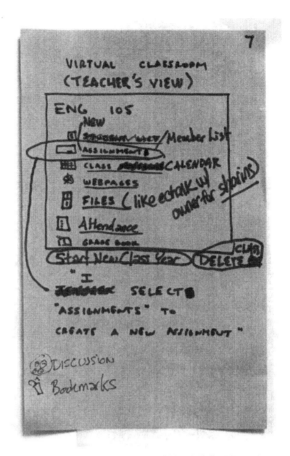

Figure 12-4: Close-up view of frame seven from eChalk, which sets the context for the frames that follow.

The top portion of the frame in Figure 12-5 is the user's screen, drawn for reference to explain what is being done behind the scenes by the system. The bottom half of the frame describes the system behavior. Note the time of day as the story of the teacher's day moves along.

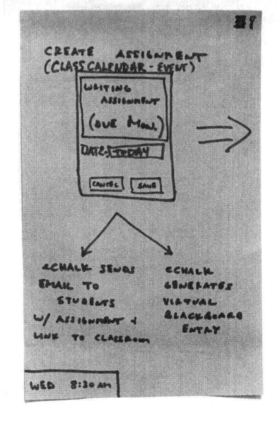
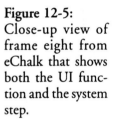

Figure 12-5: Close-up view of frame eight from eChalk that shows both the UI function and the system step.

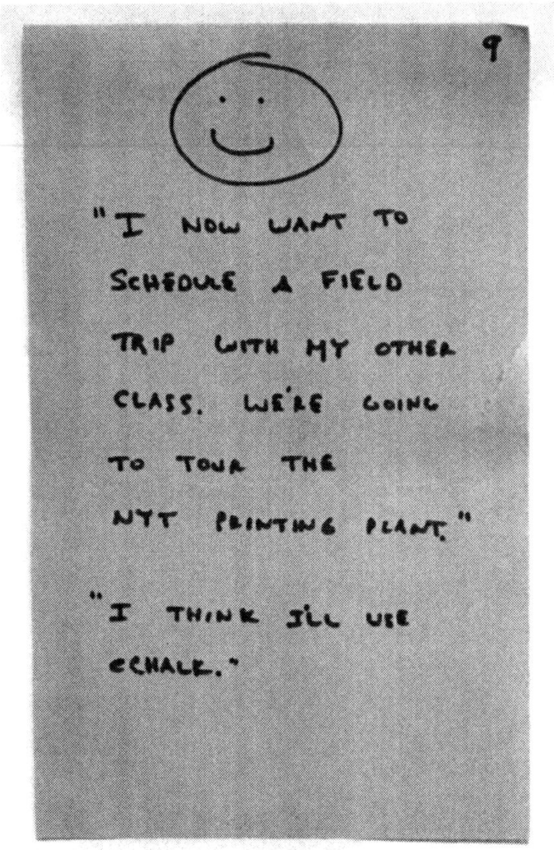

Figure 12-6:
Close-up of eChalk frame nine. This frame uses a manual step to tell the story and drive out the work the design must support.

A manual step makes the transition to the next task to be performed. Figure 12-6 shows the teacher's intent and task. It also shows how the eChalk tool is planned to be hooked into the overall process.

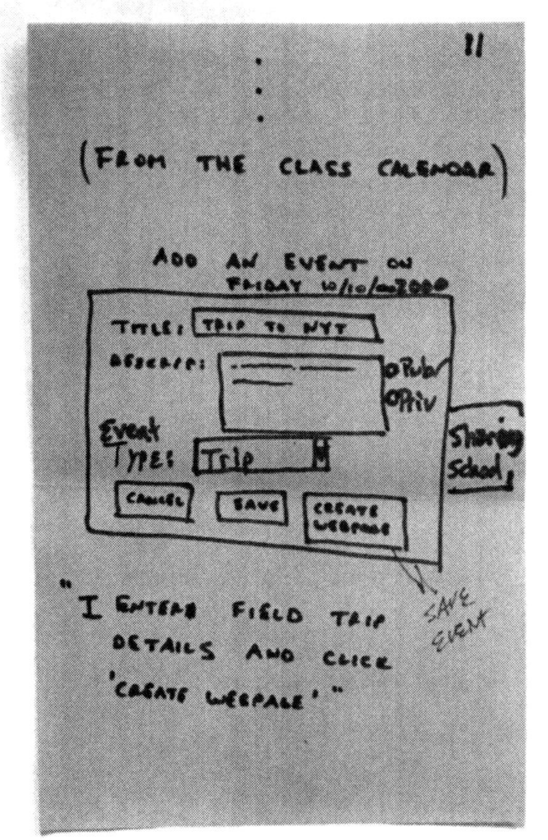

Figure 12-7:
Close-up of storyboard frame eleven. This frame is using a real case to reveal the needed function.

Figure 12-7 shows a screen interaction sketch, with real details about the field trip class event the user is creating. The details come from an actual field trip the team captured in a sequence model.

Figure 12-8 shows a more detailed view of a screen that is presented to the user, with enough UI details to make it clear what functionality needs to be available. Remember that this is not the real UI; the screen sketch is intended to capture only the functions that need to be present to do the task for the user.

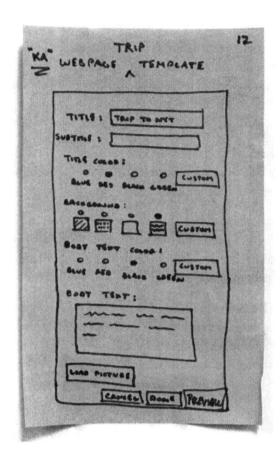

Figure 12-8:
Close-up of storyboard frame twelve that represents the needed functions without designing the actual UI.

Tips

Here are some tips about the storyboarding process.

- For storyboarding you are concerned with overall structure and function. *Do not* worry about precise language, icons, or layout. The real UI design will be created later.

- If you get stuck while drawing out the storyboard, go back and low-level vision the part you are stuck on.

- If you seem to keep generating new cases as you work out the sequence you have, ask yourself if these are cases that have appeared in the users' work and therefore must be dealt with, or if they are your idea of what might or could happen. Don't worry about logically deduced cases—get the known user cases right first.

Check storyboard against the consolidated sequence

When the storyboard is complete check it against the consolidated sequence models be sure that you have accounted for each step and intent in the sequence. "Accounted for" means that you have thought about how the step or intent will be achieved. It may be that you have decided that certain steps or intents will be supported the same way they are now with no change in your new design. Or you may have introduced new steps, new technology, or automation. This is a last pass quality check to be sure you did not break the work with your design.

Share the storyboard

If your team is larger than two people and you worked in parallel, share your storyboards after they are completed. This storyboard share is a review session to give each storyboard pair feedback on their work. Capture the issues gathered and then rework the storyboard.

If you are developing a system for in-house users, conduct a storyboard share with them. This is now a more formal presentation where you share your ideas on how their work will change and let them provide feedback and express concerns. So it needs to be planned for and moderated.

For this formal share, use a digital camera to photograph the storyboard frames and project each one in a slide show to project the storyboard in a large room. If you have been sharing the data with this group all along, there is no need for a slide show or wall walk to share the data. If you have not shared the findings and your vision do this first.

When you are ready to share the storyboard frames, project each one and capture issues by hand on each frame. You can bring along the paper storyboards and add a Post-it® to the affected frame so you can go back later and redesign to address the issues. This allows the stakeholders to feel "heard" as they publicly see you putting up their issues.

To run any storyboard share, hang the:

- Consolidated vision

- Storyboard

- Sequence that was the basis for the storyboard

For this meeting to be an effective review with your team, all team members need to be present. You don't want to do this over and over and get feedback one piece at a time. So hold one meeting and tell those that can't make it that they are giving up their opportunity for input. One way to manage time for Rapid CD is to be clear about expectations for participation.

For any storyboard share meeting identify a moderator to run the meeting. This will be one team member. The moderator keeps the meeting focused and on pace. He or she will also decide what discussions should be continued or deferred to a later time. The storyboard will be presented by two of the people from the storyboard team: the presenter and the Pen.

To share a storyboard, the presenter:

- Introduces the sequence or task that the storyboard addresses at a high level to orient the viewers.

- Walks each storyboard frame in order, describing what is happening on it.

- Listens for feedback, issues, or design ideas from the participants writing them on Post-its® and posting them to the relevant frame.

As the presenter talks, the Pen annotates the storyboard for anything the presenter says that they forgot to write on the storyboard. This is another informal quality check.

While the presenter is walking through the storyboard, reviewers should be looking for:

- Missing or confusing aspects of the storyboard
- Violations of user work practice as collected in the user data
- Inconsistency with the vision
- Opportunities for more improvement to the work
- Worries about technology or user acceptance
- Violations of planned business process change
- Inconsistencies with the business mission

Team members also can write their issues or design ideas on Post-it® notes and stick them on the storyboard frame they are related to.

Note: Resolution of issues or adoption of design ideas is the work of the storyboard team. The whole group asks questions to understand the design and the design choices, but they do not engage in resolving issues together in the share session. That's the job of the storyboard team when they rework the storyboard.

Rework the storyboard

The storyboard team takes the notes from the share session and decides how to change the storyboard, and then reworks it using the same storyboarding process.

One rework is sufficient. There is no need to reshare the reworked storyboard unless you want to. Again, remember the storyboard is on its way to testing with users through mock-up interviews. Too much rework just wastes time better spent with the user.

Go on to the next storyboard

Once you are finished with one storyboard, go on to the next piece of the consolidated vision that needs to be storyboarded. You will create a storyboard for each of your major tasks that are affected by the vision. You may have four to ten storyboards depending on the complexity of your problem, each with its own branches. Your goal is to cover the key tasks that the users will engage in to get their work done that are touched by introducing your new technology.

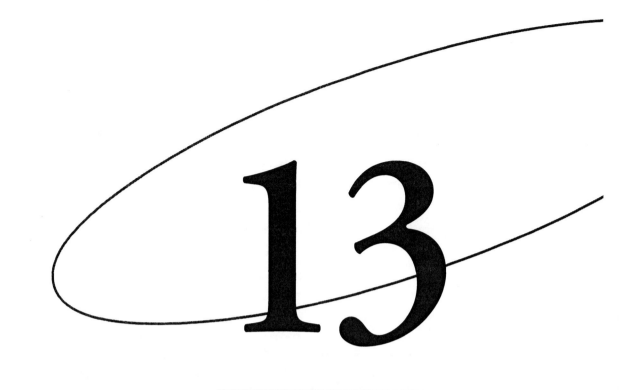

Testing with Paper Prototypes

Rapid CD Process	Lightning Fast	Lightning Fast +	Focused Rapid CD
Paper Mock-up Interviews with Interpretation		✓	✓

After visioning or developing a list of recommendations, the team will work out their first cut at how to present their redesign and new function to the users. In Lightning Fast + the team will use whatever methods they have in the past to come up with a first cut at a user interface. In Focused Rapid CD you worked out the new work practice and system in your storyboards. Now you need to abstract out the elements of the design that will define the system and the user interface (UI). Whichever process you have chosen, you need a way to define the first cut of your function and your UI.

But this function and initial layout is as yet untested with users. To test your design concepts and clarify your function we recommend constructing a paper prototype and testing it with your user population in paper prototype field interviews.

In this chapter we introduce how to build a paper prototype including how your storyboard will drive identifying the functions to include. In Chapter 14 we describe the paper prototype field interview designed to test and iterate your initial design.

A paper prototype invites users to codesign the solution with the interviewer. The unfinished paper representation that clearly is not fully designed communicates better than words that users can add to and change the design to better support their tasks. By asking users to perform their real-life tasks in the paper system, users immerse themselves in the detail of the design in the context of a real-life case. When you observe and talk with them about their response to the system, you can tell whether or not the proposed design is working. If not, the interviewer suggests design changes by physically altering the prototype in the moment. In this way the team gets feedback on the design and fleshes out final requirements for the system.

The paper prototype interview is a two-on-one interview where one person interviews and the other takes notes. Following the interview, the interpretation session captures key issues that the team needs to address. We recommend multiple rounds of interviews with two to four users to allow the team to iterate the design based on user feedback. After each round of prototype interviews the team makes changes and then tests again.

See Chapter 17, "Prototyping as a Design Tool," pg. 367, and Chapter 18, "From Structure to User Interface," pg. 381, in *Contextual Design: Defining Customer-Centered Systems.*[1]

Definition

A paper prototype is a paper representation of your product. Constructed out of Post-it® notes, various other pieces of paper, or any other materials you need to use, it allows you to test your design with the user interactively. Everything in the prototype needs to be movable and changeable because you will be adding user content, changing the interface structure, and otherwise modifying it in response to the customer trying to use it. The paper prototype is used in a paper prototype field interview conducted with the user at their work site.

Key concepts

Paper mock-up. Term used interchangeably with prototype; that is, paper mock-up, paper mock-up interview.

Paper prototype interview. Type of field interview conducted in the user's workspace using the paper prototype in a "let's pretend" situation to accomplish the user's real tasks. The interviewer manipulates the parts of the mock-up changing function and structure in response to the user's needs and tasks. There is no pre-defined user task as is common in a usability test.

Wire frame. A computer-drawn user interface that represents the basic user interaction design including layout, simple buttons, and plain content. It does not include any visual or aesthetic design. We sometimes use these in the second and third round of paper mock-up interviews to get a head start on the final user interface design. But we cut all the pieces out so it is still a movable mock-up, not a presentation of the proposed interface.

Visual design. The visual or aesthetic look of a user interface displayed on a computer screen or other device. Color, shape, size, and style are used to support and enhance the function or use of the interface.

Paper prototyping process

☐ Preparation

    ☐ Plan your rounds of iteration

    ☐ Prepare data and space

☐ Build your paper prototypes

    ☐ Walk storyboards to identify components

    ☐ Brainstorm and define UI concepts

    ☐ Share all UIs

    ☐ Build the prototypes

☐ Change the design based on user feedback

    ☐ Build subsequent prototypes to test with users

Plan your rounds of iteration

In Rapid CD you want to balance testing the vision and function with very fast iterations. In projects with new product concepts or significant new function, use three rounds of prototypes testing three to four users in a round covering two to three roles. In projects that are adding function to an existing system or where the system components being built are small in scope use two rounds of mock-ups with three to four users covering one to two roles.

In projects with three rounds of paper prototypes, the rounds should follow the following plan.

- First round—very rough prototypes with everything hand-drawn on Post-it® notes and paper. The intent is to test the vision and structure of the design and not the UI. Hand-drawn prototypes can be produced within a day and since the team does not yet know what function will be validated or changed, creating wire frames is a waste of time. (See the box, **Why build initial prototypes on paper—why not use online wire frames?**)

- Second round—more refined, but still rough prototypes with some work done online if you choose to make generating the prototype easier. The intent is to clean up the structure of the design and speed up the creation process.

- Third round—more refined, wire frame prototypes with enough definition of the UI design to test it and the content of the prototype. The intent is to make sure the user interaction design and words work for the user.

In smaller projects with two rounds of paper prototype interviews, the rounds should follow the following plan:

- First round—more refined, but still rough prototypes. We still recommend starting with paper to get a quick first version and maximize the invitation to the user to change the function and layout. But this can include more detailed function integrated with your already existing function in the current product. We assume that you are extending function in an existing system so that you are fitting in with an existing UI paradigm that will not change. We also assume that this is a less comprehensive redesign, and we do not need to test the vision and the structure of the design as thoroughly as we would in a larger project. So for some changes, if you are adding only one to two functions to an existing user interface, add a Post-it® with the function to a screen dump of the system to focus the user on the change.

- Second round—more refined, wire frame prototypes with enough definition of the UI design to test it and the content of the prototype. The intent is to make sure the user interaction design and words work for the user.

Tip: Once you start using wire frames, you can begin building up a library of reusable UI parts. This will help speed up the process the next time you have to build prototypes. But you don't want to automatically start your next prototype by building from your last one, because this could discourage you from trying a totally new approach.

Why build initial prototypes on paper—why not use online wire frames?

Paper mock-ups and paper mock-up interviews are now used everywhere for user interface development, although this was not so when we first developed CD. (Kyng's article is the classic on this topic. Snyder's book is a more recent resource.[2]) Paper mock-up interviews work as a means of testing systems because users understand user interfaces. They do not understand models like the UED or OO.[3] Nor can they easily imagine a new work practice from storyboard review. After all, if the customers' awareness of their work is tacit, they are not going to be able to articulate what might work and might not work within a meeting setting.

So to test a system's acceptance and function we take out a representation of the system in paper—complete with movable buttons, menus, content layout, and other aspects of the proposed user interface. Paper is eminently practical for helping the user focus on the structural aspects of the design—when a window is drawn by hand, it's pretty clear that icon design, precise layout, and fancy direct manipulation are not the important points. When users interact with paper they aren't distracted by fancy user interfaces; they have to focus on structure. Even house architects, who aren't constrained by writing code, prefer to communicate their first ideas to clients as sketches rather than finished drawings.

The very nature of a paper prototype invites change. When the user gets to a window in the prototype and says, "But now I need to do *this*," it's easy to add the function right on the window. It's easy to invite users into a discussion of what they need, why they need it, and which of several alternatives would better meet their need. It's easy to move into codesign of the system. No running prototype or prototyping tool can ever be as fast as paper or as inviting of codesign.

So rather than taking out running prototypes or even printouts of completed interaction or visual designs, we start with paper. After the first round or two of testing when the parts of the system and the layout start to stabilize you can build very simple wire frames with no color. But we take these wire frame representations to the user as cutouts in paper. The wire frames speed up the development of the next iteration—it is one step on the way to the final interaction design. But the cutouts and the extra parts and pens brought along to the interview still invite change.

It is important that you do not start with a finished visual design. One of the main purposes of any visual design is to support the function and content of the system. Since the function and content are not yet final, there is no way to know what the visual design should even support. If you start your visual design now, it will need to be altered every time the prototype is changed, which will result in a lot of wasted work.

Prepare data and space

To start building prototypes for a UI, hang all of your storyboards up in your team room if you have them. You will also need materials to create the prototypes. If you are building a prototype for a device or other piece of hardware you will need to adapt this list to include appropriate materials for your product.

- Cardboard poster board or card stock sheets (9x12, 11x14, or 11x17) for prototype backgrounds

- Full size (8.5x11) and half-size (5.5x8.5) sheets of paper for screens, web pages, and big dialog boxes

- Printouts of content you may want to include by cutting it up and laying it out differently, particularly useful for web page design

- Post-its® in all sizes and colors—1x2, 2x3, 3x3, 3x5, 4x6—used for everything from large buttons to pull-down menus to dialog boxes to small windows

- Post-it® flags for tabs

- Round stickers or dots for buttons

- Removable tape to stick the parts together and move them easily

- Correction fluid in case you make a mistake

- Sharpie® Extra Fine Point pens—enough blue, red, black, and green for each person. You want to use extra fine tip instead of ball point or other types of pens so your text will be clear enough to read.

- Highlighters in multiple colors

- Scissors

- Overheads to create overlays of function if needed

- For hardware or hand-held prototypes, boxes in various sizes or children's toys

- Folders or envelopes for storing different pieces of the prototype (optional)

Look at how we used the supplies to create the paper prototype in Figure 13-1. The cardboard is the base for a multi-paned design. The parts representing different concepts are placed on separate pieces of paper and movable Post-it® notes. We even made columns on paper to test information layout in a spreadsheet or chart.

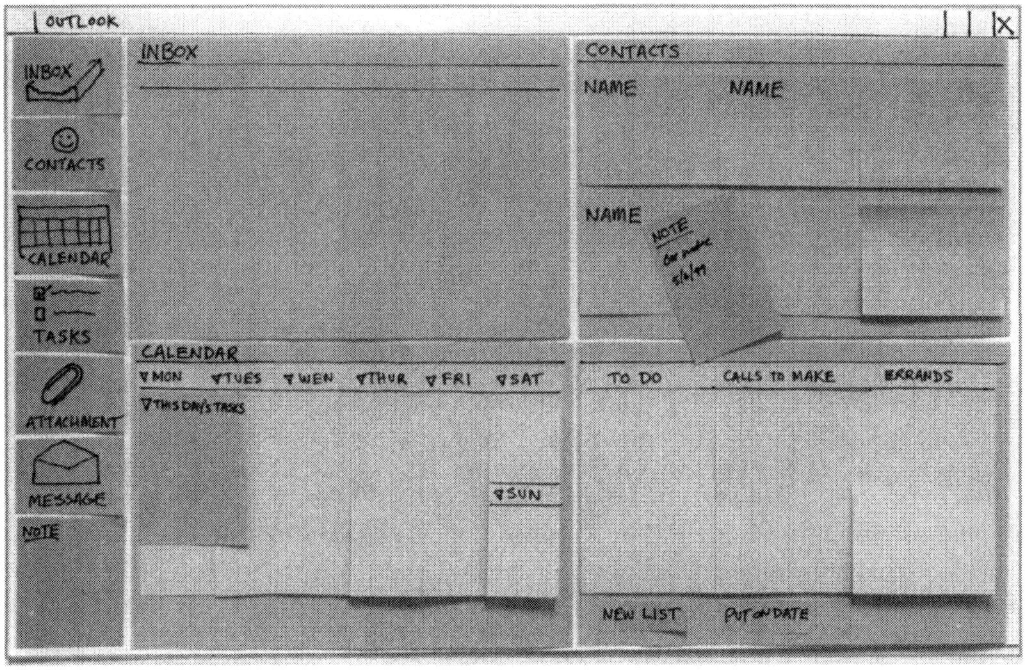

Figure 13-1: Sample paper prototype for testing function and information layout.

Walk storyboards to identify components

If you have used a different process to define your function and UI layout you will skip this step. But if you have created storyboards you are now ready to abstract out the function you need to present based on your detailed design of the new work or life process you want to introduce.

To abstract the needed function, rewalk the storyboards identifying the core components of the system represented and their function. Components will likely be used in more than one storyboard so you will need to walk them all to collect the function implied by the storyboard relevant to a certain component. Choose someone to tell each storyboard story. As you are walking through each of the storyboards write down the major parts of the new system that will be relevant to the users along with the key functions and any automation or business rules.

You can make a simple list of components with their characteristics or do quick UI drawings taken from the storyboard indicating the needed functions. But watch out, different storyboards will reuse these same components so just add to them. And be careful not to create components with overlapping function—merge components that belong together.

For Rapid CD we recommend moving straight from the storyboards to the user interface mock-ups. If you have a complex system or want a more formal specification and system layout consider using the User Environment Design formalism (see the box, **User Environment Design helps see system structure**).

When you are done you should have a set of user interface components with the initial layout implied by the storyboard filled in with the function implied in the storyboard. This is not your interface design; this is just your "notes" or specifications for the user interface.

Before you are done step back and examine the components and their content. Ask yourself:

- Does each component hang together to support a coherent task or role?
- Are there too many components, should you combine some into a more coherent interface?
- Are the links between components clear?
- Is the function within each component clearly supporting the component's purpose?
- Is it overly complicated? Can the function be simplified?
- Did you make sure you did not add functionality that is not in the storyboards or supported by the customer data?

Once you are satisfied that you have a good set of parts to start with you can brainstorm alternative user interface concepts. This is a similar process to visioning, but now you are focused on how the UI would be put together to define the function laid out in the storyboards or identified by other methodologies (see Chapter 15, "Rapid CD and Other Methodologies").

User Environment Design helps see system structure

For Rapid CD we recommend that you skip creating a formal User Environment Design (UED) and go straight to the user interface structure. But for complex projects and systems, for doing a competitive analysis, or for analyzing a planned design to find potential problems you should consider using the UED formalism.

A good product, system, or web page must have the appropriate function and structure to support a natural workflow within it. System design really has three layers. The user interface accesses the function, structure, and flow necessary to support the user's redesigned work. The implementation makes that function, structure, and flow happen. But the core of a product is that middle layer: the explicit work the system is performing. Just as architects draw floor plans to see the structure and flow of a house, designers need to see the "floor plan" of their new system. Hidden within the storyboards are the implications for the system floor plan—the UED.

The UED formalism represents a set of "focus areas" or places in the system that provide support for coherent activities. A place might be a window, web page, dialog box, or pane. The UED shows each part of the system—how it supports the customer's work, exactly what function is available in that part, and how the customer gets to and from other parts of the system—without tying this structure to any particular user interface or implementation design. The function in the UED drives functional specification and implementation level use cases. The function in each focus area becomes the specification for the part of the user interface that will support that function.

In creating a UED the team walks the storyboards and abstracts out the implications of what the system needs to provide. As the implications of storyboard after storyboard are rolled into the UED creating focus areas, functions, and links the team starts to see the best way to structure the system. This system structure now represents the system that, if built, will actualize the vision as it has been worked out in the storyboards.

But whether this system will be valued by the users has yet to be tested. And any design team can anticipate needed function only up to a point. So after working out the preliminary UED, the team mocks up each focus area in paper and tests it in mock-up interviews. Through iteration with the users, the UED stabilizes, the user interface paradigm stabilizes, and the lower level requirements are solidified.

For a thorough discussion of the User Environment see Chapters 14 through 16, starting at pg. 295 in *Contextual Design: Defining Customer-Centered Systems*.

Brainstorm and define interface components

At this point in the process the team should have members who are UI and graphics designers. If not, now is the time to bring them on-board to help you work out the initial user interface design and continue in the process to the final design. If you are bringing in people who have not been involved directly with the project, have them walk the data and share the vision and storyboards with them.

You should also already know what platform you are developing for: web, desktop, mobile, and so forth. You should also know what, if any, corporate or legal user interface standards you need to comply with and what technology constraints you have. Your goal is to develop a rough UI concept for each UI component representing the function you need to present within a reasonable UI layout.

If you have a larger team, you can break into two pairs with a user interface designer in each pair to develop components in parallel. But make sure to divide the design into discrete components or sections so the design will hang together when complete. If you have only one UI designer let him or her float between groups.

In order to develop the UI design:

- Brainstorm ideas for how to represent the component, sketching out your ideas on a flipchart so everyone can see and participate.

- Develop multiple alternatives (see Figure 13-2).

- Run through pluses and minuses for each of the brainstormed ideas.

- Overcome the minuses. Brainstorm solutions for each minus.

- If there is more than one alternative, choose one. Remember, in order to drive innovation choose the more radical of the ideas to test with users. You can include prototypes pieces for both designs if you want, so you have quick access to the alternative idea during the mock-up interview if it is needed.

- Sketch out the final user interface on a flipchart when you are finished including all the function. This will act as a guide when people are making the prototypes (see Figure 13-3). It will be difficult for UI designers to keep this rough. The natural tendency of most designers is to be very detailed so watch out and don't lose time putting in details you don't need.

- Run a real user work case through the prototype components to make sure you have all the function you need for your typical case. If you have a sequence that would use this component walk through each step and see if your mock-up can support the overall work. You can use several actual sequences to check if you have the flow and function you need to complete each task. Update the interface function if needed.

Figure 13-2:
Sample paper prototype component sketch showing two UI choices. The team chooses one to test with users.

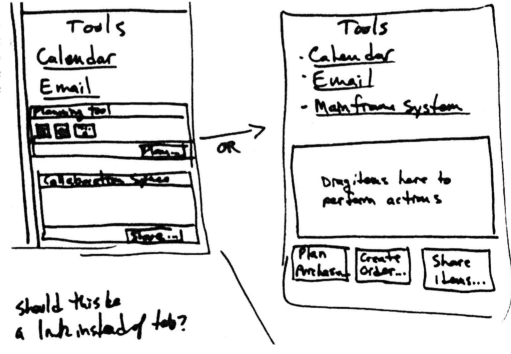

Don't spend more than a day working out the design for the first round of paper prototypes. You don't want to be focused on minor details and finishing the design at this point. You want to capture only the major components and features of the design. You only need a rough idea of placement for your UI elements. For Rapid CD your scope should be small enough to complete this in a day.

And don't get attached to your ideas. It is very common for at least some part of the design to change drastically after the first round. Users will always surprise you with great ideas that you didn't think of. The best thing about developing a UI in a day is that it is easier to let go of ideas you didn't spend a lot of time developing.

Note: The first UI design should be rough and is intended to support only the initial paper prototype. With each round of paper prototyping the UI should be refined until it's complete.

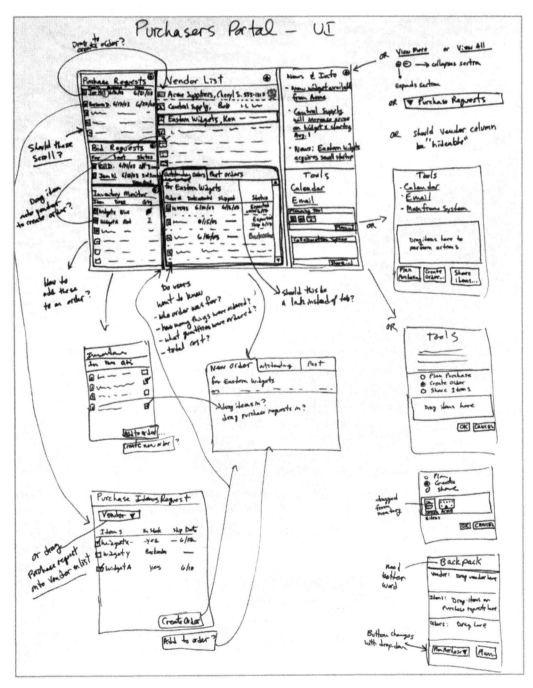

Figure 13-3: Example sketch of the final UI that will guide the team when making the prototypes.

Example: Purchasing

This sketch (Figure 13-4) shows the purchaser's portal, with multiple variations being drawn for several sections of the interface. You can see that issues and questions were also captured as the ideas were being worked through.

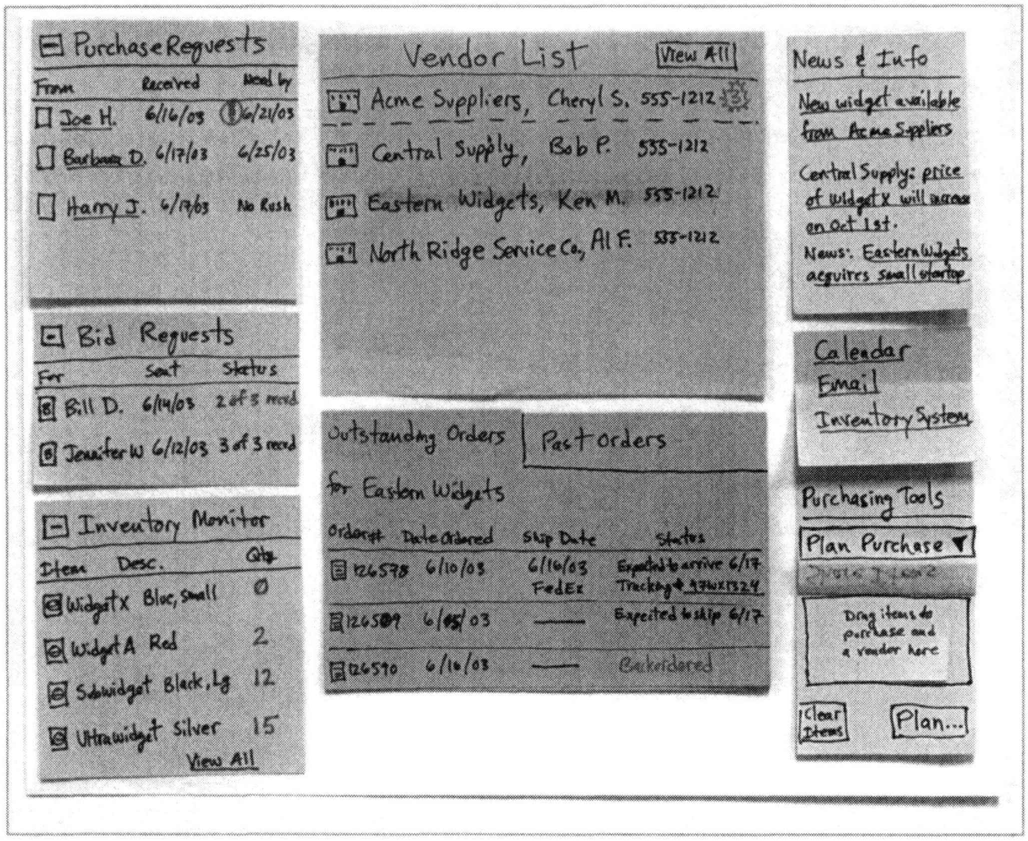

Figure 13-4:
This prototype for a purchaser's portal was hand drawn on Post-it notes, allowing the interviewers to easily move, modify, and add new content during the interview.

Share all UIs

If you have a larger team and have broken into subteams to work you need to share the designs. You can do this before you build the prototypes or after. The best time to share is before you build so that you don't have to make changes in the mock-ups. But often the design is not truly worked out until all the pieces have to be assembled. So consider running a review of the initial design and then a final review of the mock-up as well.

After each subteam completes its component of the initial UI design, it shares each design with the whole team and conducts pluses and minuses. Look for inconsistencies in paradigm and elements that were left out given the storyboards and vision. Capture the changes needed and agree upon consistency standards. But don't agonize about UI standards at this point. Minor inconsistency in paradigms and elements is not that critical in the first round. In fact, it can be useful to test different paradigms in the first round to get an idea of which will work best for the user. So if you really have two different concepts for the layout, test them both.

After you have shared and agreed on the design components you are ready to build the first prototype. Or if you have already built the mock-up, go back and make any necessary changes.

While you were reviewing the designs you may have identified key test issues—add these to your list of things to pay attention to in the mock-up interviews.

Build the prototypes

Use the various paper components to build the mock-ups. When you are building your first prototypes consider the following guidelines:

- Make sure that any part of the interface that might move or be moved is movable; for example, buttons, pull-down menus, sections of a web page that might be moved around, and so on.

- Create a link for every major UI component you are testing. You want to show a clear flow between your core parts but you do not need components for functions that are common, existing, and known functions, or other minor elements you are not really trying to get feedback about. Remember, this is a rough prototype; include what is necessary to focus the user on the parts of the system you want to discuss.

- Don't have hidden functions in the prototype UI. You have to represent each function on the prototype visually for it to be tested; that is, you can't have function represented only by keystrokes or right-clicking.

- Include example data or content, but make it removable. This content is intended to give the user a sense of context and to help them map the prototype to their current work. Don't present a bunch of blank screens with nothing on them. But, once you get in the interview, you will change the sample content to the user's real content.

- Include information content. If you are building a web site you must lay out all the content, taking out example pages for the user to test. Make sure the content and elements of the page are movable, but use real content. So if you have a product page on the site develop example product pages for the key lines and test the layout across product lines, using example pages to discuss the real product the user is looking for. Show this representative content in paper and then discuss how their particular product would be represented similarly. You can also go to the existing site to look at the real content and then discuss how it would be represented in paper.

- Create stimulus areas for new content. Sometimes the design implies presenting a new kind of content that you don't have or rewriting content in significantly new ways. You can create mock-ups that simply label sections with the type of content they will hold. For example a section called "value proposition" will stimulate a conversation about what the user would like to see. Or it can be a placeholder for the user's response to existing content of this type on the web.

After the first prototype is assembled, prior to taking it out to test with users, walk through all the parts of the mock-up it in its entirety to be sure all the pieces are there and that it hangs together. Make one complete copy of the prototype to review as a group to make sure that you haven't missed any pieces of your design (see the box, **Do you need a complete mock-up to start testing?**).

After any necessary minor changes, make enough copies for each interview you are conducting in this round. To save time, you can make the first copy by hand and photocopy the pieces for the other copies.

Before you go out to interview make sure that you organize all of the pieces and parts of the prototype so that they will be within easy reach during the interview. We often put them in manila folders labeled by component—one for each component. Use removable tape to secure components on the inside of the folder. Bring white poster board to be your screen or background and place it in front of the user.

Do you need a complete mock-up to start testing?

If your design is large and your time is short you might want to take out your components for testing in stages. Start testing the central or critical components and grow the mock-up over your rounds. Just watch out, be sure to test each component at least twice. You may need to add additional rounds if you test component by component. And be careful that you do test the system altogether or you might get good components that don't play well together.

As long as the prototype allows the customer to do at least one coherent piece of work, it can be tested. For example, the eChalk team's design had several components: e-mail, attendance taking and reporting, reporting student progress, and calendars. They could reasonably have gone out initially with any one of these pieces since each one represented a coherent task.

Example: eChalk

In Figure 13-5 you see some examples of eChalk's paper prototype from an early round of interviews. They have a combination of rough, hand-drawn elements along with pieces of prepared content photocopied and taped to the prototype.

Figure 13-5: Example of how eChalk mocked up their home page. During the interview, the user clicks on one of the buttons such as My Classes, and the interviewer opens the folded Post-it® to reveal the choices.

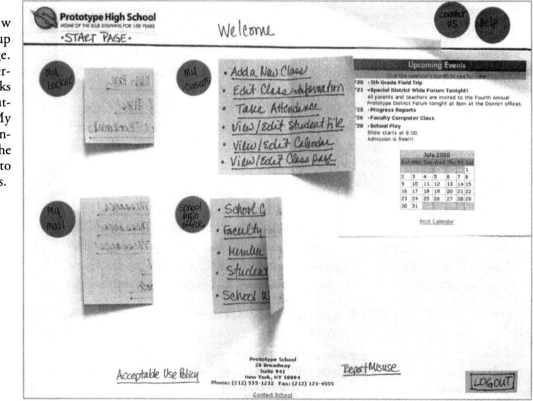

This approach let them immediately signal to their users that the prototype was meant to be changed, but saved the eChalk team time in not needing to create everything.

The eChalk team was testing the idea of being able to create events, which could be made visible to members of a group. Figure 13-6 shows this piece of their UI has all the functions designed by the team before going into the field for prototype interviews.

The UI is all on paper, including a combination of pre-existing screens or wire frames that were cut up and hand-drawn functions on Post-its®. When they went out for their interviews, the prototype was populated with the users' real world content.

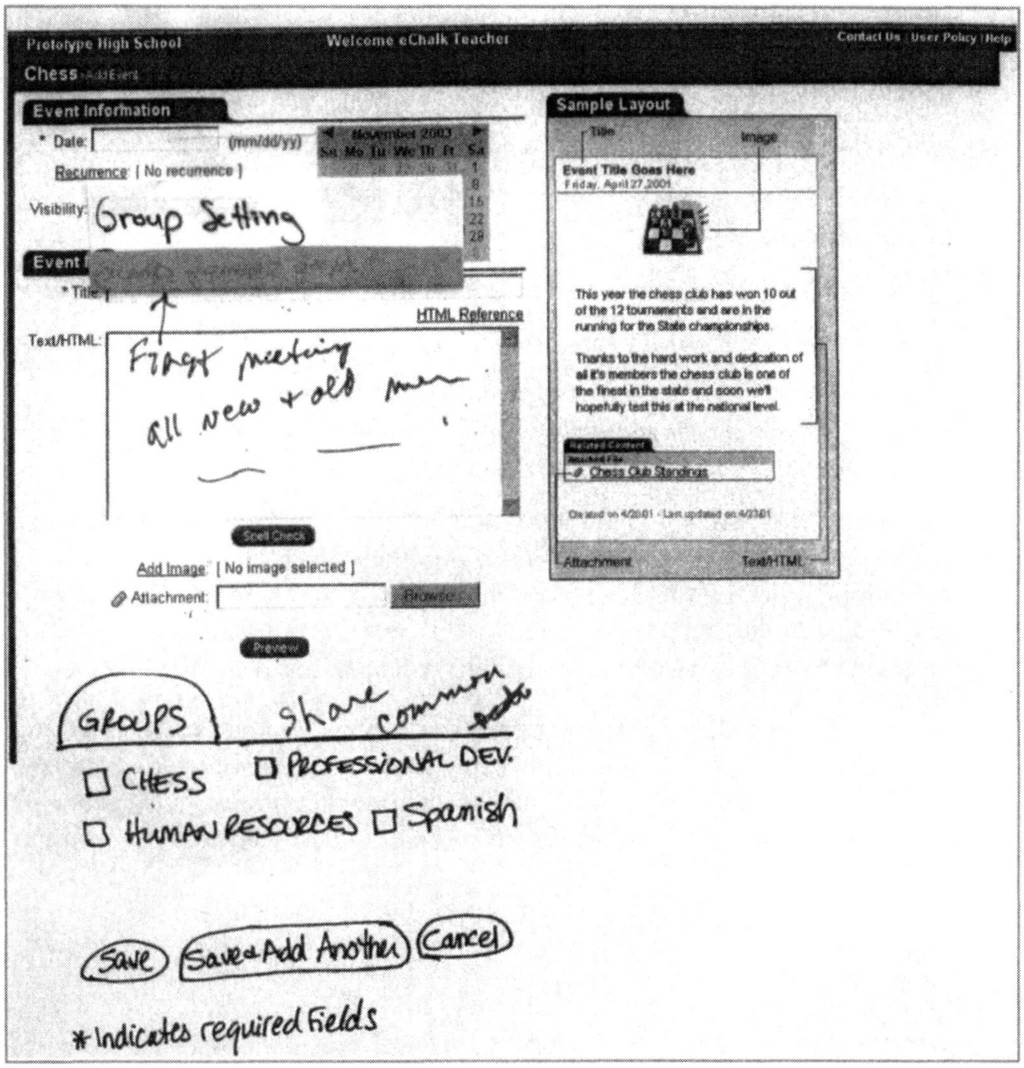

Figure 13-6: eChalk prototype that uses both wire-frames and hand-drawn Post-its®.

Build subsequent prototypes to test with users

After you complete your first round of prototype interviews and interpretation sessions (as described in Chapter 14) you will need to create the next round of prototypes. As you confirm pieces of your design you can turn them into wire frame drawings in the prototypes. Doing so allows you to get a jump on producing your final UIs. It also places emphasis on the parts of the design that you need to validate in your upcoming interviews.

If you are going to move to wire frame drawings in your prototypes make sure that you cut the pieces apart and that the prototype is still flexible enough to add users' content and change pieces of the prototype during the interview.

What is a wire frame?

A wire frame is a graphic representation of a UI element that has:

- Everything positioned as it would be in a real UI

- Relative sizes that are reasonably accurate

- Real words

- Borders between parts shown with simple lines

- Elements with simple shading for emphasis, but no gradients

- No worries about typefaces or color except to the extent that color carries semantic meaning

- No positioning to the pixel

- Minimal or no aesthetic appeal

- Simple aspects of visual design to reinforce the functions and content in the design—simple lines for borders, simple shading, and limited color to show which elements are conceptually or functionally related or prominent

As you move from the second to the third round of mock-ups continue to solidify your interaction design and layout so that the third round is much more complete than the first both in function, content, language, and layout. From here you can more easily move to the final interaction design and visual design (see the box, **Using running prototypes**). The mock-ups themselves act like specifications for the final design.

The next step in your process is to do the real visual design. You may have to rearrange content and even change some function slightly to make it work with a visual design. If you are designing to an existing GUI standard, that makes it easier. Throughout you will have been coordinating with developers to ensure that your UI design is implementable.

Using running prototypes

Toward the end of the prototype rounds, we use running prototypes to test low-level usability function that simply can't be tested on paper; for example, how well the user can manipulate a handle for an object in a drawing tool. Running prototypes help us test emulating the timing of content that updates automatically (as on a mobile device); live scanning of a web page, which is much different than scanning a piece of paper; and the physical sensation of pressing buttons and having something occur on a display screen.

$\longrightarrow$

We also use high fidelity completed web page designs displayed online to test alternative visual designs. This helps us determine optimal use of font, color, and spacing to promote scanning, test various layouts for relationship and prominence of elements and flow from one area to another, to test the "feel" of navigating from place to place, to test the physical experience of using a device such as a cell phone, and again, to test those interactions that can't be tested on paper. But these "design reviews" as we call them are not testing function; their intent is to test how well the visual design and layout support the design. Moreover, any of this testing comes after the mock-up testing has already solidified the system structure and function.

Running prototypes are also useful when you are designing a small extension to an already existing system, like a new section of a large web site. You can easily link to the existing system and test navigation, consistency, and flow between it and the new design.

Endnotes

[1] Also see Snyder, C. *Paper Prototyping: The Fast and Easy Way to Design and Refine User Interfaces.* Morgan Kaufmann Publishers. 2003.

[2] Kyng, M., "Designing for a Dollar a Day," in *Proceedings of the Conference on Computer-Supported Cooperative Work*, Sept. 26–28, 1988, p. 178. Portland, Oregon.

[3] Ehn, Pelle. *Work-Oriented Design of Computer Artifacts.* Gummessons, Falkoping, Sweden 1988, international distribution by Almqvist & Wiksell International, also Coronet Books, Philadelphia, PA.

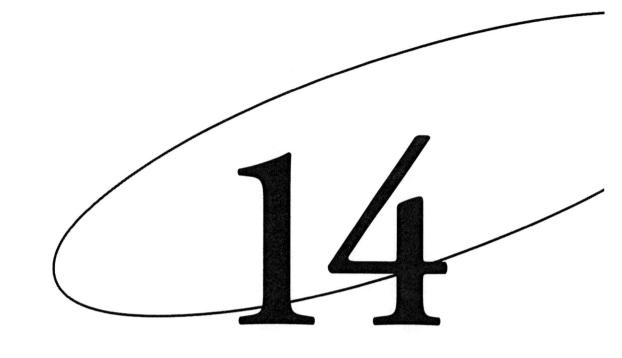

Paper Prototype Interviews

Rapid CD Process	Lightning Fast	Lightning Fast +	Focused Rapid CD
Paper Mock-up Interviews with Interpretation		✓	✓

Paper prototype or mock-up interviews help designers understand why design elements work or fail, and also identify new function. These interviews are based on the principles of Contextual Inquiry given earlier. We test the paper prototype with users in their own context, to keep them grounded in their real work practice. Users interact with the prototype by adding in their own content and manipulating and modifying the prototype. The partnership is one of codesign. As the user works with the prototype following a task they need to do or did in the recent past, the user and designer uncover problems and adjust the prototype to fix them. Together the user and interviewer interpret what is going on in the usage and come up with alternative designs.

You do not go into the mock-up interview to validate your design, but rather to work with the user to try to break it. If the prototype stands up under use, you know, in fact, that your design is good.

Conduct a mock-up interpretation session within 24 hours of each interview to capture the key issues and any new function. After each round of interviews redesign the prototype and test it again in the next round. Through this iterative process you ensure that the design has the function and the user interaction layout that best suits your users.

This chapter will prepare you for how to run and interpret a paper prototype field interview. It covers the types of information you should look for in an interview, and how to approach users and let them know what you plan to accomplish while you are with them. It also covers how to conduct a mock-up interpretation session. See Chapter 4, "The Contextual Inquiry Interview," for more information on interviewing and handling unexpected situations.

See Chapter 19, "Iterating with a Prototype," pg. 293, in *Contextual Design: Defining Customer-Centered Systems*.

Definition

Paper prototype or mock-up interviews are two-on-one interviews conducted in the user's workspace that focus on observations of the user using the prototype to do his or her work. The interviewer offers suggested design changes based on the user's response, and together they change the prototype in the moment to better suit the work's needs. Unlike CI interviews, paper prototype interviews require two interviewers, and the user will not get much work done during the interview. One interviewer runs the interview, another takes notes. In the interview the notetaker is a silent observer; the primary interaction remains one-on-one between the interviewer and the user.

Key concepts

Context. Understand user needs in the context of their work by walking through the prototype with a real-life case and physically interacting with the mock-up.

Partnership. Work with users as partners in codesign, modify the prototype as you go.

Interpretation. Create a shared understanding of the user's response to the mock-up and suggest design changes and function additions in response to user needs.

Focus. Listen and probe from a focus on how the prototype is supporting the user work, starting with a focus on structure and moving to a focus on interaction design over rounds of iterations. Challenge your assumptions about favorite design elements.

Paper prototype process

☐ Preparation

    ☐ Set up mock-up interview visits

    ☐ Schedule enough time to iterate the design and prototypes

    ☐ Get organized before you leave the office

☐ Conducting the mock-up interview

    ☐ (Optional) Give an introductory talk

    ☐ Go to the workspace

    ☐ Run the interview

☐ Conduct interpretation session

    ☐ Iterate the design

    ☐ Finalize the design

Set up mock-up interview visits

Once you complete your initial field interviews and develop your design concepts, if you are running mock-up interviews you need to set up these visits. You will want to find new interviewees with the same job roles you targeted in the initial study, but only those for whom you have designed a solution. You can reuse one or two of your participants or places but you want to expand into new users and places to ensure that your design ideas will support the population, not just those people. You do not go back to users from previous paper prototype rounds.

The mock-up interviews last the same length of time as a CI, about two hours. And like CIs, you may get pushed back from high-level managers but don't schedule anything shorter than one hour or it will be unlikely that you will have enough time to watch them work inside of the mock-up and then codesign together.

Your mock-up interviews will be conducted in two or three rounds. You want to cover each job role supported in each round. You don't want to interview more than four people in a round. The best results occur when you talk with at least three people in each job role. Plan your rounds accordingly.

As with Contextual Interviews, the day before the interview, call the user to confirm. Deal with any confidentiality issues during this call. At this point the confidentiality may be on your side—you may want them to sign a nondisclosure since you are showing them your new design.

Explain that paper prototype interviews are a pretend situation and that the user will not get much, if any, real work done during the interview. You still want to make sure that the user does not clean up and that they do have some relevant tasks to do—although it will be a "Let's pretend" situation in the mock-up.

Caution: If you are rolling out your prototype in parts you may have support only for certain tasks. Make sure that the users you pick are playing the role or doing the task that your prototype supports.

Schedule enough time to iterate the design and prototypes

Paper prototype interviews should be clustered together within a week to allow for time to interpret the interview, adjust the design, and build new prototypes. Paper prototype interview weeks could look like the schedule in Table 14-1 (see Chapter 2 for other schedule plans).

Monday	Tuesday	Wednesday	Thursday	Friday
ALL DAY Conduct Round 1, two paper prototype interviews at one location/	AM Conduct Round 1, third user. PM Interpret paper prototype interviews with at least one helper.	ALL DAY Interpret paper prototype interviews with at least one helper.	ALL DAY Determine changes needed to UI.	Rebuild paper prototype. Make copies for next week's interviews if done.

Table 14-1: Possible paper prototyping schedule.

If you are going to create wire frames between one round and the next allow more time for building the prototype. If you have a complex system with many parts, you will need to schedule more time between rounds to get the work done. Or test the prototype in parts targeted at different roles in each round and do more iterations. A Rapid CD process works best if you are targeting one to three job types; more than that will take longer.

Get organized before you leave the office

Being prepared for the paper prototype is critical. Be sure you have one entire prototype for each interview and know where to find all the individual pieces. But don't be overly worried that occasionally it might take you a few moments to find a piece during the interview. You can always tell the user that "the server or web site is temporarily slow right now, bear with me." The user will be understanding.

Have a kit of prototype supplies with you so you can modify the prototype when working with the user. Decide in advance with your interview partner who is going to be the interviewer, and who will be the notetaker. You can also decide that one of you will start the interview, and at a logical break midway you will explicitly change roles. If you are going to switch tell the user at the start of the interview and again when you are about to make the switch in the interview.

Give an introductory talk

As with the Contextual Interview, you may find it necessary to brief the users, sales, and management. If your interviews are in homes you can use the same type of introduction to the family if you are planning on interviewing more than one of them. Then just start with one person and move to the next.

This time your introduction will include telling them the progress of your project and showing them the mock-up so they can understand what is about to happen. Emphasize that this is not a demo or sales call, and that they will be doing real tasks using their real data or information but with the paper system. Emphasize that this is a codesign situation and that everything is changeable—display your extra Post-its® and UI parts.

Finally, clarify that this is a prototype, that the company will come out with new features but that the time frame is currently not fixed. One worry organizations often have is that by showing the prototype they are promising to deliver what the user sees. Ensure your own marketing department that you will emphasize that you are in predevelopment and that you will need to create a rollout plan once the design is stable. If you do have a delivery projection you can share this if it is in the interest of your business.

Keep the introduction short and informal. You are just letting the interviewees and the stakeholders at that business know what is about to happen for buy-in. If you have only one user at a business you don't need to do this step.

Go to the work space

Even though we are engaging the user in a "let's pretend" situation you still need to run the interview in their real work environment. During the interview you will enter real data, have them move between the paper and their other related systems, and you may even show them content currently on a web site and discuss how it will fit within the mock-up. So run the interviews in their workspace.

On your way to the user's desk make the most use of your time, take notes, ask questions; you may even be able to do the majority of your introduction while you are walking to the user's desk. Talk about your focus. Ask the user about the work they currently are doing.

Run the interview

Paper prototypes follow the same structure as CI interviews. They also take about two hours to conduct. This section outlines the parts of the interview.

The introduction

The introduction should take up no more than the first 10 to 15 minutes of the interview. You'll want to cover what a prototype interview is in your introduction, and you should expect to reinforce it through your actions throughout the interview.

Introduce yourself, your focus, and the interviewing method. This is the time to introduce yourself, the project focus, and to make sure the user understands what you are trying to learn. Explain to the user that you will introduce him to the prototype and ask that he "do" his work with it.

You will also explain the reasoning behind using paper. Tell the user that you expect him to make changes to the prototype, to add or subtract functionality, and to brainstorm with you solutions to problems he encounters using the prototype in the interview.

Set expectations for the length of the interview. Tell the user that you plan to be with him for the next two hours. If, prior to the interview, the user agreed to only an hour or one and a half hours use this time to find out if you can run longer.

Reassure the user that everything that is said in the interview is confidential. Tell him that his identity will be replaced with a user number and that he is free to say anything.

Identify a starting point in the prototype. If you haven't already, ask the user about his work. Get an overview of the user's background and role as it pertains to your focus, as well as any demographic information about the user or the organization that is relevant to you. Listen to the type of tasks they need to do that day or have done in the recent past. Once you find some that match what you want to cover in the prototype you are ready to transition to the mock-up part of the interview.

Establish the roles of the interview. Explain to the user that the primary interviewer will be acting as the prototype's CPU, responding to his actions in the prototype and that the second interviewer is a silent notetaker. Tell the user that you expect him to write on the prototype, move pieces around so that they make sense or are better organized, and to take pieces away if necessary.

Example script: eChalk
Let me start by telling you a bit about this project and what we are trying to do. We have been interviewing teachers, principals, and administrative staff in different kinds of schools in different cities. We observed people, including teachers like you, as they

communicated with their colleagues, parents, and students. In addition, we also observed how teachers performed other classroom tasks such as creating lesson plans, assigning homework, taking attendance, and producing progress reports. From that data we've built a paper mock-up of how we envision the work being conducted with better support from our eChalk product. We want to get your feedback on what we've developed. We'll be asking you to pretend to use this paper system to help us understand if it will work for you, and as a means of engaging you in codesign of the solution. You may get a bit of the real job done—doing it first for real and then replaying it in the mock-up—but you will not get much work done.

(Interviewer points to paper prototype, letting the user see that it is made up of Post-its®.) Before we develop this, we want to test it with people to be sure that it really works for them. That's why we have a paper system here. To be sure that it really does work for you, you'll be using this as though it was a live product. You can see that I have this bag of supplies with me (points out supply kit). This is a test of the prototype, not of you—it's our job to make the prototype work for you. If something doesn't work for you, I'll be tearing off the paper and changing it so it does work. We want to put this prototype through its paces, and "kick the tires." So, we expect to make a lot of changes to it and will be disappointed if we don't!

My partner is acting as our human video recorder, so he'll be silently writing down everything we do and say.

So, let's start by getting a bit of an overview of what you do that involves communicating with colleagues, students, and parents; and taking attendance, creating lesson plans, and other tasks.

The transition

The transition phase is a brief (two minute), but explicit part of the interview process. During the introduction you are not merely getting acquainted, you are also looking for relevant tasks or work the user performs that you can ask him or her to do or re-create for you in the prototype. The transition is a critical piece of the interview. The transition is the part of the interview where you move out of the question and answer mode of the introduction and into using the prototype.

Clearly shift from traditional interview mode to prototype mode. Introduce the new system in two to three sentences describing its basic structure. Bring out the prototype. If your prototype is easily recognizable let the user figure it out for himself. You want to give the user an opportunity to orient himself and identify the pieces and parts of the prototype without leaving him adrift and overwhelmed by what he is looking at.

If your prototype is a drastic departure from what the user is currently using you may need to introduce the prototype and its major components. Whatever you do, do not demo the prototype, or go into "do you like our product" mode. Give the user only enough information to orient him to the prototype and associate it with his work. Use the following example script as a starting place for your interview transition.

Example script: eChalk
I think I have a good idea of your role here. Let's get started using the prototype. Here is the opening screen. And here is your combination mouse and keyboard (gives the user a pen). You told me that one of your primary tasks is communicating assignments, exams, and projects to your students, and you need to assign a new project that will last five days. Take a minute to get oriented to the screen. (Pauses while the user looks it over.) How do you think you'd get started in setting up the project?

The interview

Make it clear that the user should start performing real work tasks. During this time observe the user performing her work in the prototype. Let the user do her work, but stop the user and offer interpretations about what you have observed. Suggest design ideas by bringing out or drawing new parts of the system.

Choose a starting approach for working with the user

Some users like to explore and some will start right away with a task. Pick an approach and let the user indicate which way she wants to move through the prototype.

Observe, discuss, and make design changes

You set the tone and rules of the interview session. If you start by doing a demo of the software she will act like this is a demo and ask questions. If you respond to comments about the details of the user interface—like names of things and icons—she will think you are interested in that level of response.

Since you are focused on testing the structure, function, and overall UI layout, don't follow up on those questions. Just change the work or the icon to whatever the user requests. It is very important to make those changes for the user. In fact, look for an opportunity to make a change as soon as possible. Even a small change signals the user that you really do want to change the prototype to meet her needs.

Figure 14-1 shows a marked up section of the eChalk prototype. Notice the changes that the user made, she both added and removed function from this piece of the design.

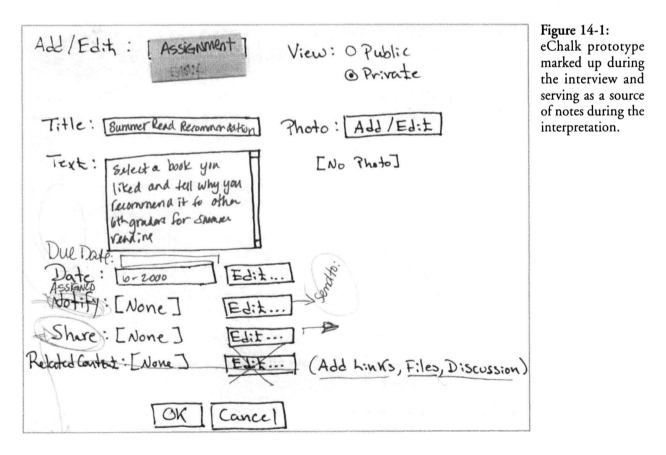

Figure 14-1: eChalk prototype marked up during the interview and serving as a source of notes during the interpretation.

If the user starts by exploring, allow her to do so. She will look at the first part of the UI and say, "What does that do?" Respond, "Click it and see," then show the UI component and discuss the user's expectations. Continue exploring in this fashion for no more than 10 minutes. Then turn the user to a task to start using the same methods as with the task-oriented person. Exploring soon turns into abstract talk and a demo, which you want to avoid. But some exploration is good because you can test how well the interface communicates its function and usage.

If the user is task-oriented put the part of the interface relevant to the task in front of her and ask, "What do you see?" This gives you some feedback on how the interface communicates. Ask, "Do you see a starting place for this task?" to see if she can get started on her own. Once she starts, put real data into the paper system or display a web page or other online content and explain how it will display in your example page.

When the user finishes one activity, ask her what she will do next and continue. If she says, "Does this button do X?" or "What does this button do?" Respond by saying, "What do you think it does?" Check the user's response against your design plan. Or say, "Try it and find out." If the user's expectation is not what the design supports, go with it and see where the user will take you. Create new interfaces and make changes that follow her tacit expectations.

But remember, the users did not step back and explicitly design with data; they simply are responding in the moment. So when you reach the end of their thoughts say, "What if I told you it worked like this instead?" Show them the planned design using, discussing, and changing it as you go.

Most of the time the users think your planned design, with some changes, is better than what they created on-the-fly. But by watching them you can change your design to better support any intents that were revealed in their tacit interaction. And you will encourage the attitude of partnership and codesign.

When you reach the end of one task, go on to another that explores a different part of the interface. Continue this way until you have covered all the major parts that relate to this user's work.

If you have time repeat similar but new tasks in the redesigned prototype to see if after one exposure she learned how to use the system. If not, it suggests that your system is still too complex.

Your overall task is to present the user with the part of the interface relevant to the work task and then present the new parts the user "clicks to" from the starting interface. Here are some circumstances you may face:

- There is no part. If the user is looking for function or a component you didn't think of, pull out a Post-it® or piece of paper and draw the part on-the-fly.

- It seems like the user wants a part that you had linked to a different component. Pull out that part and use it wherever it makes sense to the user.

- The user responds badly to one design. Change the part or design element to better suit the situation.

- The user responds badly to the design. If you have an alternative design (because this was part of your test case), pull out or draw the alternative and see how they respond to that.

- The user hates your UI theme (maybe you used tabs or a web presentation on a desktop tool). Quickly restructure the UI so that it removes these superficial details and continue. For example, tabs become pages or boxes, put menus on a web UI and take off the left navigation bar.

Your overall goal is to move through the prototype in a real usage case getting feedback, changing function, and adding components together with the user as you go. Following the user through his work may not take you to every part of the prototype. If there are specific parts of the prototype that you want to test you can point to a button/feature and ask the user what she thinks would happen if she clicked or used it.

The complexity of the prototype can increase with each iteration and round of testing. As you refine the design including more user interface elements, you should be pushing to test more complicated aspects of the function and how it impacts the user experience. Some common examples of this are testing how much scrolling of content is acceptable in panes, windows, or web pages; testing whether expanding and collapsing of content is appropriate and how it affects the rest of the layout; making sure that content-rich designs are easily scannable; and ensuring that you have the right balance between all the elements so that the important function and content is most prominent.

Take notes

The interviewer is the primary person who interacts with the user and suggests design changes and solutions. The interviewer will annotate the prototype and create new UI pieces as she goes. The marked up prototype is then referred to during the interpretation session.

The second person on the interview is acting as the notetaker. The notetaker must be very meticulous. His job is to write down in a notebook or equivalent each interaction and identify each piece of the UI that was touched and changed. The notetaker is trying to capture as literal a sequence of the events as possible so that it can be recreated in the interpretation session. User quotes are important at this point because they provide insight into what the user likes and does not.

The notetaker should not try to ask questions during the interview. This pulls the interview in too many directions; the user won't know which of you to interact with. It may also break the interviewer's train of thought or flow. Remember, the two of you can always agree in advance that you will switch roles midway during the interview and you can ask your questions then. Or you can turn to the second interviewer at the end and see if there are other issues to explore. Most importantly, the notetaker wants to stay focused on note taking—if he thinks he is supposed to participate he will stop taking those meticulous notes.

Again we do not recommend bringing in computers or video. To get the detail the video would have to be pointed at the mock-up, which is much too interfering. Audiotape also will not get the detail you need. A second person can get up and look at what is going on. He may even stand while taking notes the whole time.

The Wrap-Up

When you come to the end of the interview you will want to wrap up. Your wrap-up does not need to be more than 10 to 15 minutes. A wrap-up for a paper mock-up interview is different from that of a CI.

First thank the users for their time. Then summarize what they liked and what they didn't like about the system and the interface. Check that your interpretation of this is correct.

It is typical to not cover an entire prototype in two hours; don't be surprised when this happens. If you did not get to some parts of the system that you want a "gut feel" response to, bring it out now, introduce it and see how the user responds. You don't have the time to go into detail but you can get a general response to the value of the function. You won't get feedback on whether the system is put together well enough to support the work smoothly.

We end by testing "sales points" and forcing a prioritization of function. The user just used the system for her own work. This is the best time to check on value because now users can understand how the system will impact their work, their self-organization, and their overall productivity.

To test value directly, we ask, "Do you like this system? What would you pay for it?" or if they don't purchase, "Would you recommend this to your manager to buy?" or if it is an internal company application, "Would you tell your coworkers to use this application?" Your goal is to get them to put a number on the value and make a statement of value. If the number is high (and often it is much higher than we ever expect) you know you have delivered value. This is not a way to determine pricing—it is a measure of value. If the tone of voice is enthusiastic, you know you have a winning product. But if the response is lukewarm, you know that something is missing. Now talk directly about what they value.

To force prioritization, we ask, "If we could implement only three things in this product for the first release what would they be?" The user will respond with what they value most and with what most supports their work. Then we ask, "What if we can do only two things?" We continue until we are clear on what is the most important to the user and why.

Finally, thank the users for their help.

Example wrap-up script: eChalk

The following is a recreation from a portion of the wrap-up of one of the eChalk interviews. Notice how the user is confirming the key points and fine-tuning them. The wrap-up is a last chance for you to confirm that you really understood the big picture for the user.

Interviewer: I really appreciate all the time you've given me. As we wrap up, let me summarize some of the key points I've learned. What works well for you is the calendar feature, especially how you can use the templates, because you have to organize and communicate to students and parents about a variety of events throughout the year and you don't like having to reinvent the wheel each time. You also really liked how the calendar could be shared both inside and outside the school.

User: That's correct, that will save me a lot of time both in making calendars and in coordinating with teachers and students.

Interviewer: What also worked for you was the announcement feature, once we moved it so it is onscreen no matter where you are in eChalk.

User: That's right—be sure it is visible from any page so I don't have to worry if people went to the right screen to see it.

Interviewer: (Continues on with the wrap up)

Interviewer: Before I leave, I have some final questions for you. Based on what you saw to today, and assuming we made the changes we did together, would you recommend that your school implement eChalk? (Records answer)

Interviewer: We are going to take all your feedback to our eChalk team. But pretend for a minute that we could implement only three things. What would your top three things be? (Records answer)

Interviewer: Now I'm going to change the rules on you. You get to have only two things. What would they be? (Continues on to the number one thing)

Tips

In this section you will find examples and tips for conducting a successful mock-up interview based on the contextual inquiry principals.

Context

Remember to stay grounded in the user's real experiences. Make sure the user does his or her current work in the prototype. If necessary, replay a recent task, within the last week or so. To keep the user connected to the prototype experience, make sure that she touches and directly interacts with it. You can also alternate between the mock-up and work with real tools. Do the task in the tool first, and then repeat it in the mock-up. Or access real information online and transfer it into the prototype.

In Table 14-2 (continued on the next page), you will find tips to stay connected to concrete data rather than abstract data. These tips will help you stay grounded in the work.

Dos and don'ts for keeping context during interviews	
Don't	Do
Let the user talk in the air or talk in abstractions about what they like or don't like.	Make talk concrete: Follow the actual work and specific cases from the recent past inside the mock-up. Understand what works in the context of doing the work.
Allow the user to summarize a story.	Reconstruct a situation: Back the user up when they skip a step. Have the user walk through each step in the prototype.

Table 14-2: Tips for staying connected to concrete data during a paper prototype interview.

Table 14-2
continued:
Tips for staying
connected to con-
crete data during a
paper prototype in-
terview.

Dos and don'ts for keeping context during interviews	
Don't	**Do**
Take on the expert role: Do not demo the prototype.	Walk through a real task in the prototype. If the user wants to explore or discuss the interface ask them to user their finger to "operate" it and show them what will happen.
Discuss feature requests out of the context of usage.	Have the user walk through the task in the prototype. See the impact of a missing function on the work.

Partnership

The principle of partnership focuses you on the codesign relationship with the user. Together you and the user are engaged in exploring and using the prototype. When you get to something that doesn't work, change it. Discuss design options together and try them out. Make sure that you are modifying the prototype as you go through the interview. Use the extra supplies you brought with you to create new pieces. Act out design suggestions in the prototype together. Incorporate user design ideas on-the-fly. If the user suggests a function, add it.

The tips in Table 14-3 will help you engage the user in a collaborative relationship. These tips will help you draw the user into a working partnership with you throughout the interview.

Table 14-3:
Tips for creating a collaborative relationship during a paper prototype interview.

Dos and don'ts for creating a partnership during interviews	
Don't	**Do**
Hide your focus on improving the system.	Share your focus and tell the user you are looking for their help in verifying that you got the design right.
Create a distant relationship: Reserved attitude; sitting back. Apologetic. Overbearing.	Create an intimate relationship: Lean forward; be fascinated. Be confiding and genuine. Play up the fun aspect of paper prototyping, enjoy your CPU role in the interview. Make it fun for the user.
Demo the prototype. Take over the interview. Put the prototype in front of yourself, instead of in front of the user. Pull the prototype away from the user to work in it yourself.	Let the user drive the usage of the prototype. Only explain function if the user can't find out through discovery. Then use a few words. If it is still unclear, the function doesn't work. Encourage the user to touch the prototype and make it his own.

Interpretation

Determine meaning together with the user. Only the user can tell you why something works or does not. You may think you know, but can't be sure that the user is doing something for the reason you assume they are doing it. Listen to the work issue behind the user's reactions and suggestions. Look for the difference between what the users say and what they want. Add what they want to the design. Be wary of users who tell you what you want to hear. Watch for users' emotional reactions to the prototype; this will clue you in to their real reactions.

Throughout the interview you need to verify that you understand the impact of the system on the work you are observing. You do this by offering your interpretation of this impact and suggesting new design options. The tips in Table 14-4 provide you with ways to verify your interpretation within the context of the interview.

Dos and don'ts for interpreting during interviews	
Don't	**Do**
Just watch what happens and record it.	Look for patterns, intents, and issues. Identify the real issues behind a response to an interface. Suggest design ideas that better support an intent or need. Then watch if they solve the problem. This will confirm or disconfirm your hypothesis and check a design idea.
Just ask yes/no questions.	Offer hypotheses that invite elaboration. Ask the user what he thinks will happen in the prototype to check against the design.
Ignore nonverbal cues to the user's response.	Watch their reactions. Drawing away from an interface usually means it is too overwhelming or complicated. Simplify it to see if that works better. Leaning forward and moving smoothly through the interface means the structure, content, and flow are working well. Look for pleasure and value to identify the most important aspects of the design for the user.
Just ask the user what they want or what they want to do instead.	Remember you have been thinking about this design and about other user data for a long time, the user has not. Often users who don't know technical possibilities and who aren't designers will make suggestions for changes that come from their existing tools. Suggest changes to them and see how they react instead. Say: "What if I gave you something like this..." On-the-fly, create what makes sense for the context of your conversation.
Make a requested change to the prototype without discussing why the user wants the change.	It won't help your team if you come back with changes to the prototype without understanding why the user wanted the change. Was it the UI that they didn't like or the function? What was the underlying intent that needed to be met?
Assume you know what the user is thinking and seeing on your screens.	Ask questions like: "Look at this item, what do you see?" "Is there anything you don't care about?" "Is anything missing?" "What do you see?"

Table 14-4: Tips for verifying interpretations during an interview.

Focus

Challenge your assumptions to expand focus and see more data. Pay attention to the structure and function of the system during the first rounds of interviews; how you broke up the function into different places and what functions you provided in each place. Don't focus on UI detail. In the prototype interviews you want to know how you're design is doing in support of the user's work practice. Remember, the more elaborate the look of the prototype, the more you test the UI; the rougher the prototype, the more you test the structure. Let the mock-up help you stay on focus.

Throughout the interview you need to make sure that you are staying on track and that you are not veering off focus. Use the tips in Table 14-5 to help you direct the interview without taking complete control.

Table 14-5:
Tips for staying on focus during a paper prototype interview.

Dos and don'ts for staying on focus during interviews	
Don't	**Do**
Focus on the construction of the prototype, comparisons to the old system, or other discussions that aren't responses to the prototype.	Focus on work; identify cases to replay in the mock-up and walk through them.
Pursue issues or events outside your focus.	Expand focus based on what you see the user do but gloss over irrelevant events introduced by the user. It is NOT rude to NOT engage the user in conversation about things that are not in focus. You don't want to teach the user that you are interested in irrelevant information. Direct the user's focus to the parts of the prototype you are most interested in testing (as long as it is in the context of their work).
Focus on the UI and discuss UI preferences.	UI detail, language, icons, colors are not in your focus. Change the mock-up to suit the user. Pursue conversations about the function, the flow, and page layout, not low level detail of the user interface.
Focus on automation or how underlying technology works.	If the user is technical they may want to understand how the automation works. If you are doing a lot of automation bring a script that shows business rules or what you will be tracking so you can share that and discuss it as part of the design. Don't talk in general about the underlying technology and platform. But do collect their skepticism about whether you can provide the data they need this will be something you will need for your market message or change management plan.
Dismiss issues because you don't understand them yet.	Probe things you don't understand or are surprised by. Look for the reasoning behind the user's reactions and see if you can offer function or design change to support the issue.
Talk from an implicit list of questions you want answered.	Follow the work, discuss how the work is structured, not topics in your head. You can ask these questions at the end of the interview.

Conduct the interpretation session

Because so much is going on and the detail is so important we recommend holding the interpretation session with both the interviewer and notetaker present within 24 hours of the prototype interview. We recommend that you have at least three but no more than five people in an interpretation session: the interviewer, the interview notetaker, an interpretation session notetaker, and general participants. Designate an interpretation session notetaker before the interpretation session so that he or she can set up a word processing file before the session starts.

If you have a large team, having three to four people at an interpretation session should be easy and will facilitate sharing among the team. If you have a small team, invite your stakeholders to be helpers—they need to commit only two hours and can see the results of the interviews directly. Because there is so much detail to show and track, it will speed the interpretation session and get an outside perspective to have a helper at each session.

Prototype interpretation sessions are very similar to CI interpretations and last about the same length of time, which is roughly the length of the interview itself. The interviewer starts the session by summarizing the interviewee's biographical information and then quickly moves on to the content of the interview. Issues related to the design should be captured and organized by each prototype section.

You can capture your notes manually on Post-its® or online. For the manual process, lay a blank user interface mock-up on the table grouped by component. Write each observation, issue, or design idea on a Post-it® note and put it on the product component. Include an area for system-wide issues. Or capture notes in a document organized by prototype section or design component. You effectively are making an issues list to be addressed in the context of each component for redesign. Online capture will allow you to project the observations for all to see.

The roles for the meeting are as follows:

Interviewer. The interpretation session can be run one of two ways. The primary interviewer can walk through the prototype and the notetaker can supplement with his or her notes, or the notetaker can lead the interpretation with the interviewer supplementing the notes. In either case, the primary interviewer recounts the story, showing the pieces of the mock-up and changes as they were addressed. The silent notetaker tracks their notes to ensure the order is correct and shares quotes.

Notetaker. Notes can be taken on Post-its® or online. Capture design validations (what worked that you planned so that you don't redesign it out), issues that need to be addressed, missing function, user quotes, design ideas, and questions. If you are generating too many notes for one manual notetaker to keep up, assign another one.

Participants. Listen to the story, ask questions, indicate what to capture, and generate design solutions. Again, this is not the time to discuss solutions. Make sure that everyone has a pen and plenty of Post-it® notes to capture their own design ideas if you are capturing manually.

During the interpretation session listen to the data and determine if the issue is primarily about the user interface, additional function needed in the components you have designed, or whole new aspects of the work you haven't thought of. Label your note with UI and F (function) to remind you to handle function issues first, UI issues last, and to discuss storyboarding any new work practices. And put a V on the validations so you know to keep that in the design when redesign starts.

Example: eChalk

This example is a partial list of issues from an eChalk paper prototype interpretation session. They have organized their notes by prototype section.

Making assignments

- Needs to have fields for both the due date for the assignment and today's date, not just one date field. (F)

- Wants to be able to add or attach links, files, and discussions to the assignment when it is given to the students. (F)

- The word "notify" doesn't make sense to him because what he is doing is making an assignment. Need to change the button name to Assign. (UI)

Creating events

- When deciding who the event is going to be visible to, he makes a distinction between everyone in the group being able to see it or the group administrators only. (F)

- Being able to make the event recurring and specify when it recurs is useful for him. (V)

After interpreting the interviews for one round of iterations you are ready to redesign the mock-up.

Iterate the design

After each prototype round, walk through the notes for each design component and identify any changes that you need to make. If you had subteams developing the components they can deal with responding to the issues. Consider rotating people on the subteams so that perspectives can be shared.

At this point, the results of the interpretation session have created a list of issues for the team to address to redesign the system. Review each point and decide whether you are making a change or leaving the design alone until you complete the next round. During this meeting, update the function and layout in the components and answer the following questions:

- Is the design on track? Are the prototype interviews suggesting a change of approach?

- What parts of the design are stabilizing?

- What parts of the design are unclear, keep changing, or haven't been worked out?

- Are we challenging the design?

- Can detailed UI design and rendering start for key components of the system before the paper prototype interviews are complete?

To decide what to change, first look at any system-wide issues that cross components. If there is a systemic problem address these issues first. Ask yourself:

- Do you need a new component that you hadn't thought about?

- Do you need to reorganize components, combining two areas into one or separating one area into two?

- Is there a whole task or content area you had not thought about?

Next, resolve issues within a component at the level of function, content, flow, and general layout. These are not UI issues; add function where it is needed, put in links, and shift the overall function and content layout. Some things will be put off because they may need further investigation or seem to complicate the design unnecessarily. You may want to wait for further feedback from users before making the change.

Finally, resolve any user interface issue focusing on creating a more complete interaction design and labeling. This is the time to start thinking about creating a wire-frame-based mock-up to be printed and cut out. This will help test layout, interaction design, and content presentation.

This should not be a protracted discussion; don't spend more than 10 to 15 minutes discussing each point. If you decide to make a significant change, mini-vision the changes to work out the design in storyboards before you build the next round of prototypes. If you are using storyboards to communicate to your users or to create user stories you will need to update your storyboards and user stories as you go.

This is the process that you use between each round of mock-up interviews. When you have finished your mock-up interview rounds, spend some time finalizing the design and documenting it.

Finalize the design

Once all of the paper prototype interviews and interpretation sessions are completed, meet to walk the design a final time. The purpose of this meeting is to finalize the design and to verify that all its associated issues have been dealt with in the UI design. This is your opportunity to make sure that the design is complete and that all issues have been accounted for. You are ready to pass this on to development, document it, or write specifications as your internal methodology and processes require.

Tip: Consider presenting the final design and quotes from the users to your stakeholders to share the design and the users' responses—that way they will know why you did what you did.

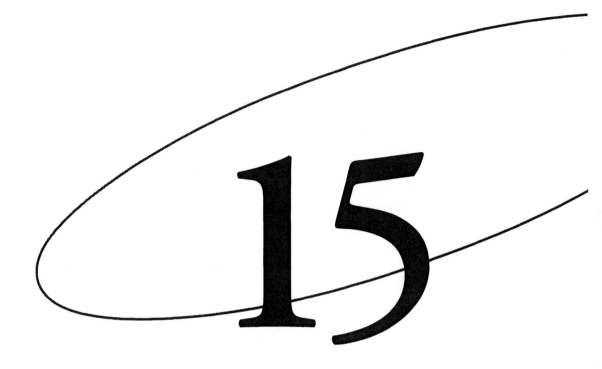

Rapid CD and Other Methodologies

The phases of Rapid CD can be broken up reasonably into three fundamental parts:

Requirements gathering—where customer data is gathered and consolidated to characterize the population needs, activities, issues, breakdowns, and potential opportunities.

Work or activity redesign—where the data is used to redesign existing work or life practices by introducing new technology both to streamline it through automation and to support it through new function organized within a user interface.

User experience design—where the system function to support that redesign is refined and a productive user interface is defined through iterative testing with users.

As we said in Chapter 2, these phases map reasonably well to any corporate or Agile methodology particularly for basic requirements gathering:

Business case. When you are trying to define a business case to show the value of introducing a new product or business system, gathering field data about your population and characterizing the needs through the affinity will reveal the difficulties that could be supported and opportunities for improvement that a system could address. Add visioning and you have the user side of the business case.

Product or system requirements gathering. Once you know the problem you want to address and the user roles that perform the targeted activities, gathering more targeted field data along with sequence models will give you the lower level detail you need to drive system definition. Add visioning to this and you have the high-level requirements for your system. This can be done just as well within an Agile process that might focus on supporting one job role and task at a time or a larger project with two to four roles and several activities.

Personas and user scenarios. In Chapter 9 we described how this same data could be used to create personas representing your core users and user scenarios representing their core tasks. These act as communication and focusing devices for development and for stakeholders, operating as the filter of the users' needs for those who may use their own methods to design a response. Or, as in the case of LANDesk, they act as a supplement to the XP process. The strength of these characterizations lay in the quality of the user data behind them as well as the clarity of the team in choosing a small, high-quality set of target job roles to represent.

Rapid CD can easily supplement or feed the deliverables required for the business analysis and requirements phases of most corporate processes. For this reason Lightning Fast CD and the first phases of Rapid Focused CD easily help drive customer data into any subsequent corporate design processes.

But methodologies like RUP[1] that require use cases in UML or XP[2] with their user stories, and even the more user-centered scenario-based design[3] use alternative design artifacts to drive their processes. Any of these methods can use the consolidated customer data to drive brainstorming of recommendations, or easily use the visioning process to generate a more systemic response to the data. Visioning is close enough to brainstorming, a known technique in any company, that it should be able to be easily adopted.

Similarly, paper prototyping has begun to be widely accepted as a means of testing design ideas and refining them. And although we recommend doing it in the field—with real user cases and not the canned test scenarios of some usability testing—paper prototyping as a technique of getting feedback from users has grown considerably over the years. Sometimes this is the best first step in getting user data into a design and letting developers and designers alike see how their systems are being received.

But how do we build a bridge between the initial user data and the eventual design response? How do we ensure that the design ideas that we are testing are really relevant to the needs of the users? If designers walk the data, the data will direct and filter their initial high level ideas. If these ideas are synthesized into a vision, the team is given direction. But to get to the detailed system function and UI structure requires a leap.

This leap is where the methodologies diverge. We suggest using storyboards to help structure the team's transition between data, redesign of activities, and user experience design. RUP requires use cases, XP requires user stories, and others employ future scenarios or future process models. But these design artifacts can be developed from storyboards. Storyboarding will focus the team on using the customer data collected to redesign the new work process directly, then transform it into the needed artifacts for your company's methodology, and then go on and prototype the design, testing it with users.

Figures 15-1 and 15-2 are examples of storyboards used for developing scenarios, use cases, and driving user stories. We also show you the LANDesk case in more detail so you can see how the customer data led to the story cards and eventual user interface design. To remind you of the storyboarding process and to provide you context for some of our examples, Figure 15-1 is an example of the Apropos call center storyboard.

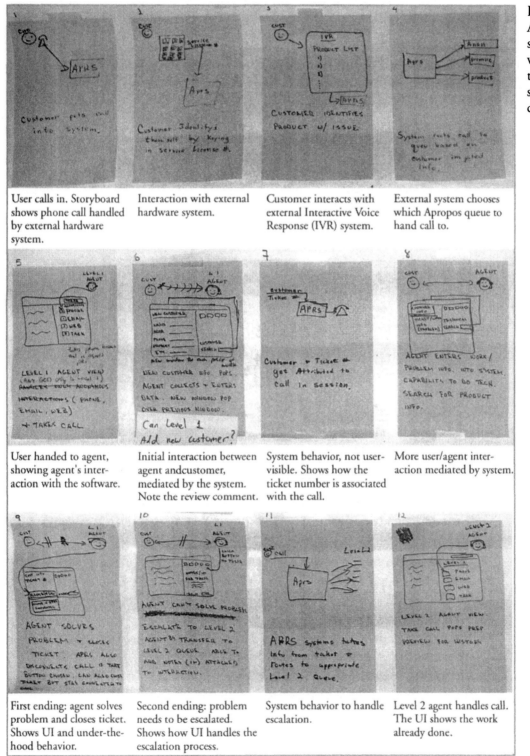

Figure 15-1:
Apropos call center storyboard example with explanation text used to create scenarios and use cases.

User calls in. Storyboard shows phone call handled by external hardware system.

Interaction with external hardware system.

Customer interacts with external Interactive Voice Response (IVR) system.

External system chooses which Apropos queue to hand call to.

User handed to agent, showing agent's interaction with the software.

Initial interaction between agent andcustomer, mediated by the system. Note the review comment.

System behavior, not user-visible. Shows how the ticket number is associated with the call.

More user/agent interaction mediated by system.

First ending: agent solves problem and closes ticket. Shows UI and under-the-hood behavior.

Second ending: problem needs to be escalated. Shows how UI handles the escalation process.

System behavior to handle escalation.

Level 2 agent handles call. The UI shows the work already done.

Storyboards drive use case cases

Storyboarding works out the details of the vision, guided principally by the consolidated sequences representing the key tasks that the system has to support. Storyboards are equivalent to high-level use case instances. Storyboards can be represented in standard use case document structure and Unified Modeling Language notation. Contextual Design artifacts easily can be used to conceptualize what needs to be done and then used as input into the development of use cases.

Figure 15-2 is a representation of the Apropos storyboard in the use case language. The following example is a use case for the storyboard illustrated in Figure 15-1. It includes the initial interaction and the two alternative endings.

Figure 15-2: Example of how the Apropos storyboard can be represented in use case language.

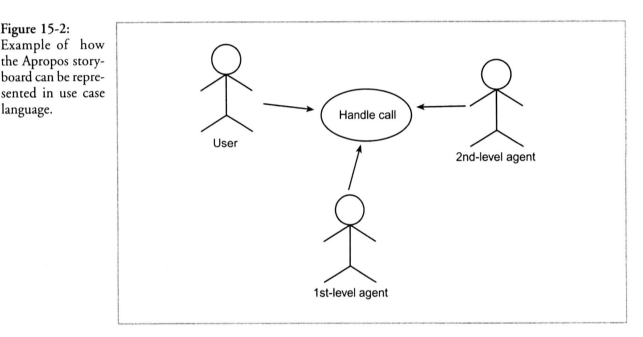

Example: Apropos use case

Preconditions
- A user has called in with a problem
- The level 1 agent has collected information about the user and problem
- The level 1 agent has attempted to solve the problem

Flow of Events
1. The user calls the center with a problem.
2. The APRS system receives the call and requests that the user identify him- or herself.
3. The user enters a service license number.
4. The APRS system determines the level of support available to the user, and the products the user receives support on.
5. The APRS system asks the user to identify the product having a problem through an IVR (interactive voice response) system.
6. The user identifies the product.
7. The APRS system identifies which queue to put the call in based on the user's support contract and product.

8. When the call reaches the head of the queue, it is routed to the next available first-level agent.

9. The agent receives the call on his headset. Simultaneously, a screen pops up showing information the system has about the user. This screen identifies how the call is being handled (phone, as opposed to IM or e-mail). The system opens a ticket and associates it with this call.

10. The agent asks the user what the problem is. As the user gives information, the agent enters it into the system.

11. The agent searches for product information.

12. The agent gives the user the solution to the problem. The agent closes the ticket. Optionally, when the ticket closes the call terminates. Otherwise, the agent concludes the call and hangs up manually.

Postconditions

• The agent is free to take the next call

• A ticket is created recording the call, the amount of time it was open on the first agent's desk, and any information that agent captured

Extension: Escalate Problem

Instead of step 12:

12. The agent determines that he does not have the knowledge to solve the problem. He tells the caller that he will escalate the problem to the next level.

13. He presses the "escalate" button on his control panel.

14. The user is put on hold, and the system identifies the appropriate queue for the call based on the service agreement with the user and the type of call.

15. The agent's screen is cleared and the agent is marked available for the next call.

Postconditions

In addition to those of the base use case:

• The ticket remains open

• The ticket shows that the call was escalated

Extension: Hot Transfer

Instead of step 12:

12. The agent determines that he does not have the knowledge to solve the problem. He tells the caller that he will escalate the problem to the next level.

13. He doesn't want this user to be put on hold again, so he checks the system to see who is working at the next level. He sees that there are two people taking calls and three people in "research" mode.

14. He knows that one of them specializes in this product. He IMs that person and asks if he can take this call. The second-level agent agrees.

15. The first agent transfers the call directly to the second. The user is not put on hold.

16. The first agent's screen is cleared and he is marked available for the next call.

Postconditions

In addition to those of the base use case:

• The ticket remains open

• The ticket shows that the call was escalated

Issues

• Can the first-level agent enter new users?

Future scenarios

Storyboards are intended to drive the design process. They provide enough process support to structure the team's thinking, externalizing it and making it concrete. But when communicating outside the team, they may not be sufficient. In a presentation it's easy enough to walk through a storyboard, fleshing it out and providing the background for those who haven't lived through the project. When you cannot communicate the design direction personally, you may want a more formal mechanism.

Future scenarios are a way to reveal the behavior of the new system—the "to-be" behavior, as some call it—in a way that anyone can assimilate. We introduced user scenarios as compliments to personas in Chapter 9, built from the consolidated data to characterize the life of the typical user before the new system was introduced. Future scenarios represent the way that user's world will change if we implement a design that actualizes the storyboards. Taken together with the persona acting in the future scenario, future scenarios give developers and stakeholders a way to visualize the implications of the new system for the work or life practice to be supported.

To create a future scenario simply write out the storyboard in text, with illustrations as needed. Like a persona it is a story and should be written like a story, with illustrative detail drawn from the actual data and the design changes implied in the storyboard. Use the storyboard as a starting point and fill in the context as you go.

A scenario typically needs an introduction, in which you describe the problem the scenario addresses and who the actors are. Refer back to personas where you can. Then the scenario should follow the storyboard, at approximately one paragraph per storyboard frame.

Where the storyboard frame shows heavy interaction with a system UI, add a sketch of that UI as an illustration. If you have done paper prototypes (see Chapters 13 and 14) use them to guide your sketches, and if you have completed paper prototype testing you can be more detailed about what the user will do in the system.

Taken together the user data driving personas, the consolidated sequences driving user scenarios, the visions and then storyboards driving future scenarios, and the paper prototypes driving future interaction with the user interface, you can paint the picture of how the users' lives will be enhanced by the new system. This representation can help development conceptualize the system, sales and marketing realize the value proposition, and the business understand the impact of the new system on their processes.

XP user stories

User stories capture the features to be implemented by the system on behalf of the user. They describe how a user will perform a task in the new system. User stories are simple and informal—usually written on an index card. The storyboard contains many individual user stories—any one of which can serve as the starting place for an XP process.

Example: Apropos

Here are some example stories that can be generated from the Apropos storyboard. Each of these cases will drive the development of one focused feature set to be tested with users.

Call center XP-style user stories

Story 1: When handing off a call, I can write a quick note saying why I couldn't handle it and highlighting any information I got from the customer that I think is relevant.

Story 2: When handing off a call, I can either just bump the call up to the next level, or I can see who's there and make sure someone's immediately available to handle it.

Example: LANDesk

LANDesk is using an XP process and used contextual data along with their XP design process to create the user stories in the preceding example. Although they did not formally storyboard, they did work out the detailed tasks that the users would have to do, guided by the consolidated sequences.

These are samples (Figures 15-3 and 15-4) of the story cards the development organization uses to estimate the work required to fulfill a particular requirement. The story card typically is written as something the customer sees or the system enables the customer to do.

Development then creates specific tasks from the story cards to guide work during an iteration. The stack of story cards that were created for a particular release is used instead of creating a large, formal, frequently outdated requirements document.

User story cards are juggled as needed to accommodate design changes based on customer feedback or new business requirements. In real use, the story cards are printed out, often handwritten, and pasted on a wall in a public work area.

Each story card is then associated with a particular UI visualization that can be tested with users first on paper or wire frames before it is coded into the product by the design team. The functional-spec level prototype shown in Figure 15-3 is typical of what the interaction design team delivers to the development team.

It tells the developers exactly how the product should look and work when coded. Testers can include this level of mock-up in their acceptance tests for the iteration. This detail of the prototype is arrived at after iterating it with customers and product marketing as well as getting feedback about technical constraints from the development team.

The story card continues to be associated with the design all the way through the process. Example 2, Figure 15-4, shows a rough visual design specification for that particular piece of the system.

This is a visioning prototype indicating how the results might look with visual design treatment in the application, sorted by successful and failed deployments. Typically this level of prototype might be passed by the customers and product marketing to see if it captures the requirement. It will then be posted to the wall with the story card to guide development.

The interaction designer works with the development team to create the final interaction and look-and-feel for the product. This all occurs after testing.

Figure 15-3:
A story card and its corresponding UI that show the success and failure of phased software deployment.

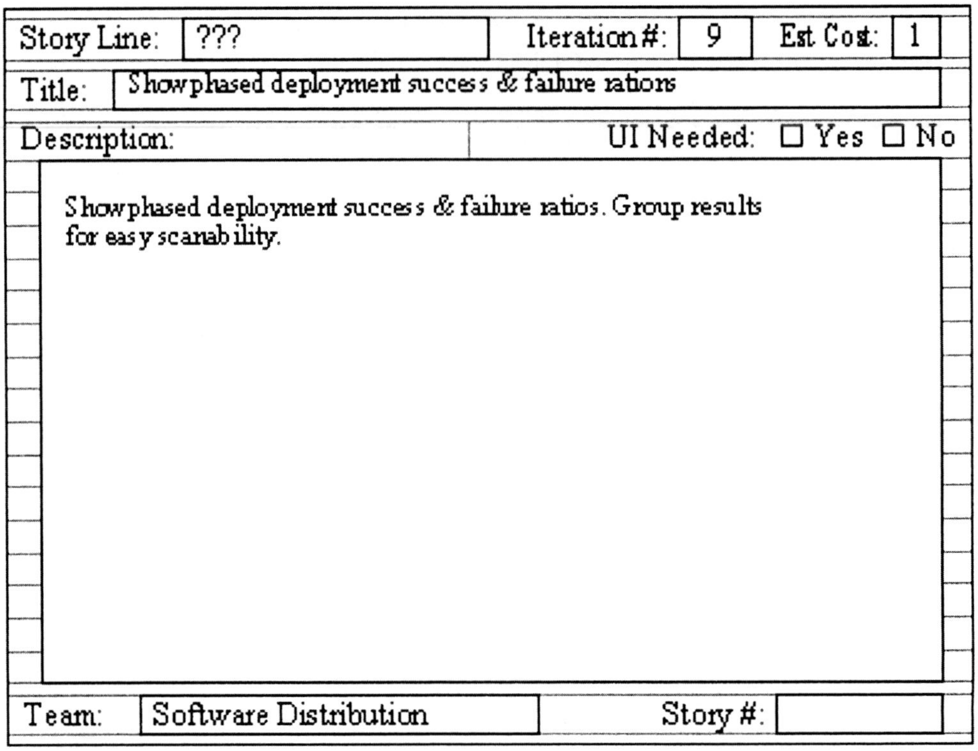

Story Line:	???		Iteration #:	9	Est Cost:	1
Title:	Show phased deployment success & failure ratios					

Description: UI Needed: ☐ Yes ☐ No

Show phased deployment success & failure ratios. Group results for easy scanability.

Team:	Software Distribution	Story #:	

This second image is the UI visualization shown to users.

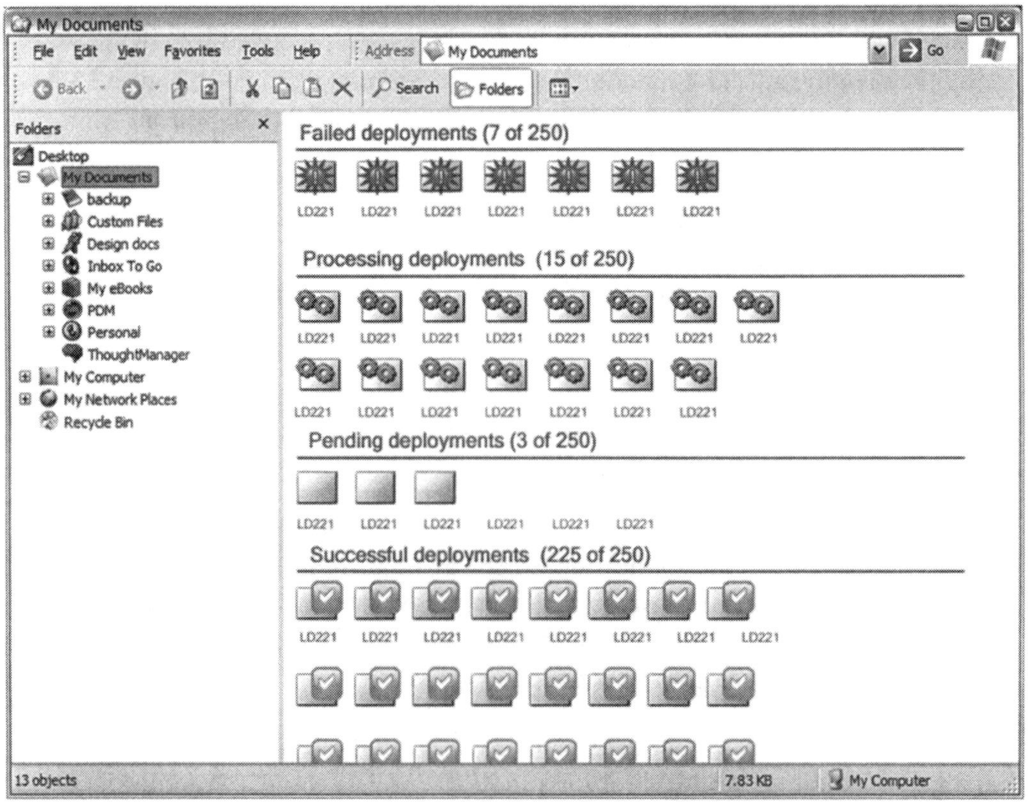

286

The second image is a more detailed, design prototype showing how the visual design could be handled.

Rapid CD for an Agile development process

User-centered design practices easily can be introduced into an Agile Software Development Methodology. Rapid CD recommends the following process, which we have developed together with LANDesk.[4]

Here is an overview of the process, step by step, with typical time estimates for each step. We assume a separate team of two UI designers working with a team of developers. The UI design team works out the details of the interface within the context of the user stories.

In practice, UI design is usually a separate skill held by different people on the team. Our experience is that this sort of handoff—once the developers have come to recognize the value of the skill—is very easy. In fact, once developers figure out how much time and effort the UI designers save them, the developers are prone to complain that the UI designers haven't told them enough about what to do and have left them with too many choices. We also find it promotes better understanding to have developers accompany the UI designer on some user tests.

Following are the steps of Rapid CD tailored for an Agile method:

Set project focus. Determine the complexity of the project and the level of innovation required. Identify the one or two key customer roles this product release will support and plan customer visits (a half-day for discussions, but expect two to three weeks to set up visits from a standing start; once you have relationships and organizational expertise, it is easier).

Do Contextual Inquiries with potential customers. Gather data from at least three people in each role. In a week, a team can do eight interviews with people from four organizations and interpret that data, producing affinity notes and sequences (as-is tasks). Ideally, this is done in a cross-functional team of UI people, marketing, and developers. In practice, we find that developers usually are finishing up their previous project and we bring them up to speed later (one week).

Build the affinity and consolidated sequences. The affinity shows the scope of issues from all customers, and sequence models (task models) show how specific tasks to be supported by the project are now done. This is a representation of the as-is user work practice (3 to 4 days).

Introduce the data to the larger team (including the full development team). Summarize key findings, then walk the team through the affinity to allow the team members to comprehend the customer environment. Ask each team member to note questions and design ideas.

Identify issues to address. The full team identifies what issues will be addressed by the project. Collect issues from the affinity, choosing the most critical issues that can be addressed within the project scope. Brainstorm ideas of how to better support the work. Record and save big ideas for future high-impact projects (2 days).

Build user stories in response to these issues. User stories are guided by the sequence models and show how the system will resolve the issues. Lightweight storyboards aid the discussion.

Run a release planning process on the user stories. Use conceptual diagrams and high-level UI mock-ups to facilitate team communication. Without a completed UI the team can't know exactly how difficult implementation will be, but within the context of an organization the team can know the typical complexity of the UIs they define, so they can supply a rough estimate. Organize the user stories into iterations, groups of stories that deliver coherent subsets of function.

Prioritize stories. Prioritize and eliminate stories as necessary to meet the resource budget for the release. We always save some budget for additional user stories that will reveal themselves once we begin getting user feedback.

Design detailed user interfaces to support the user stories in the first iteration. UI design is its own discipline—don't mix it with the implementation work of coding the user story (1–2 days).

Test UIs with users in paper with mock-up interviews. User stories are a fairly fine-grained definition of system functionality; many user stories can be covered in a single paper prototype test. Test

these UIs with three to four users and use the results to refine the design. Do a second round of tests with a more detailed UI if you have the time and resources. A third round of testing will happen with live code (2 weeks for both rounds).

Provide the user stories and completed UIs to the development team for implementation. With detailed UIs, developers can very accurately cost their work for the iteration. In addition, testing can incorporate UI mock-ups into their acceptance tests, providing development with a clear end point to their task.

Develop the second iteration mock-ups in parallel. During implementation of the first iteration, the UI team develops the UIs for the second iteration's user stories and tests them with users in two rounds of paper before the code for the first iteration is complete.

Provide the second set of stories and completed UIs to the development team for implementation. When the code for the first iteration is completed, the UI team gives developers the next set of stories and UIs and the developers start on the second iteration.

Design and test the third iteration. Meanwhile, the UI team designs the UIs for the third iteration and tests them with users in paper. Simultaneously, if desired, they test the running code of the first iteration with users to get quick feedback on the actual product. (Our projects have done this with customers every second or third iteration.)

Provide the third set of stories and completed UIs to the development team for implementation. At the end of the second iteration, the UI team gives the user stories and UI designs for the third iteration to the development team and the testing feedback is incorporated into the plan. This process repeats until the release is done.

Deal with user feedback. If user testing suggests changes to future user stories, the changes are made and the work estimate for those stories is changed if necessary.

When user feedback indicates you must change work the team has already done, plan additional user stories and schedule them in as needed. (Be aware this will happen as the system comes alive and low-level issues reveal themselves. Be careful not to schedule yourself too tight in your initial resourcing. The team will need to save some of its resource budget to accommodate these additional stories.)

Rapid CD can augment other methods

The core of Rapid CD is getting customer data and its implications into the design process and into the minds of designer and developers. It provides the data that is needed to guide business decisions, prioritize requirements, identify how to streamline work, be clear on what will be of value to the user, and produce high quality user experience.

Use the techniques of Rapid CD and adapt them to your own corporate methods, translating the design artifacts as we have shown here to ensure that you too can take advantage of the power of user data.

Endnotes

[1] Kroll, Per and Kruchten, P., *The Rational Unified Process Made Easy: A Practitioner's Guide to Rational Unified Process*. Addison-Wesley, 2003.

[2] Beck, K., Extreme *Programming Explained: Embrace Change*. San Francisco: Addison-Wesley, 2000.

[3] Alexander, I and Maiden, N., eds. 2004. *Scenarios, Stories, Use Cases through the Systems Development Life-Cycle*. John Wiley. See also Chapter 10, "Role of Scenarios in Contextual Design," *Contextual Design: Defining Customer Centered Systems*, Elsevier.

[4] Beyer, H., Holtzblatt, K., and Baker, L., "An Agile Customer-Centered Method: Rapid Contextual Design" in *Proceedings of XP Agile Universe 2004*, Calgary, Canada.

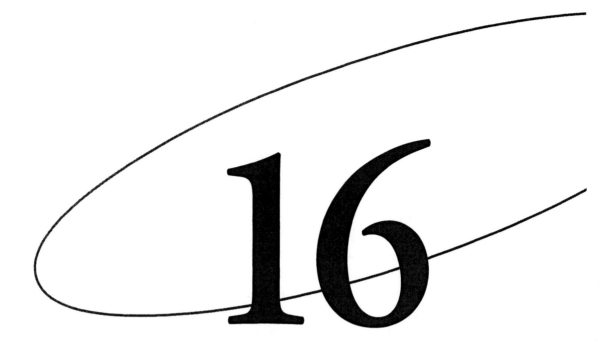

Issues of Organizational Adoption

Contextual Design helps you use customer data to produce the right design for your company. Contextual Design is also encouraging organizations to make decisions about system direction and redesigned work practice based on how real people work and live. If you have customer data, you can make decisions, you will not get bogged down in arguments, and you will have a story for your market message.

If you have processes that tell you how to collect and use customer data to produce designs, working together in cross-functional teams quickly is possible. Rapid CD processes help you get data into your design processes in as little as two to four weeks. Add on time to do some redesign and prototyping and you can produce a user-centered design within eight to ten weeks.

Some companies do not really do front-end design. They may review their enhancement database and choose the next features. Developers and designers may be expected to depend on marketing to identify features—which is often inadequate for good design. They may do some focus groups or talk with important customers in an informal way. Introducing a more structured front-end design process in which designers participate with product management or marketing may be a real time cost. But most of the time when people push back and say that the process is too time consuming or too heavy they are not talking about time and resources. They are really talking about resistance to change.

Even introducing a more robust front-end design process is a request for change. A change that will subsequently reduce development and design time on the back end, simplify requirements prioritizations, and increase the quality of the user experience, but change nonetheless.

More and more companies think they ought to use customer data in their processes. But this means organizational and personal change. In this chapter we address some of the issues that have been raised and recommend how to address them.

What project should we start with?

Dennis Allen,[1] when he worked at WordPerfect, described the water drop method of introducing Contextual Design. He would collect a little data and chat about it at lunch to key developers and managers. He would invite a few people to do an interpretation session. He arranged for InContext to come in and give a general interest talk. He collected a little more data, and told more people. He made a slide show of the data. People started to want the data. Soon the company was ready for a project. By the time we left, 10 teams from the core product set were starting to use the process—but then WordPerfect was sold. And we had to begin again. Dennis Allen knew how to create a buzz and get his company moving.

Our experience has been that the best way to raise awareness is with the water drop technique. Do something small: collect a little data, interpret it with a buddy, and share it around. Do guerrilla warfare: find some others to join you and collect a little data and interpret it without getting permission. Then share it around.

The next step is to identify a test project. Start with a project led by a manager or project leader who wants to get customer data into the design. Try not to start with a big project or the most important product in the company. A large project having a wide scope will be difficult to manage and will take longer to show results. The flagship product of the company or the core business group is often the greatest source of resistance to change. You will be going up against the cash cows—the ones who have made the company successful. They will wonder why they cannot just keep doing what they have been doing. So, if you want to get their buy-in, scope the project small and plan to attack a piece that everyone agrees is a problem. Make sure everyone is well trained and lead the project carefully. Use a Rapid CD method so it is fast and people can see results soon.

Or pick an outlying project, a new division that wants to make its mark. They will want to differentiate themselves by project and processes. They may be more willing to try new things. You still need buy-in but these teams, in our experience, are more willing to experiment and roll with the discomfort of learning something new. So start with one project success. Then move to another project. Build success a bit at a time.

How do I create a buzz?

The water drop method creates interest by simply spreading the word until it becomes part of the culture or people get curious enough to start asking about what you are doing. Companies often start with an enthusiastic set of people and invited guests to stimulate a larger discussion at regularly scheduled meetings, off-sites, or informal bag-lunch sharing sessions.

Make your project visible—it's part of organizational change. Simply talking about the impact of any customer data you have will spark the most interest. The Contextual Design process is best done with a dedicated design room that creates its own buzz. Design artifacts like the affinity diagram, the online data browser created with CDTools, storyboards, paper prototypes, and the team room to make the project visible. Others passing by will start to peek in. Soon they will want to try using customer data, too.

The environment a team room creates is so unusual that people will visit the room just to see what is going on. One team put their diagrams on an outer wall in order to lead passersby into the room. Do this with your personas—distribute them around your developers and stakeholders. Invite them to informal gatherings in your team room to see the data pointing them to parts of the wall most relevant to them. Hang up your paper prototypes and walk through them so developers and stakeholders see tangible results early on and use them to drive design review meetings.

A good design room, quick access to information online, and some internal marketing combined with the water-drop method will help create the buzz you need to get things going.

What's the ROI on user-centered design?

Most companies talk about wanting to see ROI (return on investment) before trying something new. Some of this is resistance to yet another expensive suggestion about how to improve the way things work. But most of this is also resistance to change. Few companies have metrics on how long their existing process takes to allow realistic comparisons. If you can, collect some informal metrics on existing projects and any pilot Rapid CD projects you do. If not, use questions like these to raise consciousness about the problems in your processes to get buy-in for a pilot project:

Defining requirements. How long did it take the team to agree on the requirements for the project? Were you still changing requirements up to the last week before beta testing? How long are your prioritization meetings when you have no data? How many iterations between the business and IT did it take until there was agreement that the product was desired—or does that never get resolved? Look at all the times that having data would shorten decisions—time existing meetings and then time meetings run with data and show the difference.

Time to code. Management often measures productivity in terms of lines of code. But, lines of code that keep being ripped out because of improper requirements or disagreements with management or UI designers are lines of code wasted. Do you have measures of that part of your process to compare?

Customer response. How were products with no customer data received? How many of these were cancelled by management or the business? Were sales or raves higher from customers when you did use data? What about industry reviews?

We find storytelling, when there are no statistics, humorously reminds people of the truth about their processes. Asking these questions will raise consciousness about the reality of the current process. Reminding everyone about the "hysterical version event" and other corporate stories can convince managers and teams alike of the worthiness of trying something new. For example, here is a story that many people can relate to their own experience.

> "It's the last few weeks before the release we are all working overtime night and day. The pizzas are brought in. We argue about what function we can cut to make the date. We argue yet again about what customers really need. We work hard, it's a team effort and we only slip by a few days (weeks). And then we take time off, sleep, do a little training and rise up once more out of the primordial mud. WHAT will we make in the next version, what do the customers want, which enhancements should we do next, how can we decide? And the cycle begins again."

So collect some statistics and share them with the community so we all can benefit from some numbers. Collect corporate myth and use it to help swing people toward user-centered design. But in the end one successful project will do more for organizational change than anything else.

How can I overcome resistance?

Resistance is normal. There will always be organizational resistance to new processes. Changing is difficult whether or not people want to change. People have their habits and their daily tasks that need to get done. Even if they want to change, they do not know how to fit those daily tasks into the new processes. Furthermore, change implies using different skill sets, ways of thinking, and ways of designing. For example, a coder trying to use customer-centered design has to talk to customers and build data for weeks at a time instead of coding. It is natural for people undergoing this kind of change to find themselves out of step with their work and their sense of competence.

If people really want to change they will read books, attend training, and forgive themselves their initial awkwardness while they learn new skills. But for people who think that customer-centered design is a passing fad, resistance can disguise itself in rational arguments about statistics and time. The answer to such people is not rational argument—it is an invitation to become involved. It is asking for their intelligence, experience, and help. It is valuing them.

Just as CD is about developing empathy for and listening to customers, you must develop empathy for and listen to developers. Find out what makes their job difficult, what excites and motivates them and gives them a feeling of self-satisfaction. Find out where they think the product or system is flawed or where they wish they knew more about the customer. Sometimes people resist because of their (unspoken and often even unrecognized) assumption that this new process will expose flaws in their work. One developer we worked with believed in our process but did not want to go out on customer visits—"I know they will find problems and I know I don't have time to fix them. So I don't want to go find out."

Many developers are perfectionists by both nature and training—exposing their "flaws" is difficult to take. That is why customer data is so valuable—it helps developers know what to build to be successful. It gives them back the control and choices they want and need. Another developer who we worked with had never been out to visit with customer; he was designing a product without knowledge of the content domain or the customer. Once we took him out into the field, he came back and said, "I feel like I have been designing behind a one-way mirror—everything filtered through marketing. Now I've walked out in front of the mirror; now I know what the customer wants and I'm never going back again." There is nothing more powerful than a field interview with a customer to remove resistance.

New processes are also threatening because they challenge existing processes and roles. The person who founded the process currently used by a company and created the company's profitable bread-and-butter product has no reason to change. Traditional usability professionals may feel that their work will disappear or that their value will be undercut. The marketing person may resent engineering being involved in "their job."

This is why involvement is vital when dealing with resistance. Include everyone in interpretation sessions, take them out on visits, and let them help build the affinity. Then bring them into the visioning session. Even if they are time constrained reach out. There is a lot to gain with only two hours of participation.

You especially want to be wary of getting stuck in your ivory tower. Doing something new often looks like a "secret" project. The team becomes involved with each other, talks a new language, and works a new way. If stakeholders, people on related projects, or the coders who will develop the designs think, "you act like you are so special," or if you keep telling them, "how great this process is," they will resent it and resist changing. Communicating out and bringing people in is the way to be sure you do not become isolated.

And don't be too much of an evangelist, talking about user-centered design all the time. People get tired of hearing about it and rebel by increased resistance. The best road to combating resistance is partnering and listening. Even the Lone Ranger had Tonto and the community behind him.

Leading edge companies know that to be continually successful they must evolve their processes. Past success with one process does not guarantee continued success, and it does not mean that a new process will not create more success in an ever-changing market. In our experience, people who want to create the best systems for their companies and markets will most readily adopt new processes. They already recognize that if they do not continuously improve their processes, they will fall behind.

How do I answer their questions and challenges?

In our experience, there is a standard set of questions that people ask when they are resistant to change. Here they are, with our suggested responses.

We already talk to our customers—why change?

It isn't that your existing practices don't use customer data; it's that all customer data isn't equal. Designers need detailed data to guide what they do. And they need enough data to be able to understand who the user is and how they work at a very low level of detail. Marketing surveys, focus groups, even in-office interviews, ask users to talk about the work in general. But designers need to talk about the work in detail. And people, because their knowledge is tacit, can't talk in detail. So we go to the field to watch and understand the work as it unfolds—this is the only way we know to really capture the user's actions within their own contexts. This is the only way we know to get really reliable data.

Without reliable data, gathered in an agreed upon way, people in your organization will keep arguing about the "real" requirements. But given a rational process for data collection that reveals what people are doing, how and why they do it, and what it means to them, designers and companies can make decisions.

Even usability tests that occur in the lab are "out of context." They ask users to do tasks that are not their own, in an environment that is not their own, with tools that are not their own, prescribed in an order that may not be their own. And they have no motivation for excellence. This alone makes the data suspect for requirements gatherers—it works only for testing low-level usability issues in the interface. But it will not test the viability of a product to support the real work, with the real data and performance load, with real exception cases, in the real work environment. Since real work doesn't happen in the lab, it's difficult to gather any user needs there beyond their reactions to the tool interface itself.

To help organizational stakeholders understand the issue try using this example:

> "We all know how to drive cars. But if we ask someone what all the detailed steps of driving are they can't tell us. They can say, well I open the door, sit down, put in the key, shift to reverse and go. Any lower level of detail is tacit—and we know this because when it is time to teach our kids to drive we don't know what speed to tell them to go around corners, how to change gears in a stick shift car, or how our eyes scan the dash."

If that story doesn't work ask them how they decide what to read in the newspaper or why they always buy one brand of food. Tacit knowledge is easy to understand once they understand the low level of detail of everyday life activities that is needed for design.

For marketing, real user data is the Voice of the Customer—written down, organized, and ready-to-drive product definition.

We already gathered our requirements—can't we use them?

The data we need is the detailed design data that will reveal users' tacit or latent needs. This leads to opportunities to support them better and the identification of delighters to put in our products. In our experience, standard requirements documents do not list user needs or latent requirements, they list feature requests. Feature requests need to be tracked back to an issue in the work practice—and usually marketing or business analysts, when asked, can't really do that. So requirements that are simple feature lists don't help designers understand the context in which these features will be used.

On the other hand, data from surveys, focus groups, user call centers, and other sources of user requests and complaints can be used in two ways within Rapid CD. First, review issues with stakeholders and let that help form your interview focus. Be on the watch for potential problems, or even possible solutions.

Second, if these high-level methods yield conditions that need to be satisfied, harvest them for affinity diagram Post-it® notes. Identify the source of the data as another type of user, for example, "the focus group user," and roll these notes into the affinity so that all data is included.

Give yourself a jump start—use the organizational knowledge. Just don't think that it is enough for design.

You don't have a statistically accurate sample—it's not a representative population

CD collects data from a small sample of users and we find that this is enough—talking to more customers does not result in significant new data. A lot of people (especially engineers) have a difficult time believing data from so few people. They want to see data that is statistically significant. If they hear about something you found out from a single customer interview they call it anecdotal and say "that's one user in a million."

Generally, when people raise the statistical argument they are concerned about one of two types of mistakes being made.

- The design will fail to take into account features that will be important to a broad spectrum of the market.

- The design will include features that are not useful or valued by many people.

Let's take each of these in turn.

Will we fail to include important features? The argument for the validity of contextual data has three parts: first, work practice is fundamentally similar across a market; second, even a small sample is reliable for our purpose; and third, we choose participants to maximize our view of the market.

In Chapter 3, see the box, **How can so little data characterize a whole market?**, where we talked about how, given the commonality of context and the few number of strategies people use for any coherent task, we need only interview a small number to see the basic structure of the work. Studies of usability tests have shown that after collecting data from 10 to 15 customers, you've discovered most of what you need to know and have started to reach the point of diminishing returns.[2]

We have also recommended in Chapter 3 that you maximize diversity of the participants so that you can collect this variation. And we leave room to expand our participants based on the first set of interviews where, sometimes, these interviews will reveal new members of a work group.

Even our wall walk process encourages stakeholders to look for holes in the data so that we can collect additional data if needed. In these ways we ensure that even with a small sample we are sampling the cases we need for good system design.

Will we include features that hardly matter? In design, we must invent features that support the real issues that impact the lives of the users and are seen as value propositions by consumers and businesses. But we don't depend on counting the qualitative data to determine that impact. Qualitative data is not collected randomly by any controlled process; its purpose is to drive insight, not produce statistics.

Instead we look at the consolidated data to see what matters in the users' daily lives. In one project fully half the notes on the affinity diagram dealt with setting up and tuning the system versus using the data in it. We didn't have to calculate anything to determine that the team had better simplify system setup.

In a classic example of designing a switch on a large computer we solved an engineering argument about having one or two switches when data yielded that people moved the switch through the off position to the remote position "very, very slowly—when we crashed it once we never wanted to do that again." In a 24/7 operation any unnecessary crash is devastating to the business—the number of times this error happened was irrelevant—the impact of work loss on the business made this a priority issue.

Qualitative data prioritizes implicitly by impact on life—this is the best way to identify worthwhile value propositions. Understanding the impact of the system or inefficient processes on the work creates the rationale for including function to improve it.

We have no travel budget—we can't find users

We think these excuses are smoke screens for resistance. In Chapter 3 we talked about how to get customers. For years companies have been finding creative ways to do so. And now general agencies are able to set up ethnographic visits. You can be creative too, but it may take your efforts to network and find a few users to interview before your organization sets up a process to help you out.

As to travel budget, financial constraints are real. But you aren't going to get the detailed data you need over the phone or a networked meeting. Call the organization on this excuse. You can always find users nearby to start with—call your friends in sales and marketing and get their help. Or go through your personal network until you find some customers. Even four users will yield more data than you otherwise would get. Those four users can help you get started being a customer-centered company.

Once you have a background of data from real field interviews you can check your findings more globally through phone-based field interviews like those we are starting to experiment with. But if you find a lot of differences, treat this as a red flag and get back out to your customers.

We don't want CD techniques—we want to do it our way

People have to own the processes they use; adaptation of Rapid CD is normal. All companies already are running themselves somehow. They may have very formal processes or they may be small start-ups with informal processes. They may have formal methodology groups in charge of their processes or they may have strong traditions that guide everyday work. And they may be in the middle of a Six Sigma implementation, adopting OO technology, or otherwise absorbed and overwhelmed with process changes.

So unless a founder who really wants to do Contextual Design starts a company, all introduction of Contextual Design involves fitting into existing ways of working. And any process, even if adopted by an enlightened CEO with an enlightened set of developers, will have to be changed to fit the company, the people, and their skills. Any user-centered design process will be renovated and adopted piece by piece.

Part of any adoption process is to make it your own. People will argue that they must change a process to fit their situation or to improve it. Early on in the evolution of Contextual Design we had a step called redesigned sequence models. We deliberately rewrote the steps of the consolidated sequences to reflect the vision, keeping the writing in text (no pictures). An internal CD evangelist we had trained as a coach could not get anyone to use redesigned sequence models. Instead, their people were excited about storyboarding as a technique. So the evangelist asked us, "Isn't storyboarding really just redesigned sequence models, but in drawings?" "Yes," we replied, "Do it. It doesn't matter if you rename 'redesigned sequence models' to 'storyboarding' as long as while they are storyboarding they account for the data."

Renaming or modifying a step in Contextual Design makes no difference, as long as the fundamental intents of the step are achieved. We watched what happened, saw the value of visualizing the steps pictorially, and adopted storyboarding as a part of the Contextual Design process. Now we are working with companies to adapt and integrate CD into Agile programming and Six Sigma processes. We are part of a community of people all striving to define and use processes that build the best systems for our users and our businesses. Rapid CD is part of that redefinition process.

Communicate out and give ideas away

The best answer to questions is involvement and communication. Throughout the book we have talked about how to involve stakeholders in the process and keep them informed and involved. Communication to the organization is one of the most important ways you can combat skepticism. Let the process and the data sell themselves. Let go of arguments about why it works, and let them see how powerful data can be in resolving arguments and defining successful systems. One favorite story is of a team who, when they presented their new design to their user group, received a standing ovation—the first in the history of a very large company.

Once you start to have data, share it. If you can start a pilot project get a team room and get your data online. Start working with teams at the fringe of the company rather than the bread-and-butter project. As other groups start to use customer data, the bread-and-butter project will feel left out. We have seen them pick up the baton and make it their own—all the while insisting that they know best how to do this new process.

Communication, involvement, ownership, and helping others be successful in using customer-centered techniques is why over the last 16 years more and more companies are looking for ways to make it standard practice.

Focus on success

To change, people need to know exactly what to do to be successful. They need to know the techniques, how to work together, and how to fit this work into their daily lives. With this Rapid CD handbook we hope we have given you the step-by-step guidance you need to make user-centered design successful in your company.

Change looks like taking on one new technique at a time. Most companies start by going to the field to gather customer data and proceed from there. Start small and focus on your success—not the resistance that will come with each new attempt. Each person you get to listen is a success. Each infusing of customer data into the design process is a success. Each technique tried and altered is a success. Recognize your success and celebrate it.

Another favorite story is of a team that we coached in a Contextual Design project who worried that the 600 coders they worked with would not adopt their designs. So they identified and targeted friendly coders, asking them for help with prototyping, for their feedback on design ideas, and so forth. Next, in the interest of rolling out the process and the design, these designers gave ownership of the designs to the friendly coders, asking them to write the specifications, prototype the design, and give the prototypes to their managers. Soon the coders were coming to them because they wanted the designs. And when the team required them to go to the field with them, they were willing—this was the beginning of organizational change.

Share your successes and challenges

We have provided you with the tools, techniques, and arguments to help you move your company toward using customer data in your design process. Whether you are working for a product company or making software to support your businesses you will face challenges and reap the rewards of success if you start using the data from real people's lives to drive design excellence.

Contextual Design has been a part of changing the industry from being engineering focused to being user-centered. That has only happened because people like you took up the challenge.

So use the tools we have offered, try them, argue about them, and change them to suit your needs. Please, share your progress. Call, send email, and read each other's stories:

www.incontextenterprises.com

We are looking forward to watching the next wave of the voice of the customer influence systems, products, web sites, portals, consumer applications, and your organizations.

Endnotes

[1] *"Succeeding as a Clandestine Change Agent,"* C. D. Allen in "Requirements Gathering: The Human Factor" (special issue), *Communications of the ACM*, May 1995, Vol. 38, No. 5. K. Holtzblatt and H. Beyer, eds.

[2] "Problem Discovery in Usability Studies: A Model Based on the Binomial Probability Formula," J.R. Lewis. In Human-Computer Interaction: Applications and case studies. Proceedings of the Fifth International Conference on Human-Computer Interaction, Orlando, FL, Volume 1, 1993. M. J. Smith & G. Salvendy, eds.; "The Trouble with Computers", T. Landauer. MIT Press, Cambridge, MA, 1995. Page 311.

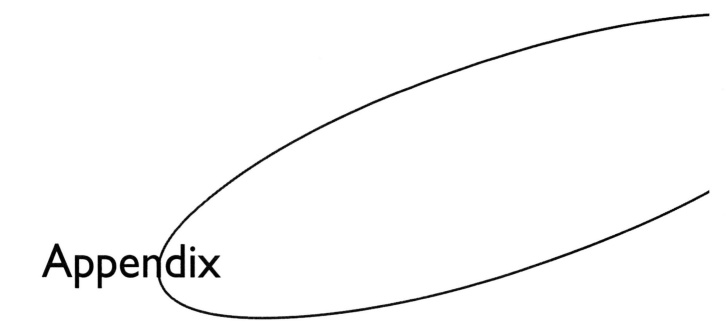

Appendix

Suggested Supply List

Exactly what supplies, and how much of them you need, can vary widely from project to project, but this list will give you a starting place for initial ordering. We've segregated the supplies for paper prototyping so you can easily put together paper prototyping kits in large envelopes that can be transported to the interview site.

In some cases we recommend specific brands that we have found work particularly well. One final hint: Keep an eye on how many pens you have and how sharp they are (using dull pens can make it difficult to read the models); you will go through them faster than you can imagine.

What	How Much	When Used
Microcassette tape recorders	One per interviewer	Contextual Inquiry Interviews
Microcassette tapes	Two 90-minute tapes per interview	Contextual Inquiry Interviews
Batteries	Two fresh sets per tape recorder	Contextual Inquiry Interviews
Spiral bound notebook	One per interviewer	Contextual Inquiry Interviews
Pens for taking interview notes	Two per interviewer	Contextual Inquiry Interviews

Table A-1:
List of supplies for the interview, interpretation, affinity building, visioning, and storyboarding processes.

Table A-1
continued:
List of supplies for
the interview, inter-
pretation, affinity
building, visioning,
and storyboarding
processes.

What	How Much	When Used
Computer for capturing interpretation session notes in either CDTools or word processing	One per interpretation session. If you are running parallel interpretation sessions, you will need one device per team. If you are capturing your sequence models online, a second computer is recommended.	Interpretation Sessions for Contextual Inquiry Interviews
Data projector or large monitor for displaying interpretation session notes	One per interpretation session. If you are running parallel interpretation sessions, you will need one device per team. If you are capturing your sequence models online, a second computer is recommended.	Interpretation Sessions for Contextual Inquiry Interviews
Flipchart paper. Try to avoid using Post-it® brand removable flipcharts. The adhesive on the back of each one makes them very difficult to store once you remove them from the pad, and Post-it® or sticky notes do not adhere to the sheets.	Minimum of three pads. If you are capturing work models in addition to the sequence model, increase the quantity by at least one more pad.	Interpretation Sessions for Contextual Inquiry Interviews. Visioning. Storyboarding.
Flipchart easels	One for each interpretation team. One is usually sufficient, unless you are running parallel sessions. If you are capturing work models in addition to the sequence model, increase the quantity by at least one more easel per interpretation team.	Interpretation Sessions for Contextual Inquiry Interviews. Visioning. Storyboarding.
Blue Sharpie® Fine Tip pens	36 (3 boxes)	Interpretation Sessions for Contextual Inquiry Interviews. Affinity Building. Model Consolidation. Data Walks. Visioning. Storyboarding.
Red Sharpie® Fine Tip pens	12 (1 box) each color	Interpretation Sessions for Contextual Inquiry Interviews. Model Consolidation.
Green Sharpie® Fine Tip pens	12 (1 box) each	Interpretation Sessions for Contextual Inquiry Interviews. Affinity Building. Model Consolidation. Data Walks.
¾ inch 3M removable tape	8 rolls	Interpretation Sessions for Contextual Inquiry Interviews. Affinity Building. Model Consolidation. Visioning. Storyboarding.

What	How Much	When Used
Tape dispenser for removable tape	One minimum	Interpretation Sessions for Contextual Inquiry Interviews. Affinity Building. Model Consolidation. Visioning. Storyboarding.
Post-it® Note sheets for laser printers. These sheets can be difficult to find. They are rarely available from your local office supply store, so try searching for them on the Internet. If you can't find them, you can always format the notes, print them on regular paper, cut them, and use Post-it® removable tape.	Assume you will have 50-100 notes for each interview.	Affinity Building.
3x3 blue Post-it® Notes. We recommend using Post-it® brand sticky notes. Other, cheaper brands (including other 3M brands) have less adhesive and are more likely to fall off the wall.	10 pads	Affinity Building. Model Consolidation.
3x3 pink Post-it® Notes	6 pads	Affinity Building. Model Consolidation.
3x3 green Post-it® Notes	4 pads	Affinity Building. Model Consolidation.
3x5 yellow Post-it® Notes	12 pads	Affinity Building. Model Consolidation. Data Walks. Visioning. Storyboarding.
Scissors	1 pair	Affinity Building.
Masking tape	1 roll	Affinity Building. Model Consolidation.
White, waxless butcher paper or white kraft paper (the brown paper is too porous; if it's waxed the notes fall off) for papering the walls for the affinity. It is also useful for model consolidation.	2 rolls	Affinity Building. Model Consolidation.
½ sheets of paper (blue or white)	Minimum of 100 half sheets	Storyboarding.

Table A-1 continued: List of supplies for the interview, interpretation, affinity building, visioning, and storyboarding processes.

Paper Prototyping Kits

We suggest you create prototyping kits by enclosing in the supplies in a large manila envelope or see-through plastic envelope. You may also need to a large envelope, art portfolio, or some other item for transporting the prototype itself. One word of caution: If you are flying to the paper prototype interview site and carrying the kits in your hand luggage, remove the scissors before trying to go through security.

You need to create one prototype for each interview team, and keep the kit restocked for each interview. That means you need to increase the quantities you see here so you have enough for each team doing interviews, plus the equivalent of one additional kit for the actual building.

These supplies are a suggested starting place, and what you actually need depends on the kind of prototypes you are building.

Table A-2:
List of supplies for the paper prototype interview kit.

What	How Much
1x2 Post-it® Notes-any color	1 pad
2x3 Post-it® Notes-assorted colors	1 pad of each color
3x3 Post-it® Notes-assorted colors	1 pad of each color
3x5 Post-it® Notes-yellow	1 pad
4x6 unruled Post-it® Notes-yellow	1 pad
Highlighters-assorted colors	1 of each color
5" scissors	1
Sheet of multi-color dots	1
Blue Sharpie® Extra Fine Tip pen	1
Black Sharpie® Extra Fine Tip pen	1
3M removable tape	1 roll
Poster boards (legal size)	2
Sheets of overhead transparency sheets	4
Sheets of 8 ½x11 white paper	4

In addition to the kit supplies, you may want to have the following items for building the prototype.

Table A-3:
List of supplies for the paper prototype building process.

What	How Much
Manila folders for organizing prototype pieces	Multiple depending on the prototype
Scissors	1 per person building prototype

What	How Much
3M removable tape	1 roll per person building prototype
Tape dispenser	1 per person building the prototype
Removable glue stick	1
Correction fluid	1 bottle or pen
Ruler	1

Table A-3 continued: List of supplies for the paper prototype building process.

Index

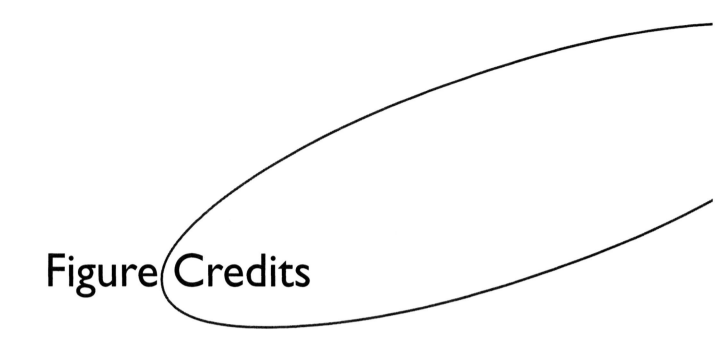

Figure Credits

Figures 6.1-6.3, 7.1 adapted from eChalk (www.eChalk.com)

Figures 6.4 courtesy of Agilent Technologies (www.agilent.com). Photography courtesy of Marty Weiskoff.

Figure 6.5, 11.5, 12.3-12.8, 13.5, 13.6, 14.1 courtesy of eChalk (www.eChalk.com). Photography courtesy of Marty Weiskoff.

Figures 7.2-7.6, 8.1, 10.1 11.3, 13.1-13.4 Photography courtesy of Marty Weiskoff.

Figures 6.6, 7.7, 11.1, 11.2, 12.2, 15.1 courtesy of Apropos Technology, Inc. (www.apropos.com). Photography courtesy of Marty Weiskoff.

Figure 9.1 copyright © 2004 LANDesk Reprinted with Permission.

Figure 9.2 copyright © 2004 Comstock Images. Reprinted with Permission.

Figure 15.2 adapted from Apropos Technology, Inc. (www.apropos.com)

About the Authors

Karen Holtzblatt is the visionary behind InContext's unique design approach to ddesign with user data.

Recognized as a leader in the design community, Karen has pioneered transformative ideas and design approaches throughout her career. At Digital Equipment Corporation Karen introduced Contextual Inquiry—the industry standard for gathering field data that enables understanding how technology impacts the way people work. Contextual inquiry and the Contextual Design processes based on it provide a revolutionary approach for designing entirely new products based on deep understanding of the context of use.

Karen co-founded InContext Enterprises in 1992, delivering customer-centered designs and coaching product teams in the Contextual Design process throughout the industry. The book *Contextual Design: Defining Customer-Centered Systems* is used by companies and universities all over the world. InContext's CDTools product launched in 2004 is the first tool suite to support teams in doing customer-centered design. Karen's extensive experience with teams and all types of work and life practice provides the back bone to the innovation and reliable quality consistently delivered by InContext's teams.

Karen has more than 20 years of teaching experience, professionally and in university settings. She holds a Ph.D. in applied psychology from the University of Toronto.

Shelley Wood manages InContext's consulting services and CDTools product. She brings more than 15 years of experience in the software and electronic publishing industries, and has held senior management positions in product management, product development, and business development. Before joining InContext, Shelley used Contextual Design on several projects, ranging from minor product fixes to major releases to developing entire new business directions. She now coaches client teams to use Contextual Design for their projects and products, and has worked with teams in a wide range of industries and applications.

Jessamyn Burns Wendell has six years of experience as a technical communications professional and project leader. Prior to joining InContext Enterprises, she worked as a contract writer, editor, and document designer within the medical, legal, and advertising communities in the greater Cincinnati area.

Jessamyn joined InContext in 2000 as a project team member, within six months she was working as a Project Lead on several major projects including the design of enterprise portals, a project leader environment, CDTools™, and a document management system. While at InContext, she also assumed primary responsibility for documenting clients' designs and InContext policies and procedures for running projects. Jessamyn is currently completing her Master's of Technical and Scientific Communication at Miami University (Ohio).

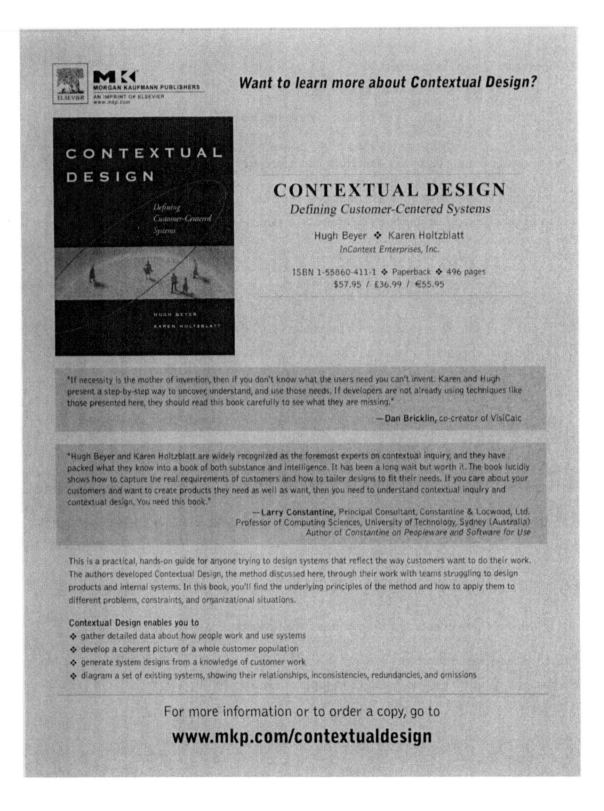

Lightning Source UK Ltd.
Milton Keynes UK
UKOW011528140612

194381UK00002B/2/P